"Here Is Hell"

Grant Dawson

"Here Is Hell":
Canada's Engagement in Somalia

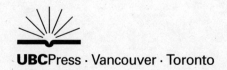
UBCPress · Vancouver · Toronto

15 14 13 12 11 10 09 08 07 06   5 4 3 2 1

Printed in Canada on ancient-forest-free paper (100 percent post-consumer recycled) that is processed chlorine- and acid-free, with vegetable-based inks.

Library and Archives Canada Cataloguing in Publication

Dawson, Grant, 1972-
    "Here is hell" : Canada's engagement in Somalia / Grant Dawson.

    Includes bibliographical references and index.
    ISBN 0-978-7748-1297-9 (bound); 0-978-7748-1298-6 (pbk)

    1. Somalia Affair, Canada, 1992-1997. 2. Canada – Armed Forces – Somalia.
    3. Canada – Politics and government – 1984-1993. 4. Canada – Politics and
    government – 1993-. 5. Canada – History, Military – 20th century. I. Title.

FC633.S6D39 2006   971.064'7   C2006-903948-8

Canadä

UBC Press gratefully acknowledges the financial support for our publishing program of the Government of Canada through the Book Publishing Industry Development Program (BPIDP), and of the Canada Council for the Arts, and the British Columbia Arts Council.

This book has been published with the help of a grant from the Canadian Federation for the Humanities and Social Sciences, through the Aid to Scholarly Publications Program, using funds provided by the Social Sciences and Humanities Research Council of Canada.

Printed and bound in Canada by Friesens
Set in Stone by Blakeley
Copy editor: James Leahy
Proofreader: Gail Copeland
Indexer: Annette Lorek
Cartographer: Eric Leinberger

UBC Press
The University of British Columbia
2029 West Mall
Vancouver, BC V6T 1Z2
604-822-5959 / Fax 604-822-6083
www.ubcpress.ca

Contents

Illustrations

Acknowledgments

Anyone who has completed a project like this will understand the large number of debts accumulated. I appreciate this assistance, which is outlined below, more than I can express. This book is dedicated to my mother and father, whose love and encouragement sustained me during the long years of research and writing. I am grateful to my brother, Glen, and girlfriend, Adria, who encouraged me when my energy was flagging.

This book has evolved considerably from its humble beginnings as a doctoral dissertation accepted by Carleton University in 2003. In the process, parts were presented to the Society for Military History annual meeting in Calgary (2001), the Canadian Historical Association 81st annual conference in Toronto (2002), and the International Studies Association 45th annual meeting in Montreal (2004). The book would not have been completed without the help of Professor Norman Hillmer, my former doctoral adviser, and I deeply appreciate his constant support and friendship. Thanks are due to Professor J.L. Granatstein, whose comments improved sections of the dissertation and book; to Professors Tom Vadney, my MA adviser at the University of Manitoba, and Alan James, both of whom provided valuable counsel; and to Vice-Admiral (ret'd) Larry Murray, who spoke with me several times and arranged interviews with high-ranking Canadian and United Nations officials. I am also indebted to Johnston Smith, who proofread and tightened the manuscript, and to Professor Sandi Cooper and my cousins Jacqueline McFadyen and her husband Chi-Wen Ho and Deidre McFadyen for hosting me during my research trip to the UN headquarters in New York.

Many busy people reviewed parts of the manuscript, sat for multiple interviews, or provided documents. Tim Addison, Paul Addy, John de Chastelain, David Cogdon, Lou Cuppens, Jim Cox, David Huddleston, Robert Fowler, Robert Johnston, Serge Labbé, Robert Oakley, Mark Moher, Reid Morden, and Glen Shortliffe commented on excerpts or draft chapters. Eighty-five different people were interviewed over seven years for this book. Paul Addy, Anthony Anderson, John Anderson, Ernest Beno, John Bremner, Jim Gervais,

Bruce Johnston, Robert Johnston, Mike Houghton, Robert Oakley, David Malone, Mike O'Brien, Serge Labbé, Mark Moher, and Edward Willer agreed to sit for more than one interview (there were about 110 interviews in total). Mohamed Sahnoun deserves special mention for driving from Wakefield, Quebec, to Ottawa so that we could talk in person. John de Chastelain answered three letters of questions, and Mike O'Brien patiently responded to many e-mails on top of the interviews. Tim Addison, Al Balfour, Jim Cox, and Serge Labbé provided unpublished documents, and Ted Kelly managed the excellent Foreign Affairs Informal Access process in an unfailingly flexible and helpful manner.

Research funding and production support were received from several sources. This project would have been much harder to complete without the Department of National Defence / Security and Defence Forum PhD Fellowship, which I received in 2001-2 and 2002-3, Carleton University Graduate Scholarship, Manitoba Bursaries, and funding provided by the Centre for Security and Defence Studies, Norman Paterson School for International Affairs, Carleton University. The University of British Columbia Press reviewers did an excellent job. Emily Andrew, Senior Editor at UBC Press, was patient and supportive and ensured that the editorial process flowed smoothly.

I thank Lieutenant-Colonel Rod Mackay, Lieutenant-Colonel Jeremy Mansfield, and CFB Petawawa Military Museums, Department of National Defence, for kind permission to publish photographs.

I am lucky to have obtained so much assistance and co-operation. If anyone has been forgotten, I hope he or she will accept my sincerest apologies. Of course, any errors of fact or interpretation remain my responsibility.

"Here Is Hell"

Introduction

This book presents a critical examination of Canadian government decision making with respect to its contribution of military forces to Somalia in 1992-93. The senior decision makers in Ottawa initially showed little enthusiasm for a role in Somalia's civil war and humanitarian crisis, but this changed as media and public interest steadily grew during the latter half of 1992. The expansion of the United Nations Operation in Somalia I and subsequent establishment of the US-led Unified Task Force coalition created opportunities for the government to reflect this interest and support multilateralism by offering Canadian Forces capabilities and personnel. Canada made three commitments: to the UN humanitarian airlift in August, to the UN peacekeeping mission in August, and to the US peace enforcement coalition in December. Canada decided against participation in the United Nations Operation in Somalia II, a large enforcement mission that succeeded the American coalition, and pulled its contingent out of Somalia in June 1993.

The argument for involvement is that although Canada had no traditional interest at stake in Somalia, Progressive Conservative prime minister Brian Mulroney (1984-93) decided that Canada should commit to the first UN mission and then the US coalition because this furthered the government's domestic political interests. The media had made the Somalia peace operations a high-profile issue, and Mulroney was being pressured to engage. He also wanted to pursue Canada's interest in multilateralism and human rights and, later, in smooth Canada-US relations.

Canada's mission to Somalia ended in recrimination and scandal. The involvement of Canadian troops in widely publicized, suspicious Somali civilian deaths embarrassed the country and pitched the armed forces into one of its darkest periods. Most assessments have been harshly critical of Canada's commanders and troops in the field and senior military leaders in Canada. This study challenges that interpretation of pre-deployment decision making and of the Canadian operations in Somalia. It finds fault and assigns responsibility but avoids retrospective and absolute judgments.

The rest of this introduction discusses the government's Somalia-related decisions and the context in which they were made. The first decision occurred in April-May 1992, when the United Nations asked Canada to contribute five unarmed military observers plus the chief military observer for a peacekeeping mission to be based in Mogadishu, Somalia's capital. Canadian officials had observed that the credibility of UN-led multilateralism was not threatened in April-May because the operation was just getting under way and media criticism of the Canadian and UN effort was muted. Ottawa therefore refused, officially because its personnel would be exposed to excessive risk. The prime minister did not intervene decisively in the government decision-making process to ensure Canada engaged. Nor, owing to the limited prime ministerial interest, did the bureaucracy assign a priority to Somalia.

Driven by mounting media attention and the realization that the Somalia crisis was becoming a major international security issue, Ottawa decided to offer troops and aircraft in August to bolster the UN's expanded peacekeeping and famine-relief plans. Mulroney provided these forces, without first being asked, in order to get the operation established as soon as possible. The government had become concerned once UN Secretary-General Boutros Boutros-Ghali and newspapers like the *Globe and Mail* and the *New York Times* began to stress that the international community was neglecting Somalia while pouring resources into the effort to resolve the Yugoslavia crisis. The prime minister wanted a more credible operation in Somalia so that Canada's and the international community's peacekeeping would appear to be balanced. Mulroney's decision to participate was opportune for three reasons: peacekeeping was experiencing a renaissance in the minds of experts and its relevance to world problems was increasing; there was no reason to believe that the UN mission would not be successful; and he wanted to show Canadians that his government was doing something about the shocking reports of starvation and massive suffering in Somalia.

By December, it was clear that the UN force and the relief effort as a whole were failing. Contributing to the US-led coalition allowed Canada to support US participation in multilateralism. Canada usually worked within broad-based and rule-bound bodies like the United Nations, but when its mission failed there was no alternative to the United Task Force. The ad hoc coalition model was acceptable to decision makers because it was multinational in dimension.

The government was not troubled by the United Task Force's enforcement mandate. Its commitment showed that Canada would use force as a last resort to ensure that the international community's will was effectively expressed. For Ottawa, the coalition was an extension of established peacekeeping practices in keeping with the other new roles being assigned to UN-mandated forces and necessary because of Somalia's disorder, warlords, and overabundance of weapons. Government leaders believed that Somalia required more determined multilateralism. The coalition's robustness was inspiring because it suggested that the international community could organize powerful coalitions to grapple with complex humanitarian emergencies.

Whether the Canadian Joint Force Somalia should stay in the Horn of Africa after the United Task Force's withdrawal became the government's final problem. The transfer of command to the second UN mission would take place on 4 May 1993. Canada could authorize a second rotation, extend the tour of its in-theatre personnel, or depart. This decision was made by the prime minister. He decided that Canada should withdraw with the coalition for four reasons: first, the UN's peace enforcement mission was expected to be a long-term mission with doubtful prospects; second, the Canadian Forces could not sustain its role; third, Canada did not have national interests at stake in Somalia; and finally, public support for an extension was lukewarm.

To put these decisions into context, one needs to keep in mind the government's foreign policy ideas and optimism for the United Nations. Government leaders sought to capitalize on the surge in confidence for UN peacekeeping in the early 1990s. They pursued this policy despite the ominous conditions of the Somalia crisis, which involved mass famine, clan militias engaged in civil conflict, unaffiliated armed bandits, and the lack of a central authority to impose order or co-operate reliably with third-party mediators. Canadian officials urged the world body to show leadership because they saw the Somalia crisis as a crucial test of its post-Cold War effectiveness. The United Nations had to experiment with several techniques – diplomatic peacemaking, peace observation, peacekeeping, peace enforcement, and peace building – in the midst of an unfamiliar, unfinished internal war. It could not help Somalia as quickly as Canada and other countries wanted and expected because the armed factions refused to respect the principles – consent, impartiality, and nonviolent behaviour – on which traditional UN peacekeeping missions depended. Paradoxically, Canada's support of multilateral solutions to world problems led it to encourage UN involvement in a situation where the organization could only be discredited.

The prime minister's multilateralism,[1] another key element of the decision-making context, grew from his belief in internationalism. Internationalism had been the dominant Canadian foreign policy approach since the late 1940s and is commonly associated with Lester B. Pearson, a secretary of state for External Affairs (1948-57), Nobel Peace Prize winner (1957), and Liberal prime minister (1963-68). Pearson defined internationalism as a constructive engagement with the world through multilateral institutions. Participatory internationalism was needed because Canada could not count on its geographic location to protect it from wars, and the great powers, if left to themselves, would try to manage world affairs on their own. Pearson believed Canada could cope with these problems by using multinational organizations, which were seen as instruments of political interaction that facilitated the sharing of international decision making.[2]

The government would strengthen Canadian sovereignty by engaging in world affairs and balancing its US, Commonwealth, Francophonie, and other connections. This was in the national interest because in few countries "are the requirements of interdependence so closely related to the maintenance of independence."[3] Pearson's vision was that internationalism not only heightened Canada's external profile but it also advanced the national interest in global peace and stability. It was "more important," Pearson wrote, "to use your sovereignty to protect and advance your own legitimate interests by establishing relations of friendship, good-will, and agreement with other countries."[4] He knew this had popular backing. Pearson said that Canadians wanted a foreign policy that inspired "hope for a better country and a more secure world"[5] rather than one strictly concerned with trade.

When Mulroney took power, the three pillars of internationalism – nationalism, humanitarianism, and multilateralism – represented not so much a policy as a bipartisan core set of principles.[6] The Nobel Prize, won by Pearson after the creation of the first UN Emergency Force (1956-67), was a national talisman.[7] Mulroney was a Pearsonian who regularly quoted Pearson,[8] and he believed that multilateralism was something real, something more than just a counter to continentalism. Mulroney was "a multilateralist" who "believed a lot in the United Nations," in human rights, and "in peacekeeping." He "thought it was an entirely appropriate role for Canada to get involved in United Nations peacekeeping and more aggressive United Nations Chapter VII operations" because this type of activity fulfilled Canada's "responsibility for the good management of international relations [which] was in our interests."[9]

The potential for multilateralism grew after Pearson left office. The United States remained globally dominant, but the increase in state interdependence, in the number of nongovernmental organizations (NGOs), and in ad hoc multilateralism (such as summitry) made power in the state system more diffuse and difficult to manage. The new order afforded Canada more opportunity to collaborate with states and follow an independent foreign policy.[10] There were, it was true, forums like the United Nations, where Cold War tension had stifled co-operation. This was disappointing for the government, which favoured the UN as the world's leading multilateral organization, with a near-universal membership and a mandate to protect international peace. Canada needed multilateral bodies like the UN because it could not address conflict by itself. According to secretary of state for External Affairs Joe Clark (1984-91), "powers our size have no choice but to work within international organizations." As a result, "making the world work together has become the Canadian vocation."[11]

The Mulroney government wanted to improve conflict resolution mechanisms. Effective multilateral arrangements, argued Canadian diplomat Geoffrey Pearson, "provide a means to exert influence on major allies and powerful neighbours as well as help to maintain peace."[12] During the civil war in the former Yugoslavia (1992-95), Canada's leaders vigorously supported the attempts at "instigating and redefining new co-operative security arrangements" within the Conference on Security and Co-operation in Europe, the United Nations, and the North Atlantic Treaty Organisation (NATO). They sought to demonstrate the relevance of these bodies and contribute constructively to conflict management in the Balkans.[13] A similar goal – aiding the United Nations and ad hoc coalitions – was important to Canada's engagement in Somalia.

Because of the government's support of multilateralism, crisis responses were sometimes not driven by specific trade or strategic interests.[14] Peacekeeping commitments could be made to further broader national interests such as global peace and stability. In the Balkans, Canada had little at stake except for a desire to strengthen the multinational response so that the fighting and human rights abuses would stop.[15] Somalia represented a similar case. Canada lacked economic interests in Africa and had almost no relations with Somalia at all. Somalia's civil war briefly became a foreign policy priority partly because of Canada's interest in multilateralism and peace.

The Canadian peacekeeping tradition was another part of the context for the government's decision making. The United Nations had asked Canada for blue helmets (the name sometimes given to UN peacekeeping troops because of their distinctive headgear) during the Cold War because it could represent the West, it possessed capable armed forces, and it was a medium-sized, noncolonial power.[16] Canada deployed peacekeeping troops to project power for national security interests, most of which related to supporting the Western alliance in the Cold War.[17] Yet the activity gradually became a national fixation and the subject of mythmaking. Nationalists preened over Canada's superior moral character, which they said was behind the UN requests. Canada's record of participation in all blue helmet operations up to the UN Angola Verification Mission I (1989-91) was a source of pride. Peacekeeping made Canada appear different from the United States since it was "something we could do and the Americans could not."[18]

The risky and multifunctional internal missions that emerged after the Cold War did not undermine Canada's love affair with peacekeeping and the self-image peacekeeping fed. Such an image was tied in with Canada's "self-congratulatory rhetoric about its traditions of kindliness, compromise and the negotiation of difference."[19] Canadians admired their blue helmets so much that the government featured peacekeeping in its unsuccessful public relations campaign before the October 1992 constitutional referendum on the Charlottetown Accord.[20] Ottawa contributed to operations in Namibia

(1989-90), El Salvador (1991-95), Cambodia (1991-93), Yugoslavia (1992-95), and Somalia (1992-93) partly because the myth that Canada invented peacekeeping made it difficult to say no.[21] For too many Canadians and their governments, the cry "send in the peacekeepers" had become a substitute for rational policy and thought.[22]

This context – the Canadian peacekeeping tradition, optimism for the United Nations, and support of multilateralism – informed all four decisions. The rest of this book examines these decisions chronologically. The importance of this study is clear when one reflects on the large number of subsequent deployments into civil conflicts, the UN's replacement by coalitions as the military manager of peace operations, the stabilization and peace-building mission in Afghanistan (2002-present, NATO-led since 2003), and the US prison-abuse scandal in Iraq in 2003. While focused on the Somalia crisis, this book deals with a number of Canadian foreign and defence policy issues. These include the Mulroney government's support of a strong UN-centred security architecture and of peacekeeping, Canada's relations with the United States and the UN and the ability of coalitions and the Canadian Forces to stabilize failed and fragile states.

Political and military judgments are dealt with separately in the chapters that follow. Chapter 1 examines Canada's diplomatic moves before the establishment of the UN peacekeeping mission. Chapter 2 looks at the Joint Staff, a staff structure created to accelerate Canadian military decision making, and its recommendation that Canada stay uncommitted. Chapter 3 discusses the decision to make Somalia a priority. The Canadian Forces' participation in a UN airlift is the subject of Chapter 4. Chapters 5 and 6 examine the troop commitment to the peacekeeping mission and the Canadian Forces' selection of the Airborne Regiment and its attempt to define its task. The decision to engage in the US coalition and the military preparations for that operation are considered in Chapters 7 and 8. Chapter 9 looks at the government's decision to not contribute to the second UN mission to Somalia and the Somalia scandal, and Chapter 10 examines the Canadian Forces operations on the ground in Somalia, the disturbing incidents involving Canadian soldiers, and the withdrawal.

1

Food for Thought: Multilateral Humanitarianism and the Somalia Crisis to March 1992

The Canadian government did not pay much attention to Somalia during the Cold War. In the early 1990s, Prime Minister Brian Mulroney changed Canada's approach because Somalia's total collapse, mass famine, and civil conflict had attracted the world's attention, and the end of the Cold War had removed the bipolar political constraint that would have made a rescue effort impossible. A spirit of co-operation had seized the UN Security Council. Ottawa was inspired by a "new" internationalism characterized by greater interdependence, co-operation between states, and reliance on multinational institutions. The government wanted to strengthen and encourage the use of world bodies in times of emergency.

Yet Canada's response to the Somalia crisis was more cautious than might be expected considering the extent of the suffering and disorder in the Horn of Africa. Government leaders were troubled by the crisis, but their main concern was UN multilateralism. An effective multilateralist response was needed so that Canada would have opportunities to influence the diplomatic agenda and help alleviate suffering. Although it encouraged the United Nations to press forward, the government was interested in supplying food aid to the international effort. It did not want to contribute troops to the planned United Nations Operation in Somalia I.

Ottawa's actions were underpinned by its belief that the UN was entering into a period of renewed relevance and vitality. Ambassador Yves Fortier, Canada's permanent representative to the United Nations in New York from 1988 to 1992, recalled that the Cold War had resulted in the "virtual paralysis" of the UN. The thaw of the Cold War, starting in fall 1988, was "nothing less than an earth-shattering revolution."[1] With permanent members co-operating rather than competing, the Security Council became a more effective forum for dispute resolution. The United Nations was more willing and able to deal with conflict, although it remained essentially an instrument of persuasion.[2] The UN's legitimacy was on the rise because it was managing more complex missions and its success rate was increasing.[3] The coalition

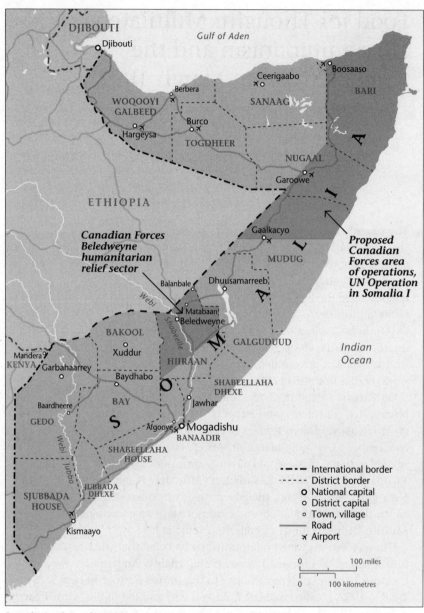

Somalia in the early 1990s

victory in the Persian Gulf War (1990-91) suggested to some officials that a new multinational peace and security architecture was on the horizon in which the UN would be in a position to mobilize political will and act decisively. Decision makers "felt that things could be done through the United Nations that were not possible before." There was "atmosphere, optimism, a belief that you [could] make a difference through peace operations and the use of military force."[4]

The government's foreign policy response, "new internationalism," was more than old internationalism. It was an attempt to take advantage of the increased freedom and potential for activism on the world stage. "Multilateralism has been a long-standing Canadian mantra," Secretary of State for External Affairs Barbara McDougall stated in 1992. "What is new is the growing willingness of other countries to use multilateral institutions."[5] The government wanted to apply the collaborative spirit to civil conflict control and humanitarian relief. These situations concerned Ottawa as threats to peace and because they could increase refugee flows. Improvements in telecommunications and the emergence of twenty-four-hour global media networks would make the viciousness of internal war vividly, widely, and immediately known. The prime minister believed his government could not afford to ignore civil strife. Mulroney observed in a September 1991 speech that Canada "favour[s] re-thinking the limits of national sovereignty in a world where problems respect no borders."[6]

New internationalism saw intervention as a moral imperative in cases of intra-state disorder and massive human rights abuse. "Canada," Mulroney said, "would like to see the United Nations become still more effective, more of an actor in international affairs," since "there are certain fundamental rights that all people possess ... [and] sometimes, the international community must act to defend them."[7] The government recognized that these were strong words. What made the policy "new" according to McDougall was its assumption that human rights in sovereign states was a legitimate subject of debate and action by multilateral forums. This was "a quantum leap in the evolution of international relations and law." Peacekeeping could further this end. McDougall signalled Canada's intention to play in the establishment of the new order, noting it had "special competence" in that activity.[8]

Most of Canada's experience was in "traditional" UN missions based on principles set down by 1958. Secretary-General Dag Hammarskjöld had argued that peacekeeping troops could be deployed only "in the interest and with the consent and co-operation of the host government." Impartiality was also essential: "The Force should not be used to enforce any specific political solution of pending problems or to influence the political balance decisive to such a solution." A further principle stated that "the operation may never take the initiative in the use of armed force, but is entitled to respond with force to an attack with arms."[9] Alan James, a noted peacekeeping scholar, argues that consent, impartiality, and nonthreatening behaviour "constitute the very core and essence of the activity."[10] Peacekeeping missions usually involved military officers or formed units monitoring ceasefires or force separations. Post-Cold War peacekeeping, in contrast, was more intrusive, comprehensive, and multifunctional.

Canadian officials tended to focus on UN peacekeeping's advances and downplay the links between the old and new versions of the activity. The political functions the new missions performed or attempted to perform – the diffusion of tension, stabilization of a situation, and the resolution of disputes – were the same as before. Internal tasks were not a unique phenomenon, although there was a heavier concentration on this type of activity in the early post-Cold War era.[11] Those in the government were more concerned with peacekeeping's renewal and potential. The multifunctional UN Transition Assistance Group to Namibia (1989-90), an internal operation with humanitarian, military, and political aspects, was, McDougall hoped, "a harbinger of events to come."[12] The Department of National Defence was attuned to the "revival" of peacekeeping and the emergence of "new challenges and opportunities." The April 1992 defence policy update prepared by the department stated that Canada should "preserve and advance this new approach to international problem-solving."[13]

Peacekeeping moved into many new areas in the early 1990s. The UN Transition Assistance Group demilitarized and administered Namibia and oversaw the election that created its first independent government. Its most important legacy was the formation of a link between traditional missions and those of the multifunctional "second generation."[14] The UN Observer Group in Central America (1989-92) was the first deployed to the Western hemisphere and to disarm and demobilize a guerrilla army (the Contras).[15] Blue helmets in the UN Observer Mission in El Salvador (1991-95) were the first assigned human rights monitoring as a primary mandated task.[16] The UN Transitional Authority in Cambodia (1992-93) dispersed throughout that country; exercised "direct control" over its federal and provincial departments of foreign affairs, national defence, finance, and public information; and organized its inaugural democratic election in spring 1993.[17]

Government interest in international peacekeeping led to commitments in the former Yugoslavia. The UN Protection Force (1992-95) deployed into a civil conflict without a stable ceasefire and encountered trouble because the disputants did not respect peacekeeping's principles. In April 1992, Canada became the first country to contribute troops. Forces based in Germany were sent into Croatia "because the reality of human suffering is so compelling" and "because peace and security in Europe are essential to peace and security in Canada."[18] Senior officials may not have fully appreciated the operational difficulties inherent in such deployments.[19] Humanitarian aid to one ethnic population was seen as having partial effects, and the UN Protection

Force could not manage the fighting because local consent was unreliable. The mission hurt the cause of political settlement and served as a prelude to further violence by enabling Croatia and the Bosnians time to regroup and concentrate on certain fronts.[20] But at the same time, it is questionable whether the UN could have avoided deploying. The UN decided that the consequences of failure were less than the harm that would be done to peace and stability if it did nothing.[21]

In contrast with Yugoslavia, the government was much less vocal about Somalia in the first half of 1992. Statements even touching on that civil conflict were rare until late summer, when more international attention and resources began to be directed at it. Canada's bilateral aid to Somalia in 1990-91 reflected this situation. Assistance was limited to the Canadian International Development Agency "Canada Fund" administered by the High Commission in Nairobi (which was accredited to Somalia). About $100,000 to $150,000 was available. Chris Liebich, an agency official assigned to the High Commission, allocated funds to a Somali-Canadian-run orphanage in Mogadishu and other humanitarian projects. By the end of 1990, Somalia was on the verge of collapse after years of worsening instability, and even that level of bilateral aid became impossible.[22]

The descent into civil war and factionalism occurred because dictator-president Mohamed Said Barre, in power since a 1969 coup, had turned the Somali "clans" system against his regime. The Somali people were made up of six clan families (the Daarood, Isaaq, Hawiye, Dir, Rahanwayn, and Digil) that shared similar customs and traditions and a single culture. They were homogeneous religiously (the Sunni branch of Islam), ethnically (out of an estimated population of 6.5 million, about 98.8 percent were ethnic Somali and 1.2 percent Arab or Asian), and linguistically (they spoke Somali, a Cushtic language).[23] However, the clan families and many clans and sub-clans that branched out from them were prone to rivalry and internecine conflict. Barre had kept these tensions subdued for ten years by making meritorious appointments, by not excessively favouring the clans related to his family, and by seeking to replace the influence of Islamic leaders and clans in Somali political life with state nationalism.[24]

In order to promote nationalism as a substitute for clan allegiance, Barre had adopted a policy of irredentism. Uniting with the ethnic Somali regions in neighbouring countries had been an extremely popular idea in Somalia since it became independent in 1960, and Barre used irredentism to draw support and attention to the state and away from the fractious clans. Two points of the five-pointed star on the Somali flag were said to represent its northern and southern regions and the others the "unredeemed territories" in Ethiopia, Kenya, and Djibouti.[25] All prospects of realizing this ambition vanished with Somalia's defeat in a 1977-78 war over Ethiopia's ethnic Somali Ogaden region. After the war, clan favouritism became more pronounced, disillusionment and dissatisfaction with Barre among certain clans who felt politically deprived grew, repression of these clans began, and a vicious and violent cycle leading within ten years to full-blown civil war was started.[26]

Barre was overthrown on 27 January 1991 by three rebel militias or "factions" loosely associated with a clan family: the Somali National Movement (the Issaq of northern Somalia), the Somali Patriotic Movement (the Ogadeni in Ethiopia, part of the Daarood clan family), and the United Somali Congress (the Hawiye of central Somalia). These armed groups were not under clan control or direction. For the faction leaders, it was politically expedient to identify their movements with clans or sub-clans, but in truth factions included members of different clans and the same clan could spawn multiple factions supporting opposing sides in the conflict.[27] The Somali National Movement switched from raids to continuous open conflict against Barre in mid-1988, and the other two movements joined the civil war in 1989 and 1990, respectively. The United Somali Congress, whose home territory and forces were nearest Mogadishu, delivered the final blow by seizing the capital.

The faction leaders did not cease hostilities. In the south, which became the locus of civil war, they made preparations for a new round of fighting to decide who would be president. It was widely accepted that the new order would be established not through dialogue but by meeting on the battlefield.[28] The southern leaders loathed each other and competed so viciously and aggressively for several reasons.[29] The south's susceptibility to chronic conflict and "warlord politics" is partly explained by its political culture, which since pre-colonial days has had no room for egalitarian values, human rights, and indigenous development, and has been extremely coercive and hierarchical, in contrast with the political culture of the north.[30] The conditions of post-Cold War government collapse gave faction heads incentives to contest rather than compromise with state power.[31] The loss of superpower patronage had made new incumbents weaker and less able to stave off challengers, and the opening of global arms markets made it possible for insurgents to vie for power on more level playing fields than had existed before. The Somali faction leaders had ready access to arms and were determined to defeat their rivals to secure control of the depleted but still remunerative apparatus of the former state.[32]

The clan's segmentary lineage system could not cauterize these wounds as it might have in the past. The patrilineal clans performed integrative (they were a rallying point against external threats) and disintegrative roles in Somali society.[33] Traditionally, clan disputes had been mediated by two social practices: *xeer* (or social contract), which prevented clashes by inhibiting the excessive economic stratification of society, and *dia,* which constrained violence by requiring "blood money" payments to a victim's clan.[34] But as a loose political system of checks and balances, the clans had been displaced by imposed colonial administrations and then the independent Somali state.

By the time Barre's regime imploded, the clans had essentially become social institutions. They were manipulated by faction leaders, who exploited clan connections to create constituencies for personal political agendas.[35]

Competition for power and state revenues caused the United Somali Congress to split into two factions associated with the Hawiye clan family. Ali Mahdi Mohamed (Abgal clan), a hotelier based in north Mogadishu who was sworn in as interim president on 28 January 1991, led one of the groups. The other was controlled by Brigadier-General Mohamed Farah Aidid (Habr Gedir clan). He had commanded the forces that seized the capital and was now headquartered in south Mogadishu. Ali Mahdi did not consult with Aidid about his appointment, and Aidid therefore refused to acknowledge or accept it. Each underestimated the other: Aidid believed his followers were the real force that toppled Barre and that the more urbanized Abgals would fold; Ali Mahdi's self-confidence in dealing with Aidid arose from his financial liquidity, arms purchases, the support he received from Italy (one of the former colonial powers), and his conviction that other Western states would come to his aid. A war of attrition developed.[36] Ali Mahdi and Aidid joined in full-scale combat from November 1991 until the United Nations brokered a ceasefire in February 1992 (it was signed on 3 March). The fighting destroyed the capital, disrupted the meagre humanitarian assistance effort, and inflicted over 25,000 civilian casualties.[37]

Barre's attempt to retake Mogadishu deepened the crisis. His forces, regrouped under the banner Somali National Front, got within thirty kilometres of the capital before Aidid turned them back at Afgooye. During the first six months of the September 1991-April 1992 campaign, Barre's faction occupied and plundered the Somali breadbasket in the south between and along the Jubba and Shabeelle rivers. They interrupted farming, damaged irrigation systems, polluted wells, and were the main cause of the catastrophic famine that overtook Somalia.[38] Considerable suffering was inflicted on the resident Digil and Rahanweyn clan families, the Banadir costal town dwellers, and the Gosha and other minorities of slave heritage also called "Bantu." These peoples were politically isolated and looked down upon because they were sedentary cultivators or urbanites in what was an overwhelmingly nomadic society.[39] Their hardship was a reflection of the faction leaders' lust for power and land, as well as race and class status, and was not simply about clan rivalry.[40] These poorly armed groups could not resist Barre. They were powerless before Aidid and the other factions who later sought to dominate the area.

Despite the seriousness of the situation, the UN response was weak throughout 1991. Although a UN narrative states that the World Food Programme and UN Children's Fund were "fully engaged" by March, each withdrew on several occasions for extended periods because of safety concerns.[41] Nor was the UN proactive diplomatically. It did not try to support the June and July reconciliation conferences sponsored by Djibouti. Mohamed Sahnoun, the first special representative of the secretary-general in Somalia (head of the UN Somalia mission), believed these were missed opportunities that could have given the peace process a promising beginning.[42] A key reason for the UN's reluctance was that Djibouti's initiatives lasted for only a limited time and were not supported by Aidid. Conflicts usually appeared on the Council's agenda when there was an internationally driven peace process and a set of disputants who wanted help.[43] Meaningful UN involvement was delayed until the crisis attracted a higher profile in the West.

Similarly, Canada's initial role in the Somalia crisis was not extensive. The government's engagement reflected the prominence of humanitarian values in its foreign policy. Mulroney told Commonwealth leaders at the 1991 Summit in Harare that human rights was a "concrete factor" in determining development assistance allocations.[44] The Department of External Affairs and International Trade Canada had been making a "major effort" to encourage human rights and democracy through stepped-up political dialogue and concerted action with other donors.[45] To Ottawa, Barre's successors were suspect because they lacked good democratic and human rights records. It urged Ali Mahdi and the leaders of Somaliland, the new name for the northwest part of Somalia, which had seceded from the south in May 1991, to behave more humanely. Otherwise, Canada would not recognize either party. Ali Mahdi's interim government was denied an official visit to Canada and told that an informal tour was unwelcome. Somaliland was informed that new bilateral ties depended on budgets and "in Somalia's case [on] the policy approaches it adopts."[46]

The government was active on the multinational humanitarian front. Ambassador Louise Fréchette, Canada's permanent representative to the United Nations in 1992, noted that Ottawa had "been much involved in the development of instruments related to the United Nations co-ordination of emergency humanitarian assistance."[47] External Affairs noted that "Canada regard[ed] humanitarian assistance as an obligation, and will therefore help Somalia." Multilateral assistance was provided because bilateral relief was exceedingly difficult to deliver.[48] A leading instrument was the UN Special Emergency Programme for the Horn of Africa, a regional emergency response co-ordinating body formed in September 1991. Canada paid some of its start-up costs, contributed to its first field mission and December interim appeal, and promised to help fund its February 1992 appeal.[49] The UN Children's Fund, World Food Programme, and nongovernmental organizations (NGOs) received $5.3 million in 1991 and $22.8 million in 1992 to further Somalia relief efforts.[50]

While Somalia's suffering was a growing concern, the credibility of UN-led multilateral action became the government's priority. The International Committee of the Red Cross started to attack the UN publicly in January

1992. During a New York University seminar on 6 January, President Cornelio Sommaruga described the UN's role as "reserved" and a "retreat from action." He stressed that UN leadership was required.[51] These comments had special weight because the International Committee of the Red Cross was one of the few organizations to maintain a presence in Somalia throughout the emergency. It had developed a famine relief system that took advantage of the country's long coastline to filter in foodstuffs and had deployed thousands of mobile kitchens to dispense these supplies. This achievement put moral force behind its criticism and illustrated that world opinion was not impressed with the UN's attempts to excuse itself by pointing to the security risks.

US Congressional representatives provided specific suggestions for improving UN conflict resolution in Somalia. Two members of the Senate Subcommittee on African Affairs, Senators Paul Simon (the Chair, Democrat-Illinois) and Nancy Kassebaum (Republican-Kansas), wrote in the *New York Times* that, although the crisis was complex, the "lack of clear answers does not excuse inaction, neglect and apathy."[52] Simon and Kassebaum called for the appointment of a UN diplomat to negotiate a ceasefire and for the imposition by the Council of an arms embargo. Canadian officials feared the impression of UN passivity and ineffectiveness would deepen. "Indeed," the Permanent Mission in New York noted, the "harsh criticism of UN performance on Somalia by United States administration officials can be expected to spread to other capitals in [the] weeks ahead."[53]

Canadian and US media saw Somalia as a test of UN Secretary-General Boutros Boutros-Ghali (who assumed his post in January 1992), the "new" peacekeeping, and the revived Security Council. A *Winnipeg Free Press* article from the *New York Times* wire service noted that the UN's "failure to act would inevitably arouse comparisons with the Council's failure to address the long war between Iraq and Iran until it was almost a decade old."[54] The *New York Times* editorial board picked up this argument a month later, observing that Boutros-Ghali would fail to meet his crucial first test unless he received more US support.[55] Mulroney might well have been exposed to these views since he read the *New York Times* daily,[56] and it is probable that he agreed since he had made similar points before Somalia became a concern to the international community. "If the UN is to succeed," the prime minister said in Harare in October 1991, "the Security Council will need the authority and the means to intervene ... And the Secretary-General will need support to play the activist role the times we live in require."[57]

The government privately pressured the United Nations to engage with more determination. McDougall referred to Somalia when she met Boutros-Ghali on 15 January to discuss the strengthening of the organization's world role.[58] She said that Canada was dissatisfied with the low UN profile in Somalia and was eager to send aid, but could not because the UN was not positioned to receive it.[59] During a meeting on the 20 January, Permanent Mission staff repeated that Canada expected the UN to take the lead and saw the "Council resolution expected later this week as only the first step in what must be effective (repeat effective) United Nations efforts to encourage [a] cease-fire in Somalia." In a March letter to Boutros-Ghali, Fréchette said Canada would send food aid to Somalia as soon as the UN could assure delivery.[60]

The government agreed with Simon and Kassebaum's UN-centred conflict resolution suggestions. It was pleased when the Council decided on resolution 733 (23 January 1992), which imposed an arms embargo under Chapter VII of the UN Charter and asked the secretary-general to press for a ceasefire.[61] Officials saw the embargo, which was "due in part to our initiative," as a breakthrough because it was "the first time such action was taken in relation to an internal conflict."[62] This exuberance was premature. Somalia was already awash with weapons from its former armed forces, and its borders were open to smugglers. Arms were essential to survival and possessed by all who could afford them. The UN could do little to enforce the embargo beyond seeking assurances from member states that they were not selling weapons to Somalia. At best, the arms embargo may have temporarily sparked the faction leaders' interest in a ceasefire. In approving the resolution, the Council's true purpose may have been to deflect criticism surrounding its inaction while still doing nothing.[63]

Canadian officials were frustrated because bandits and faction members were blocking the UN relief effort by looting the food coming into the country without fear of arrest. So much was being stolen or impeded that UN humanitarian agencies considered breaking with procedure and feeding the gunmen so that their needs could be met without their disrupting the entire aid program.[64] The view from Ottawa was different. The government was growing concerned that the UN's inaction was "crippling ... [its] credibility in the humanitarian assistance field."[65] Officials wanted to act under a UN umbrella and called for a more determined UN engagement because Somalia was "the most prominent current element of the international humanitarian agenda with which Canada is strongly identified."[66]

Despite the criticisms, the United Nations believed caution was justified. Its personnel were not used to working without protection, and Somalia was especially bad in this respect. UN Children's Fund representative Caroline Tanner recalled that "you didn't have any respect for working for the United Nations. Everything went out of the window ... Nobody really knew how to handle that."[67] UN organizational culture was different from that of the NGOs and International Committee of the Red Cross. While equally conscientious, UN personnel were not driven by the same adrenal temperament and sense of adventure and camaraderie.[68] The Special Emergency Programme for the Horn of Africa and UN union were sensitive to the irrationality associated with exposing people to excessive risk in order to save others. One of the co-ordinating unit's draft reports pointed out that "it has to be recognised that the lives of our colleagues are not less important than those we are supposed to help and assist."[69] Staff Union president Ronald Hewson touched on the UN Children's Fund case in an interview with the circular *Secretariat News*. The "purpose of UNICEF is to look after children," he said, "but that should not involve making orphans out of UN staff members' children."[70] This view spread to the top of the UN hierarchy. Under-Secretary-General James Jonah, the lead UN diplomat for Somalia until the peacekeeping mission was established in April, told Canada's Permanent Mission in New York that he wanted to be replaced because his wife was concerned for his safety.[71]

The UN's hesitancy and ineffectiveness were directly related to the operational challenges in Somalia. The collapse of Somalia's government meant that the UN had to deal with faction leaders since they were the most powerful figures on the ground. There was no central authority to sign a peace deal and ensure it was honoured, which made it difficult to secure an agreement that could serve as the basis for further diplomatic peacemaking, peacekeeping, and humanitarian relief.[72] Jonah said that "nothing short of a peacekeeping force would be acceptable as a solution," but he was "not optimistic" one would deploy because Aidid maintained the crisis was an internal affair.[73] This posed a dilemma for the United Nations. Peacekeeping missions are creatures of the political environment and conflict environment in which they are created. The activity was unsuited to the Somalia crisis because the conflict situation lacked much of what peacekeepers require to be successful.[74] Without local consent, for example, the force could be perceived as lacking impartiality, and this would sharply reduce its calming and stabilizing effect. The context into which a UN force was sent, more than any other factor, determined whether it would be a success or a failure.[75]

The United Nations felt caught between the expectations for action and its concern about deploying into a highly insecure country. Jonah noted that "I don't think we should put all our staff at risk, but if we have no presence there, our image in the world is at risk."[76] A Special Emergency Programme for the Horn of Africa *Consolidated Inter-Agency Appeal* (February 1992) admitted that "the UN must look for ways to ensure its own staffing and procurement processes are better able to adapt to swiftly changing situations which are both complex and hazardous."[77] The UN decided to send volunteers to get around its rules barring staff deployments to perilous areas. This may not have been what it seemed. Hewson complained in a letter to the UN Children's Fund executive director, James Grant, that its "staff members have been nudged to 'volunteer' for this dangerous assignment."[78]

The establishment of a peacekeeping mission in Somalia was complicated by the inexperience of the United Nations when it came to dealing with subnational authorities in a constantly changing and chaotic setting. It had deployed without a ceasefire once before, to El Salvador in 1991, but at the request of the disputants.[79] In Somalia, conditions were much less favourable. On 14 February, representatives of Aidid and Ali Mahdi reached an agreement after UN-brokered talks. The United Nations revealed its greenness, however, by conferring legitimacy on the faction leaders, who were unelected gunmen in possession of territory seized by force of arms. The UN peace process made them the central power brokers, while at the same time excluding the voices of women, civil society, and clan leaders.[80] The UN did not try to pin down specifics in order to conclude a deal. A short (102 words) and vague agreement was produced as a result. The ceasefire did not signify a true commitment to peace, and it led Aidid and Ali Mahdi to different interpretations of key issues, such as whether the UN or Somali clan elders would serve as the monitors.[81] Despite this, the UN hoped for a calming effect from the ceasefire, which was signed by Aidid and Ali Mahdi in Mogadishu on 3 March and included a provision for a fifty-person UN observation mechanism.[82]

Shortly thereafter, Boutros-Ghali laid the foundation for the first UN peacekeeping mission in Somalia when he connected this political and military task with the relief effort. In his 11 March report to the Council, he called for troops to escort aid deliveries out of Mogadishu. Peacekeepers had not been employed that way before, and, the secretary-general admitted, "this exercise represents an innovation that may require careful consideration by the Security Council."[83] Boutros-Ghali's recommendation was acknowledged (but not approved) by Council resolution 746 (17 March 1992), which authorized the deployment of a seventeen-person Technical Mission to conduct negotiations on ceasefire monitoring procedures and to "develop a high priority plan to establish mechanisms to ensure the unimpeded delivery of humanitarian assistance."[84]

In deploying the Technical Mission, the United Nations did not show Aidid the respect he demanded. These teams were created routinely so that the United Nations could determine the modalities for a new peacekeeping operation. The assignment was delicate because Jonah and Aidid had not discussed the use of UN troops to protect humanitarian aid and workers during their ceasefire talks, and now an armed peacekeeping unit would have to be "sprung" on Aidid. Jonah told the Permanent Mission that, while he questioned whether Aidid would accept the need to protect relief workers, he thought that with determined Council support and a strongly worded resolution, Aidid could be pushed into accepting the idea.[85] This showed that the international community was prepared to assume compliance from and to underestimate the faction leaders. It reflected a willingness to push forward with multilateral peacekeeping, even if some local disputants were opposed to this, because of the serious humanitarian need.

Canada had followed these developments, but it was primarily concerned with finding a multilateral famine-relief role. Fréchette had highlighted the government's priorities in her March letter to Boutros-Ghali. She welcomed the fact that the 3 March ceasefire required a small monitoring mechanism but did not offer unarmed military observers on behalf of Canada. Instead, Fréchette concentrated on the situation inside Somalia, "the humanitarian aspects of which are a matter of great concern to the Government of Canada." Fréchette was writing to stress "the gravity of the situation in Somalia and the need for the UN to provide as rapidly as possible an adequate level of humanitarian assistance, particularly food supplies."[86]

By calling for more effective humanitarian peacekeeping action, Canada passed too easily over the risks associated with operating without firm support on the ground. A possible reason for this, Norman Hillmer suggests, is that the success of the coalition during the Persian Gulf War had ratcheted up expectations for UN-led operations to unrealistic levels and "did the UN a disservice by creating the impression that it could become a powerful and visionary organisation."[87] The groundbreaking deployments to Namibia, Central America, and El Salvador reinforced this optimism. This was significant because government officials tend to be strongly influenced by their experiences in previous operations.[88] Decision makers in Ottawa were not troubled by the uncertainties relating to how to help government-less Somalia, the UN's inexperience, or the risks associated with acting without the consent of all disputants. The principal issue for them was getting the UN to act because the situation was intolerable.

Canada's position differed from that of France, the United Kingdom, and the United States. These countries agreed that more needed to be done for the starving, but they were reluctant to send peacekeepers into a still-simmering civil war where they might not accomplish much. All three believed it was too soon to deploy a force to protect relief deliveries.[89] The United Kingdom and the United States clearly expressed this belief when the Council gathered to consider the draft of resolution 746 on 16 March. The UK permanent representative, Sir David Hannay, was openly sceptical about the provision calling for the deployment of a Technical Mission. "It is all summed up in the little phrase," he said, "You can't have peacekeeping if you haven't got a peace to keep."[90] US Deputy Permanent Representative Ambassador Alexander F. Watson concurred: "The United Nations cannot perform effectively in a situation where the parties to the conflict are unwilling to create the conditions necessary to enable it to do so. No United Nations monitoring mechanism to supervise a cease-fire can be put into a situation where there is no effective cease-fire. The United Nations cannot deliver humanitarian assistance where an active conflict is underway."[91]

Canada's officials disagreed because they wanted the United Nations to respond effectively to humanitarian crises and believed that a monitored ceasefire that had the respect of the parties would enable the UN to make progress in this area. During an informal discussion with Council members on 17 March, government representatives stressed that the Technical Mission "needs to be given a strong hand to negotiate monitoring of the ceasefire as a first step to ensuring effective humanitarian relief."[92]

Despite the objections of leading Council members, by mid-March the United Nations had to become more deeply involved. According to Ambassador Peter Hohenfellner, Austria's permanent representative to the United Nations, the Technical Mission needed to go to Somalia "to discuss arrangements to stabilize the cease-fire." The agreement, he said, "has not yet been fully respected ... [and this] clearly indicates that further efforts are necessary."[93] The Technical Mission's recommendations would serve as the basis for Boutros-Ghali's report to the Council on how the UN should proceed.[94] The secretary-general noted on 19 March that the Mission would "prepare for monitoring the cease-fire and providing humanitarian assistance in conformity with Security Council resolution 746."[95] This led to the establishment of the United Nations Operation in Somalia I.

Conclusion

The Canadian government welcomed the revival of UN peacekeeping in the late 1980s and early 1990s. With the relaxation of Cold War tensions, decision makers believed that the UN would be able to take a leadership role in maintaining international peace and security. The Mulroney government adopted a new internationalist foreign policy that stressed multinational co-operation and intervention. It wanted to make multilateral institutions as strong and relevant to world conflict as possible because they provided Canada with opportunities for influence and engagement. The chief goal of government policy was to support UN-led activities like peacekeeping in the belief that this would generate confidence in the organization.

Ottawa's priority during the first months of 1992 was to encourage and support UN-led humanitarian action in Somalia. The senior leaders believed that safety concerns should not dissuade the UN from establishing a ground presence. The government had linked its foreign policy with a multilateral humanitarian agenda, and it needed the UN to get involved so that Canada could be seen supporting it. The decision makers' optimism regarding the effectiveness of co-operative military action, which stemmed from the Gulf War and recent peacekeeping achievements, led them to pay less attention to the obstacles in the way of success in Somalia.

The United Nations, of course, could not ignore the operational difficulties. The unconventional situation – particularly the lack of a central government to guarantee order and abide by a peace deal – forced the UN into unfamiliar territory. It had to learn how to deal with faction leaders like Aidid and marry ceasefire monitoring with humanitarian aid protection. The international organization showed its inexperience by deciding to surprise Aidid with its intention to deploy peacekeepers. This was not the best way to approach the situation, for Aidid was a key figure and this sort of move could breed confrontation.

Canada disagreed with the United States, the United Kingdom, and France on peacekeeping in Somalia. The three permanent Council members expressed doubts about the viability of peacekeeping in Somalia. They called for delay in mid-March since there was no stable ceasefire. This was a reasonable argument, but it did not change the fact, recognized by Canada and the secretary-general, that a UN engagement was becoming unavoidable.

2
The Canadian Forces and the Recommendation to Stay out of Somalia

Up to 1990, the National Defence Headquarters had concentrated mostly on the management of scarce defence resources and tended to staff operations in an ad hoc way. The national headquarters did not acquire command experience and a system to staff operational needs rapidly until the Oka crisis (1990) and Persian Gulf War (1990-91). The Canadian Forces Joint Staff, established in July 1990, made National Defence Headquarters an operational headquarters. The Joint Staff was focused on the principle of operations primacy, which meant mission requirements always had precedence over routine headquarters issues. Relying mostly on officers at the colonel/captain (navy) level, the Joint Staff sought to co-ordinate and accelerate priority staffing issues through special joint cells and meetings of the Joint Staff Action Team (JSAT).

Somalia was one of the first crises handled from beginning to end by the Joint Staff. Initial consideration of the UN Somalia operation was left to middle-ranking Joint Staff members. Canada's political leaders were not strongly concerned about the Somali civil war in March to May 1992, and they wanted humanitarian not peacekeeping roles (see Chapter 1). The government's detached approach was a direct reflection of the attitude shown by permanent members of the UN Security Council, many of whom did not want to engage or to make Somalia a priority. The staff work was straightforward and not very time-consuming during this stage, but the Joint Staff's functioning is noteworthy since the same procedures and mechanisms were used later in the year when Somalia became an enormous priority and the requests much more urgent, large, and complex.

The strongest resistance on the Council to peacekeeping in Somalia came from the United States, which as a permanent member could block decisions using its veto power. According to Assistant Secretary of State for African Affairs Herman Cohen, Somalia was "out of luck" because the explosion in peacekeeping operations had drained the US government administratively and financially.[1] The State Department's Bureau of International Organization

Affairs had been overwhelmed by the number of Cold War missions to the Middle East, India-Pakistan, Cyprus, the Golan Heights, and Lebanon and 1990s missions to Iraq-Kuwait, Western Sahara, Angola, El Salvador, Cambodia, and Croatia.

The United States, along with other permanent members of the Security Council, did not want the UN mission in Somalia funded collectively through the assessment process. When a peacekeeping mission was funded by assessment, the cost was spread across the UN membership, but the United States was responsible for the largest share (30 percent of the total in 1992).[2] Congress did not want to finance another operation given its concern over the dramatic rise in costs associated with the activity,[3] including the $1.7 billion, 22,000-person UN Transitional Authority in Cambodia.[4] The United States and Russia objected to a Somalia mission for financial reasons because both were massively in arrears in their peacekeeping dues,[5] and the United Kingdom and the United States did not want Somalia recognized as a threat to international peace and security because then it would fall under the Council's mandate. These countries wanted the Somalia operation paid for voluntarily through appeals as aid initiatives traditionally had been.[6]

Some Africans argued that the Council's reluctance to do more for Somalia was discriminatory. The arms embargo that had been imposed on Somalia in resolution 733 (23 January 1992),[7] did not protect the members from charges of racial bias. Fatun Mohammed Hassan, chargé d'affaires of Somalia's Permanent Mission to the United Nations, wrote in early February that her country was being "neglected by the powerful members of the international community [either] because it had lost its strategic value" now that the Cold War was over, "or because of its being African."[8] Following the creation of the UN Protection Force in the former Yugoslavia and the UN Transitional Authority in Cambodia in late February, African intergovernmental organizations began demanding equal treatment for Somalia. Otherwise, an Organization of African Unity representative informed the Council on 17 March, "Africa will be left with no other impression than that its problems are of limited concern to the international community ... Africa deserves the same qualitative and quantitative attention which has been paid to other regions."[9]

Despite these statements, the Council would only consider a small peace-keeping mission to Somalia. Resolution 746 (17 March) called for a Technical Mission of about twenty military and civilian personnel to visit Mogadishu and prepare operational plans for the protection of aid deliveries in and around the capital and the monitoring of the UN-negotiated ceasefire of 3 March.[10] As noted, Somalia was not a promising environment for peacekeep-ing because of the civil war and lack of government, but the UN hoped it could calm the situation and alleviate suffering. The UN's concern, that Somalia was too insecure, was shared by the National Defence Headquarters

Joint Staff. The Joint Staff had to assess the operation's viability and offer Canadian military and political leaders a recommendation on participation.

In most militaries, the "joint" in joint operations stands for the close operational co-operation of two or more national services. In the case of the single-service Canadian Forces, it referred to the combination of at least two military doctrines.[11] To enable these doctrines and the related forces to work together, joint operating procedures and a Joint Staff were needed. Unfortunately, the Canadian Forces had failed to "integrate the three service doctrines and practices into a tri-service base of fundamental beliefs, values, and collective sense of purpose."[12] Almost no joint training took place, and joint doctrine did not exist and was not envisioned.[13] The development of a joint culture and methodology was impeded by defence commitments that could be addressed by one Environment. The land, maritime, and air force roles in the North American Aerospace Defence Command and North Atlantic Treaty Organisation (NATO) nourished single-service cultures and outlooks.[14] Before the Persian Gulf War, the three Canadian Forces Environments were more comfortable co-operating with their foreign counterparts than acting with each other.[15]

The absence of joint missions impeded development of a joint staff. The three Environments were present in National Defence Headquarters, but there was no joint activity or focus, in the sense of soldiers, sailors, and aircrew working in unison on a single mission or goal.[16] Joint staffing existed in the headquarters only as an idea in a draft mobilization plan called National Defence Headquarters Operations Plan (HQDP 900 for short). HQDP 900 authorized specialists to gather temporarily to manage a specific crisis. It created ad hoc, unified staff networks, only to have them dissolve after deployments or missions.[17] The "matrix" was the permanent and dominant structure in the headquarters.[18] It worked like a pyramid, staffing problems from the wide bottom up. Building consensus, typically through committee, was crucial if an issue were to move up the hierarchy to the decision makers. The national headquarters worked more like a regular government department than a military operations centre. While it reacted to operational pressures when it had to, the matrix was almost exclusively concerned with managing resources and ensuring that the departmental budget was used to buy the right equipment in the right order.[19]

After the Cold War, the Canadian Forces was thrust into a more unpredictable global security environment. The new era was one of "civil wars, ethnic or even tribal conflict, and frontier disputes"[20] that could suddenly emerge as international priorities, often after they had resulted in humanitarian catastrophe. Military leaders soon realized that National Defence Headquarters needed a joint rapid-planning capacity to handle governmental and operational demands. Government leaders wanted to react quickly because of the seriousness and strong media interest in these humanitarian crises and conflicts, and Environmental co-operation was required so that contingents could be deployed to distant locations, be supported in harsh situations, and function across a broad spectrum of operations.[21] Commodore David Cogdon, chief of staff to the J3 (deputy chief of the defence staff) from 1991 to 1993, noted that "there was a recognition that we will be more and more into contingency ops ... [in which] things would come upon us pretty quickly, [and] we would have to be able to react more quickly than the system was capable of doing at that time ... [This] was really the genesis for the joint staff system."[22] Three important and unforeseen operational taskings – in Haiti, in 1988, and in Quebec and the Persian Gulf in 1990 – vividly demonstrated this point.

Operation Bandit, a proposed deployment to Haiti in spring 1988, showed that National Defence Headquarters was incapable of quick responses. The Canadian Forces had been asked to plan the evacuation of Canadians from Haiti, which was experiencing internal turmoil. National Defence Headquarters had no process to enable the Canadian Forces to act quickly, and in the end it produced nothing – nothing workable or doable.[23] Lieutenant-General John de Chastelain, then the assistant deputy minister (Personnel) and senior army officer at National Defence Headquarters, advised the chief of the defence staff, General Paul Manson, that the operation should be cancelled and the plan redrafted.[24]

The Gulf War and the armed standoff near Oka, Quebec (July-September 1990), a small-scale but politically sensitive confrontation between Mohawk Natives and the Canadian Forces, were even more important in terms of the development of the Joint Staff. The weight attached to both by the government required that responsibility for planning and force employment stay with the national headquarters since it was close to the political centre of authority and the source of strategic military advice. Oka "was such a politically charged activity, that it had in certain respects to be run from Ottawa," recalled David Huddleston, then a lieutenant-general and deputy chief of the defence staff. "It did not really cause the Joint Staff to blossom as the Gulf War did, but it started the process, and the one ran into the other."[25] It was obvious that National Defence Headquarters could not cope with the speed at which Oka and the Gulf War were happening and that reform was necessary to prevent the occurrence of another Operation Bandit. The Joint Staff – the Canadian name for the continental European staff system that most Western nations, including the United States, were using or adopting – was seen as the solution.[26] It was created in the national headquarters in July 1990 and improved upon before Somalia in 1992.

The Joint Staff worked as a system within the matrix. Officers took the European staff structure, in which the main military functions were separated and numbered alphanumerically, and overlaid it on top of the matrix structure. The matrix had been divided into six Groups: Personnel, Deputy

Chief of the Defence Staff (Operations) Group, Material, Finance, Policy and Communications, and Defence Information Services. With a "J" designating joint in front, these were retitled as follows: Personnel was J1 Personnel; the Deputy Chief of the Defence Staff Group was J2 Intelligence and J3 Operations; Material became J4 Logistics and J4 Material; Finance was called J4 Financial; Policy and Communications was J5 Policy, J5 Public Affairs, and J5 Legal; and Defence Information Services was J6. J3 Operations, known as the centre or central staff, was the heart of the system. National Defence Headquarters considered its members to be "purple," meaning that their loyalties were no longer to their Environment and its uniform colour – navy blue, sky blue, or green – but to the mission.

The Joint Staff emphasized "operations primacy." This meant that the "focus [of] all staff effort [was on] the aim of the operation."[27] The Deputy Chief of the Defence Staff could shortcut the normal procurement process "to identify priorities for the provision of material and services in support of operations."[28] The mission was given precedence over routine matrix duties. Chief of Staff to the J3 Commodore Bruce Johnston (Cogdon's predecessor) said that under operations primacy "to support a Commander in the field, the Joint Staff will assume that every staffing requirement is urgent unless subsequently proved otherwise."[29] The responsiveness of National Defence Headquarters was also improved by concentrating responsibility for operations on the Joint Staff alone – it handled them all and did nothing else – so that deployed commanders, Environmental Commands, and the functional Groups inside the national headquarters knew where to turn with questions or comments.

Operations primacy recalibrated the influence exercised by the three informal officer networks in National Defence Headquarters. These associations existed at the colonel/navy captain level, and two- and three-star general/admiral ranks. The first network, the Joint Staff Action Team (JSAT),[30] became most important. It was made up of roughly twenty-five colonels who filled important posts in the Groups and who also headed "J" cells. The team members in 1992-93 are shown in Table 1. The JSAT's importance reflected the standing of colonels in the national headquarters: they possessed detailed, current knowledge of their professions, and they had access, because they were senior enough to have the right contacts to their two-star superior.[31]

Either J3 Peacekeeping or J3 Operations would be named the office of primary interest and given responsibility for a new mission. For the UN mission to Somalia, J3 Peacekeeping Colonel Mike Houghton was given the task. The selected cell also served as the Joint Staff contact point for deployed commanders. JSAT meetings took place to "deal with staffing problems at an appropriate rank level to ensure their rapid and co-ordinated conclusion."[32] The JSAT ensured that the matrix staff met the priorities and timelines it

Table 1

Joint Staff Action Team, June 1992-June 1993

Category	Matrix location
J1 Personnel	**Personnel Group**
J1 Co-ordinator	Lieutenant-Colonel L.R. Larsen
J1 Medical	Lieutenant-Colonel Peter Green
J1 Dental	Colonel Peter McQueen
J2 Intelligence	**Deputy Chief of the Defence Staff (Operations) Group**
J2 Operations Co-ordinator	Colonel Vic Ashdown
J2 Security Ops	Colonel Al Wells
J3 Operations	**Deputy Chief of the Defence Staff (Operations) Group**
Chief of Staff J3	Commodore David Cogden
J3 Peacekeeping	Colonel Mike Houghton
J3 Plans	Captain (N) Ken McMillan
J3 Operations	Colonel Mike G. O'Brien
J3 Co-ordinator	Major Terry Melnyk
J3 Arms Control Verification	Colonel Gary George
J3 Training and Chemical/ Biological/Nuclear Warfare	Colonel Art Nielsen
J3 Doctrine	Colonel William (Bill) Morton
J3 Security	Lieutenant-Colonel Peter MacLaren
J3 Engineering	Colonel Merv Lougher-Goodey
J3 Reserves Co-ordinator	Lieutenant-Colonel P.D. (Dave) Montgomery
J3 Organization	Lieutenant-Colonel Lavigne
J3 Air Co-ordinator	Colonel David Jurkowski
J3 Maritime Co-ordinator	No fixed representative in this period
J3 Land Co-ordinator	Unknown
National Defence Operations Centre	Commander John A. Keenliside
J4 Logistics/Material/Financial	**Material and Financial Groups**
J4 Logistics	Colonel Les White
J4 Movements	Colonel William (Bill) Fletcher
J4 Financial Co-ordinator	Colonel Don Ferguson
J5 Policy/Public Affairs/Legal	**Policy and Communications Group**
J5 Policy Operations	Colonel John Bremner
J5 Public Affairs Co-ordinator	Colonel Geoff Haswell
J5 Legal Co-ordinator	Commander William (Bill) Fenrick Lieutenant-Colonel Kim Carter
J6 Communications and Information Systems	**Defence Information Services**
J6 Co-ordinator	Colonel E.M. (Mel) MacLeod

had set. Typically, about thirty-six hours were allowed between the time of identifying a task and the time when it was supposed to be completed, and the centre was to be informed of the result. At the same time, team members kept their superiors informed of what the Joint Staff was doing or proposing. If a two-star had a problem, the colonel responsible had to resolve it within the time limit allowed unless that officer took the matter up directly with the deputy chief of the defence staff.

The one- to three-star officers, in contrast, tended to be marginalized by the speed of the new system. Unless they held key Joint Staff positions like the chief of staff to the J3, brigadier-generals/commodores (one-stars) were generally cut out of the planning process because there was not enough time to consult them. The Battle Staff, the two-star network, was bypassed. Although supposedly a senior advisory body to the chief of the defence staff, there was never time to convene the Battle Staff to discuss Somalia.[33] The three-star/assistant deputy minister network decreased in significance. It was composed of the "Group Principals": the military assistant deputy minister (Personnel), the three-civilian assistant deputy ministers (Finance, Material, and Policy and Communications), and the vice chief of the defence staff.[34] This network was too important to be side-stepped, but the JSAT made most of the urgent decisions and the three-stars were not central to the day's activities.[35]

Under the Joint Staff, capability-based planning replaced the old practice of preparing for North Atlantic Treaty Organisation or North American Aerospace Defense Command commitments that had been fixed beforehand at the political level.[36] Capability planning involved consideration of the "what ifs" of an envisioned scenario or existing crisis. It enabled senior officers and officials to know the options before they were recommended, permitting the decision making on each new contingency to be based on the actual capacity of the Canadian Forces.[37] J3 Plans included the results of this work in a catalogue of possible "force packages." The government could then draw on them either singly or as part of a custom-built contingent when a joint or combined operation was desired.[38] Capability planning was primarily a J3 Plans responsibility, but small missions such as the United Nations Operation in Somalia I were left to the J3 Peacekeeping cell. J3 Plans continuously checked with the Environmental Commands to keep up to date and co-ordinated with other Joint Staff members. Input from J4 Financial and J4 Move was needed to ensure that a plan was affordable and that unit response times were correct, and J1 Personnel would determine whether augmentees were required (and how many, and from where).

Since the Joint Staff's function was co-ordination, it did not do much paperwork besides this crucial national-level planning role. The Joint Staff was "a single high volume artery and vein connecting the organs (Groups) to the brain (senior management). The organs do the staff work. The Joint

Staff co-ordination cell(s) are the interface between the Joint Staff and the Matrix."[39] Breaking out from JSAT meetings where the timings and priorities were established, the Joint Staff worked by passing information and instructions to and from the appropriate matrix staff through the relevant joint cell.[40] The J3 Co-ordination cell was especially important, for it received and distributed all operational correspondence entering and leaving National Defence Headquarters and identified the actions and decisions required based on direction, messages, or discussion emanating from the JSAT.[41] Detailed operations plans for Somalia and other missions were prepared by the matrix, which would work with the Environments to determine the specifics of Canada's military response. Once staffed, the item returned to the Deputy Chief of the Defence Staff (Operations) Group, where it was passed up the reporting chain for decision makers' information or final approval.

Some Groups complied with the new system by developing special mechanisms to accelerate their share of the staff work for an operation. Initially, it was assumed that joint cells would alone handle the co-ordination between the Groups and central Joint Staff. They were supposed to serve as a "fabric or spider's web within National Defence Headquarters," acting "as a horizontal staff action agency in times of crisis."[42] What transpired was that three of the groups developed or strengthened their own "crisis action teams." Each body – the National Defence Operations and Intelligence Centres in the Deputy Chief of the Defence Staff Group, the National Defence Personnel Control Centre in Personnel, and National Defence Logistics Control and Movement Control Centres in Material – was the Joint Staff "engine" in that particular group.

A weakness with the Joint Staff during Somalia was that the three Environmental Commanders of Commands were not based in Ottawa. This meant that they could be left out of the loop when operational decisions were being made. The opportunity for them to provide advice might not be taken or extended.[43] Commanders relied on "Environmental Staff Chiefs" to represent them in National Defence Headquarters. To the matrix, these two-star officers were called the Chief of Land/Air/Maritime Doctrine and Operations; their Joint Staff designations were J3 Maritime/Air/Land. These two-stars were marginalized by the Joint Staff's acceleration of the operational staff work because there was seldom enough time for their advice to be sought. The other point of Environmental input into the new system was at the colonel/navy captain level. Three officers headed, in addition to their matrix roles, special cells that plugged into the JSAT. Called J3 Air/Land/ Maritime Co-ordination, they provided service-specific input to the Joint Staff. However, these officers concentrated on operational-level details and were too low in the military hierarchy to provide the chief of the defence staff with strategic component advice on behalf of their service.

In short, the chief of the defence staff essentially commanded operations that had been planned using one leg (the Joint Staff) instead of two (the

Environments and the Joint Staff.[44] This complicated the national head-quarters staff work. It made vertical and horizontal synchronization more difficult and built a time lag into all Canadian Forces deployments because tight co-ordination had to be maintained with the Environments.[45] But it was not the case, as Charles Oliviero has said, "that the 'Joint Staff' at National Defence Headquarters was neither joint nor a true staff."[46] By the time of the Somalia mission, the Joint Staff was a tri-environment reality that had enabled the headquarters to become an operational organization.[47]

Despite being fully functional, the Joint Staff had not been monitoring events in Somalia until the United Nations started organizing its Technical Mission to Mogadishu in mid-March 1992. Joint Staff involvement usually began when Dr. Kenneth Calder, the assistant deputy minister (Policy and Communications), or Colonel John Bremner, the J5 Policy Operations, learned of a situation that could lead to a Canadian Forces role. But there had been no consideration of assisting UN ceasefire monitoring and famine relief in Somalia. Houghton was surprised when he was ordered to join the Technical Mission, even though he was a logical choice as the head of J3 Peacekeeping. He assumed that the decision to send him had been prompted by a 5 March episode of the Canadian Broadcasting Corporation's *The Journal*.[48] The nationally televised world news program had aired a special report from British Broadcasting Corporation correspondent Michael Burke that described Somalia as a place where there was "no government, no law, no order – just madness, anarchy and death." In the interview that followed with the CBC's Brian Stewart, Burke said he had "never seen such heavily armed anarchy ever. You know, Mogadishu ... is desperate and it's destitute and it's destroyed and people ... people are just living like rats there ... [It is] a test case for international intervention in this new brave post-Cold War world. There is no more desperate case for intervention by the outside world, there's no more treacherous place where the outside world should intervene."[49]

Just thirteen days after this telecast, Houghton was given two days' notice to move – he was ordered to depart, in other words, "on extremely short notice" – to Nairobi, the mission staging area.[50] Canadian Major Ken Klein, who was serving with the UN Disengagement Observer Force in the Golan Heights, was transferred (with Ottawa's concurrence) to serve as Logistics Officer.[51]

Houghton's view that military leaders and the Joint Staff were unconcerned with Somalia, and that therefore the media must have had a role in prompting his tasking, is only partly correct. Within the Joint Staff, for example, there was almost no information available to help Houghton prepare. Among his own seven-member staff, one officer constantly monitored world problems that potentially might involve Canada. Since there had been almost no indication of government interest, Somalia had not been identified as one of the possibilities.[52] Houghton asked for a briefing from the J2 Operations Co-ordination cell. All it could provide was the Burke report, and

Houghton was invited to watch the videotape, which he did. Bremner's cell had not been monitoring Somalia. Two airlifts, one in the late 1980s and the other in the early 1990s, had familiarized his six or seven international policy officers with the Horn of Africa (though Somalia itself was largely unknown), but by necessity the only conflicts they tracked were those that could or did have Canadian Forces involvement. The policy file usually built up quickly. But had Houghton asked for information that day, only basic sources, like a few pages from the United States Central Intelligence Agency *World Factbook* and telegrams from the Canadian High Commission in Nairobi, would have been available.[53]

Houghton knew he would be the mission's chief operations officer, but specific duties remained unclear until he met the mission leader, Robert Gallagher, a retired Canadian lieutenant-colonel and former military representative at Canada's Permanent Mission to the United Nations, on 20 March in London. Only then, to his great surprise, did he learn that he would be expected to write the security plan for the protection of humanitarian aid delivery in and around Mogadishu.[54] The formal channel for information about the mission was to Houghton from External Affairs and J5 Policy. Houghton could have kept himself apprised through a backchannel to Colonel Douglas Fraser, the military representative with the Permanent Mission in New York, had they both known that the UN was actively considering operations in Somalia. Houghton's reaction indicates that the informal and formal processes were not utilized, and the policy and peacekeeping cells had not examined the secretary-general's 11 March report to the Council or resolution 746, which both outlined the technical team's tasks and responsibilities.[55]

Contrary to Houghton's recollection, Canada's role in the UN preparatory mission took place as a result of a normal request from the Department of External Affairs and International Trade Canada. External Affairs received a UN request via the Permanent Mission in New York, which it then discussed with the Department of National Defence. In this case, Michael Brock, the acting director-general of the International Security Bureau, wrote to then Rear-Admiral Larry Murray, the associate assistant deputy minister (Policy and Communications), on 18 March, the day after passage of resolution 746. Brock hoped that National Defence would respond favourably to the UN request for an officer because this would be consistent with the government's recent encouragement of UN efforts and would not be costly. He asked National Defence to accede because Canada "has been among the leaders in encouraging the Secretary-General and indeed the Security Council to play an active role in Somalia." Brock shed light on the government's attitude, in particular its desire to avoid an unwanted peacekeeping commitment, when he added that "our involvement would be without prejudice to any future Canadian commitment."[56]

The Joint Staff interpreted the UN Technical Mission as a sign that Somalia could potentially involve the Canadian military in the future, but it did not prepare for such a role in March to May 1992. The creation of the Technical Mission indicated that the international community was growing increasingly concerned about Somalia. According to the Chief of Staff to the J3 Commodore David Cogdon, Houghton's secondment to the UN mission "certainly gave us an indication that something may come down the road." There was now "a consciousness of Somalia as [having] potential for the future," but the Joint Staff "had no indication at all what it would be or if, in fact, it would involve Canada."[57] A contribution of peacekeepers to Somalia was neither anticipated by Canada nor even discussed at this point. Houghton has noted that peacekeeping was not mentioned and he was not given any instructions related to this activity before he left for Africa.[58]

In April, the United Nations asked Canada for ceasefire observers for its Somalia mission. UN Secretary-General Boutros Boutros-Ghali, in his 21 April report to the Council, recommended that a peacekeeping operation be established in Mogadishu with security and peace observation components.[59] Fifty unarmed military officers were needed to monitor the ceasefire in accordance with the arrangements negotiated by the Technical Mission. Boutros-Ghali called for five hundred armed security personnel to conduct light vehicle patrols and provide UN relief convoys with a muscular escort to deter looters. The UN approached Indonesia and Pakistan for the troops, and it informally asked Canada, Finland, and Austria from the "Western Europe and Others Group" of states to supply the monitors. Each was asked to contribute five observers (the organization needed only one country from this group to agree, but turning to several at once increased the chances of a positive response), and the UN hoped Canada would provide the Chief Military Observer.[60]

Houghton, head of the J3 Peacekeeping cell, did most of the staff work. If the United Nations had requested a battalion (as it did in August), the Joint Staff would have been more broadly and deeply involved. In that case, he would have conferred with Bremner, who would have been getting information about the task from his informal network, and with J3 Plans Captain (navy) Ken McMillan, to get a sense of the Canadian Forces' capabilities.[61] Houghton would have developed an estimate with J3 Plans and prepared a memorandum with other Joint Staff cells for the deputy chief of the defence staff on possible military responses to the UN request. McMillan would be asked to inquire with the Canadian Forces' land, maritime, and air elements to see whether they had the capability, keeping in mind the need to sustain existing operational commitments, to meet the UN's request. The questioning would revolve around generalities such as "Are we capable of providing a logistics unit?" or "Do we have a signals regiment available?"[62] As Houghton testified before the Somalia Inquiry, "What I would be doing is going to

McMillan and saying: 'What is our capability to provide this particular kind of a unit, because it would appear that the United Nations is interested in Canada providing it.'"[63]

But in April, the staff work did not progress far or involve many people because the request – the Chief Military Observer and five observers – was small, and the viability of the UN's Somalia mission was doubted. Houghton's cell received advance notice of the UN requirement through an informal network that originated with Fraser, in New York.[64] The question of whether Canada should agree required close co-ordination between Houghton and Bremner. Houghton also consulted with his immediate superior, Cogdon, the Chief of Staff to the J3, before his recommendation could be passed up to the Canadian Forces decision makers. Colonel Mike O'Brien, the J3 Operations (he had responsibility for all non-peacekeeping missions), generally stayed aware of developments related to the United Nations Operation in Somalia I but had no direct input.[65] Otherwise, the staff work was largely limited to Houghton. His opinion on the advisability of contributing observers was asked for, but he did not brief the JSAT or prepare an estimate on the issue.[66]

Houghton recommended that the Canadian Forces not participate because the UN had chosen to deviate from the operational plan he had written. The way the UN had chosen to proceed seemed too risky considering the lawlessness on the ground. Houghton had called for the deployment of the observers, followed quickly by the security force, and only then the aid. He was not confident that the UN would follow these steps. Houghton worried that aid would be delivered first, ahead of the security battalion and observers, meaning that "the warlords would have control of the humanitarian assistance and the international community would have lost control of the situation before it started."[67] He was proven correct. Even though the troops' arrival was potentially a long way off, Boutros-Ghali deployed the ceasefire monitors and redoubled the relief effort because the nongovernmental organizations (NGOs) wanted to act immediately.[68] Houghton informed Cogdon that UN's Somalia mission was unsafe, and likely would not succeed, because the change in plans called for the unarmed observers to work without protection in a city awash with loosely controlled gunmen.[69]

The UN plan contained significant and questionable assumptions that may not have been clear to National Defence. The secretary-general decided to deploy the observers with the expectation that it "would be the responsibility of the forces of the two sides to ensure their security at all times."[70] Mohamed Farah Aidid and Ali Mahdi Mohamed (the main faction leaders in the capital) promised to do so.[71] In reality, there were so many factions and bandits, and Mogadishu was so chaotic, that no group could reliably make such guarantees. The leading disputants had less power and control over events than they pretended.[72] This would become clear when they failed to deliver on their promises. Boutros-Ghali admitted that the main threat to the UN force "comes from a variety of armed elements – many of which are not under the control of any political authority"[73] but did not clarify how it would cope.

The difficulties experienced by the United Nations when it tried to establish its Somalia mission confirmed Houghton's fears. Council resolution 751 (24 April) created the operation and authorized the deployment of the monitors. It approved the security force only "in principle," to allow time for additional discussion among the permanent members and for negotiations with Aidid, who would not consent to their deployment.[74] Determination to see the mission go ahead in some form from the Africans at the top of the UN hierarchy – Boutros-Ghali (Egypt), James Jonah (Sierra Leone), and Kofi Annan (Ghana) – influenced the decision to deploy observers without security.[75] Negotiations with the leading factions in Mogadishu were required to determine whether the observers would be armed and uniformed and to secure consent for the larger security force. Gallagher's biggest challenge was convincing Aidid that UN forces would only protect relief workers and not prop up Ali Mahdi.[76] The latter welcomed everything the UN proposed, but Aidid did not want troops or uniformed monitors.[77] Aidid did not consent to the deployment of the observers until 21 June, and they did not deploy until late July. As Houghton anticipated, the aid groups became enmeshed in a "protection racket" with the Somali gangs and factions in order to deliver a small amount of food.

The Joint Staff policy branch shared Houghton's concerns about the feasibility of the UN Somalia operation. The policy staff articulated its views in light of the National Defence "criteria" for accepting or rejecting new tasks. Policy officers were responsible for producing the aide-mémoire for Minister of National Defence Marcel Masse on whether the Canadian Forces should engage. They had to consult the rest of the Joint Staff and review the seven "criteria" in the *1987 Defence White Paper*. According to Deputy Minister of National Defence Robert Fowler, these points made more sense in the predictable context of the Cold War. By 1992, the criteria were little more than general guidelines that National Defence staff officers took into account "somewhat" but "not in any particular detail."[78] Colonel Bremner said they "were never intended to be a checklist, a set that if we can't complete these we won't do it, or if we do meet these we will do it; that was not the point. It was to give us something to guide our policy process."[79]

Nevertheless, the United Nations Operation in Somalia I did not qualify under several criteria. The need for a mission to have "a clear and enforceable mandate" was not met since it was not clear that the faction leaders in Mogadishu could control their fighters. The requirement to have a "size and international composition [that was] appropriate to the mandate" was in doubt because Aidid had not consented to the five-hundred-member security force, and in any case the Council had not yet approved it. An equitable financial arrangement, which was another criterion, did not exist. The United States and United Kingdom did not believe, as Canada did, that funding should be provided via the assessment method normally used for peacekeeping.[80] The stipulation that a mission be "likely to serve the cause of peace and lead to a political settlement in the long term" was questionable in this case since Somalia's problems were so pervasive.[81] These shortcomings did not guarantee that Canada would refuse the UN, but because of them the mission looked unpromising. "I recall the policy analysis of this," said Bremner, "we had significant concerns about the viability of sending fifty unarmed observers into a place like Mogadishu."[82]

National Defence would only advise against a new peacekeeping role if it would expose the Canadian Forces to an unacceptable level of danger. Cost was a concern, but if the political will existed to make the deployment happen, then the money would always be found.[83] Safety was a more serious consideration, and the UN mission in Somalia failed to meet the required standard during the period March to May 1992.[84] The government position did not change, even though it was the only country to refuse to assist out of the approximately sixteen informally approached by the United Nations. Pakistan filled the Chief Military Observer position, and monitors were accepted from Finland and Austria, the other two countries in Canada's geographic grouping.[85]

Most important in terms of how the criteria were interpreted was the cautious attitude that prevailed in Ottawa regarding the UN Somalia mission. Government and military decision making was suffused with an atmosphere that helped to prioritize issues.[86] Brian Mulroney led the way and his instinct was to help. On 4 May, Paul Heinbecker, the chief foreign policy adviser in the Prime Minister's Office and assistant secretary to Cabinet for foreign and defence policy in the Privy Council Office, instructed External Affairs to agree to the UN observer request. He would never have intervened without Mulroney's specific request.[87] External Affairs was surprised because it was unaware that the prime minister was taking an interest in this issue. "Although we had previously explained our position," Brock commented, "we explained again that we were not saying 'no' to participating, but rather 'no' to doing so under current arrangements."[88]

Mulroney allowed the External Affairs/National Defence recommendation to stand. One of the prime minister's strengths was his willingness to listen to advice and reverse directives and "decisions" if that advice was convincing, and this was one case where it was. Senior officials probably persuaded him that Canada should not get involved because Mogadishu was so insecure that the operation's prospects seemed dim.[89] Hugh Segal, then Chief of Staff in the Prime Minister's Office, has argued that Mulroney would never ignore a concern like excessive risk to the Canadian Forces,[90] and this was the reason for the Joint Staff recommendation. Yet the prime minister offered Canadian troops to an expanded UN Somalia mission in August, when the security situation had not noticeably improved. Mulroney's unwillingness to push for a role suggests he found the Somalia crisis deeply troubling, but not yet so intolerable as to demand immediate corrective action. In addition, there was almost no media pressure to act, and the credibility of multilateralism was unthreatened since the UN mission had just been created.

The Joint Staff recommendation that Canada not contribute was passed up the Deputy Chief of the Defence Staff Group reporting chain. The Joint Staff settled back into a low level of activity with respect to Somalia. The recommendation was presented to Defence Minister Masse, having been seen by Chief of Staff to the J3 Commodore Cogdon, Deputy Chief of the Defence Staff Vice-Admiral Bob George, General de Chastelain, and Deputy Minister Fowler. A similar recommendation was sent by External Affairs officials to Barbara McDougall, the secretary of state for external affairs. Officials in both departments would have considered it a failure if the ministerial briefs did not agree.[91] This process was complete in May, which was when Calder remembers the first flurry of Somalia-related work having occurred.[92] As noted in *Dishonoured Legacy*, the report of the Somalia Inquiry, afterwards National Defence Headquarters "continued only to monitor the situation."[93]

Conclusion

Three permanent members of the Security Council – the United States, the United Kingdom, and Russia – opposed the deployment of a large peacekeeping mission to Somalia in April because of cost. Somalia's representative at the United Nations and the Organization of African Unity pointed out that the Council had authorized large missions to Cambodia and the former Yugoslavia but was unwilling to do the same for an African country. The Council did not feel pushed to respond to this charge of discrimination. For the United Nations, Somalia was not a priority between March and May 1992.

In Canada, the crisis response was handled by the recently established Joint Staff. Joint planning procedures did not exist, work had just begun on an options catalogue, and the system marginalized the Environmental Commanders. Despite these shortcomings, the Joint Staff was able to successfully muddle through and produce accurate and timely advice that took into account both the operational context and the general view of the government. The effectiveness of the Joint Staff's response is evident from the fact that its advice was accepted as the government's position. Its recent creation did not reduce the effectiveness of the National Defence Headquarters.

During March-May 1992, the Joint Staff was not attentive to Somalia. This was a reflection of the UN's reluctance to engage and its decision to deploy a very small mission (fifty observers, with the security personnel agreed upon by the Council only "in principle"). The UN Somalia mission was consequently not a major concern for the government. Mulroney's first instinct was to help, but officials persuaded him that the mission was too risky. The prime minister was not fully engaged because he did not yet find the crisis unbearable, the peacekeeping mission was just starting, and the credibility of the activity was not being questioned. During this period, Mulroney was not being pressured by domestic media to commit Canada to a role.

The government was concerned about the UN Technical Mission and whether Canada should provide five ceasefire monitors and the Chief Military Observer to the UN operation in Somalia. Houghton remembers no discussion or serious consideration of a peacekeeping role prior to April, when Canada was informally asked to contribute. Bremner and Houghton handled the staff work related to the UN request. After a policy analysis that dealt with force protection issues and whether the UN Somalia mission was a good mission for Canada to join, the Joint Staff recommended that Canada not get involved. External Affairs was interacting and collaborating with National Defence, and it provided similar advice to McDougall.

The Joint Staff's work demonstrates that the government had not been closely following the Somalia crisis and that the possibility of peace observation was not seriously considered in the period between March and May. The Joint Staff's role was to provide decision makers with a recommendation on whether to engage. The UN mission did not appear viable to the military, which was, in part, a reflection of the fact that the international community had not made Somalia a high priority. As long as this attitude prevailed, the prime minister was likely to think that the crisis was not Canada's crisis.

3

"Do Something Significant": Government Reconsideration of the Somalia Crisis

In August 1992, Brian Mulroney committed Canada to the United Nations Operation in Somalia I. He was being pressured to make this decision because he had engaged aggressively in Yugoslavia in 1992 and had reached out to Balkan refugees later that year but had not moved to assist Somalia. UN Secretary-General Boutros Boutros-Ghali, the *New York Times*, and Canadian newspapers argued that Somalia was being neglected while Yugoslavia received considerable attention from peacekeepers and diplomatic peace-makers. The difference, it was true, was stark: in July 1992 there were 13,600 combat-capable blue helmets deployed with the UN Protection Force in Bosnia-Herzegovina and Croatia, while the Somalia mission had only fifty unarmed observers.[1] The heightened media coverage and the UN plan to expand the Somalia operation demonstrated that the Somalia crisis was becoming an international priority, and in this light the government decided it should contribute to the UN-led airlift and the mission to deflect sugges-tions of Eurocentric bias away from itself and the practice of peacekeeping. Senior officials supported the United Nations because a strong and effective multilateralism would provide Canada with the means to achieve its inter-national ends, and they shared the UN's determination to press forward with humanitarian efforts.

The prime minister was the principal driver behind Canada's decision to commit itself to the Somalia mission. It has been argued that peacekeeping's popularity in Canada made it impossible for Mulroney to resist a policy of energetic participation,[2] but what this overlooks is that he decided how active this engagement would be. Mulroney had spent over seven years in power by 1992, and according to Hugh Segal, his chief of staff, the prime minister was "prepared to push the envelope, to make sure we did what we should."[3] Mulroney's actions support this characterization. Despite fiscal constraints, Mulroney made 1,200-1,300-person commitments to Croatia, Bosnia, and Somalia in 1992. His pragmatic side was revealed by the 25 February federal budget, which called for the withdrawal of all Canadian Forces members stationed in Europe with the North Atlantic Treaty Organisation and the 11 December announcement to end what would be a twenty-nine-year commitment to the UN Peacekeeping Force in Cyprus in mid-1993.[4] Both decisions freed forces for use elsewhere. His view was that Canada had a responsibility and an interest in constructively engaging with world problems, despite the government's deficit reduction concerns.

Mulroney's conduct of Canadian foreign policy was facilitated by the decision-making structure he established. Instead of a collegial or bureaucratized system, he preferred a centralized "process-empty bilateralism," which diminished the relevance to decision making of the public service and the unwieldy full Cabinet (it grew to forty ministers, the largest among Western democracies).[5] Mulroney's family was extremely close, and one of the few people he could implicitly trust when mulling a decision was his wife Mila. She came from Yugoslavia and was familiar with the tensions there, and her strongly held views on the role of women and human rights internationally carried considerable weight with him.[6] Mulroney also relied on the telephone and a worldwide network of contacts that included state leaders (many known on a first-name basis), generals, ambassadors, advisers, journalists, and regular Canadians.[7] He used the calls to obtain advice, get the view of the person on the street, and talk out his own decisions before and after making them. Lead ministers would always be contacted and involved when important decisions had to be made. His personal bilateralism was facilitated by communication improvements and indicative of the concentration of power in the federal government. Power once wielded by line ministers and departments had moved to the government "centre," and within the centre power had shifted to the prime minister, key ministers, and a few political and public service advisers from central agencies and away from Cabinet and Cabinet committees.[8]

Initially there may have been a political motive behind this personalization of decision making. The public service managers whose influence Mulroney diminished were Liberal appointees in almost every case. Early in his government's tenure, some Progressive Conservatives in the Prime Minister's Office suspected that these officials remained loyal to the Liberal style of governing and distrusted them.[9] Mulroney might have obtained more independent advice by working around the public service during those years, but his relationship with senior mandarins improved considerably after a period of familiarization.[10] It is noteworthy that Derek Burney, a career public servant, became his chief of staff in 1987. The prime minister's habit of forming confidences outside government circles continued, however, and left him vulnerable to betrayal and embarrassment years after leaving office.[11] Mulroney's evolving partnership with the public service notwithstanding, decision making on Somalia was centralized and instituted from the top down. Clerk of the Privy Council Glen Shortliffe stressed that the "leadership on this at the end of the day was very much in the hands of the Prime Minister. It was the Prime Minister's views that prevailed in terms of what we did."[12]

Shortliffe supported Mulroney by convening regular ad hoc meetings of senior officials to discuss options and share information. For Somalia, the usual participants (the "/" indicates a change in office holder in summer 1992) were: Reid Morden, Jeremy Kinsman/Gäetan Lavertu and Mark Moher from External Affairs and International Trade Canada; General John de Chastelain, Robert Fowler, Dr. Kenneth Calder and Rear-Admiral Larry Murray from the Department of National Defence; and Paul Tellier/Glen Shortliffe and Paul Heinbecker/Jim Judd from the Privy Council Office.[13] Depending on the issue, the Department of Employment and Immigration and Canadian International Development Agency would be invited. After a meeting, Shortliffe would be in a position to brief Mulroney on where the government stood on Somalia. The Privy Council Office's purpose was to guarantee that the prime minister's decisions were based on the highest-quality information.[14]

For the first half of 1992, however, there was little for the prime minister to decide upon because the UN Security Council was not paying attention to Somalia. In July, Boutros-Ghali observed that if the "Council continues to concentrate its attention and resources to such an extent on Yugoslav problems, this will be at the expense of the Organization's ability to help resolve equally cruel and dangerous conflicts elsewhere, e.g. in Somalia."[15] Like the Council, Ottawa's energy was focused on the civil war in the former Yugoslavia. Canada's permanent representative to the United Nations at the time, Louise Fréchette, said this was because the Balkans seemed to be in constant crisis, whereas Somalia was much quieter.[16] Senior officials believed Somalia was "totally secondary, totally minor" compared with Yugoslavia, said Jeremy Kinsman, the assistant deputy minister (Political and International Security). Somalia involved "a totally different and less comprehensive operation, and at a much lower level of priority in terms of interests and profile and everything else."[17]

External Affairs was highly critical of the Somalia operation's weak financial foundation and the lack of protection for the observers, and it agreed with National Defence that Canada should not participate. The Canadian Forces had deployed to risky situations before (most recently on 6 April, when it moved into United Nations Sector West in Croatia), but the planned deployment of the observers without security caused External Affairs to have "great difficulty with the totality of the Somalia package."[18] Clerk of the Privy Council Paul Tellier (Shortliffe's predecessor) noted that it was extremely unfortunate that financing issues had contributed to the security battalion's delay. In a memorandum to the prime minister, Tellier wrote that the battalion would have made the mission safer and alleviated its logical and medical shortfalls.[19]

Secretary of State for External Affairs Barbara McDougall was actively involved in these policy discussions and aware that something had to be done about Somalia given the political climate. On 6 May (the same day as Heinbecker's intervention; see Chapter 2), she informed Michael Brock, the acting director-general of the International Security Bureau in External Affairs, that "it is difficult to avoid politically the issue of our being in Yugoslavia and hanging back in Somalia." McDougall urged her Department to stress to Boutros-Ghali and the Canadian public that the government hesitated only because the risks were too great. She said the message should be that "we *are* committed to go but *cannot* without security."[20] Government leaders worried that their handling of Somalia might be perceived or represented as official disinterest, and the media would intensify this concern in the months that followed.

Although Ottawa decided not to engage, the prime minister made the occasional attempt to bolster the UN-led multilateral humanitarian effort by encouraging states to throw their support behind the Somalia mission. Mulroney publicly highlighted Somalia's plight and indirectly criticized the powers that he thought were holding up the UN operation. At the International Conference of Young Leaders in Montreal on 24 May, the prime minister expressed disgust at how "in Somalia, marauding gangs are shooting their country back into the stone age," and he called attention to the UN's "struggles to enlist the political will of member countries and their resources to end the suffering there."[21]

The bureaucracy shared his commitment to multilateralism. For Morden, the undersecretary of state for External Affairs (the deputy minister), the situation in Mogadishu was clearly unlike traditional peacekeeping in which disputants normally agree to stop fighting. However, the bottom line was that the UN was playing a role in Somalia and Canada wanted to assist.[22] Another top External Affairs official at the time believed that the Pearsonian tradition of being helpful was a Canadian foreign policy axis and that Canada served its interests when it made responsible contributions to the protection of peace and security and the alleviation of massive humanitarian suffering.[23] A former high-ranking National Defence bureaucrat recalled that almost no one in the public service resisted helping Somalia.[24]

The government's latent peacekeeping desires flared up because of events in the Balkans in June. A daring new mission to Sarajevo, Bosnia's besieged capital, added lustre to peacekeeping. A Canadian Forces battlegroup stationed in Croatia was ordered to cross through the Bosnian war zone and enter United Nations Sector Sarajevo, which was under the command of Canadian Major-General Lewis MacKenzie. They opened the airport to vital humanitarian traffic in July. According to senior officials like Kinsman, this was "a little moment ... where it seemed that United Nations peacekeeping was having some effect and might be pertinent." Somalia "had as its backdrop the challenge to the United Nations in the Balkans. Those two things were somehow psychologically connected for some people."[25] Blue helmets appeared to be making a difference, but this was not all that energized the government. A Somalia role would address media complaints over the UN's neglect of Somalia and, as McDougall observed, balance government actions in the former Yugoslavia.

The excited and expectant atmosphere made it easier for the media to politicize Somalia and partially account for the July-August decision to engage. Several studies have observed that the impact of print and television journalism on decision makers, while difficult to measure precisely, is strongest when government policy is uncertain and that, when the opposite is true, this influence decreases.[26] The media had a "push" effect on the government's Somalia decision making. Mulroney was so concerned with what the press was saying about him that engaging the media became the priority. He monitored the coverage his ministry garnered extremely closely and was acutely sensitive to criticism, which he found painful, frustrating, and worrisome.[27] When the government committed to the peacekeeping operation, it was responding to the evening newscasts that featured the suffering of the Somali people and the challenges facing the United Nations.[28] Once a growing domestic constituency was demanding involvement, decision makers recognized the need to be seen as responsive to the now-public crisis.[29]

Somalia was a "black hole" with which Canada had no ties,[30] but the media drew attention in Canada and the West in general to its myriad problems. Journalists were "one of Somalia's most powerful allies" and "an invaluable facet of the humanitarian relief effort."[31] Television transmitted the most vivid and shocking images. And yet it was concerned chiefly with the effects of starvation. Western publics were largely ignorant of Somalia. Moralistic narratives that personified and sentimentalized pain and hardship were the only way foreign correspondents could connect with viewers.[32] The Somali famine and civil war troubled Canadians and made them want to help, but this was a shallow and cathartic interest.

The media depoliticized and de-emphasized the causes and context of the crisis. The local political dynamics, the goals of the fighters, and the preconditions for a sustainable peace became less significant because coverage revolved around individual victims and the victimizing factions.[33] Canadians saw quiet and resigned faces of suffering, like those described by the Canadian Broadcasting Corporation's Gillian Findlay: "Children grow weaker. Old people seem to wither away."[34] They heard of people "dropping like flies" and of a "living hell" where Somalis were "praying for food."[35] Crises could become interchangeable when viewed through this fuzzy humanitarian lens. In January 1993, for example, a Canadian television network broadcast pictures of what it thought was Somalia, only to admit the next day that they were from Mozambique.[36] This moral and pitying gaze was not the foundation upon which a domestic political constituency could be built for long-term and expensive UN diplomatic peacemaking and peace building, even though such roles were vital for lasting stability. The government's humanitarian engagement made it seem as though Canada was doing something, but its declining official development assistance budget revealed how detached it was from peripheral nations like Somalia.[37]

The news stories tended to be from wire services like Reuters, since the danger and difficulty of access led most journalists to avoid the country.[38] During late summer, no reporters were resident in Mogadishu, and Canadian Rick Grant received no inquiries from Canadian journalists while working as the principal spokesperson for CARE USA (the group's country co-ordinator for Somalia and one of the few NGOs then in Somalia).[39] What coverage there was on television and in newspapers increased public anxiety. CARE Canada raised about $1 million for Somalia relief during the summer.[40] Shortliffe informed the prime minister in mid-August that the humanitarian situation was deteriorating dramatically and press attention and public interest were growing daily.[41]

Media interest in the Somalia crisis grew because of its proximity to Ethiopia, which had experienced famine in 1984-85. The simultaneous occurrence of many disasters can result in an emergency being crowded out of the news, but when the mass famine in Somalia became severe, it had been years since Western publics had heard of this type of human drama in that part of the world, and this helped make Somalia a compelling story.[42] Journalists comparing the crises were struck by the fact that while the Somalia famine was more severe than Ethiopia's in absolute and proportional terms, no effective assistance effort was in place for the former. A million had perished in Ethiopia (out of a population of forty million), whereas in Somalia one-third of the people (estimated at 6.5 million) were at risk of death.[43] The *New York Times* wrote that "unlike the Ethiopian famine," which "also occurred during a civil war, there have been no Live Aid concerts, no chorus of pop stars singing 'We Are the World.'"[44] Médecins sans Frontières nurse Brigitte Doppler said Somalia "was worse than Ethiopia. There it was mostly confined to one region. Here it is the whole country ... We are losing an entire generation of children here."[45] Geoff Loane, the country co-ordinator for the International Committee of the Red Cross in Somalia, said, "Here is Hell ... I thought I would never see Ethiopia again, and I didn't think we would allow it to happen again."[46]

Canada had remained a leading food aid donor to Ethiopia.[47] It had contributed about $500 million to Ethiopia up to August 1992, but that year sent only $22.8 million to Somalia.[48] The government wanted to avoid the suggestion that the next Ethiopia was being ignored so soon after the multinational coalition's triumph in the Persian Gulf War (1990-91) in pursuit of a strategic end (Kuwaiti oil). "There was a sense," said Jim Judd, then the assistant secretary to Cabinet for foreign and defence policy, "that if it could be done for that kind of a reason, why couldn't something smaller be done for an issue that was even more desperate in terms of its impact on the human beings involved." Live Aid had been created by a NGO/private citizen movement (spearheaded by Bob Geldof), and there "was a non-strategic humanitarian kind of imperative that had to be played out to address this kind of tragedy."[49]

The media called attention to what Canada and the United Nations were doing in the Balkans and not doing in the Horn of Africa. By July, Canadian newspapers were publishing public-opinion-influencing editorials that were critical of the government. The *Montreal Gazette* argued on 22 July that the UN should stop ignoring Somalia. Referring to the Sarajevo airport reopening and the thousands of blue helmets in Croatia and Bosnia, the newspaper said "Lord knows, Yugoslavia needs the world's help. But so, urgently, does Somalia."[50] The *Globe and Mail* contrasted Canada's decisive action on Sarajevo and the Council's support of the UN Protection Force with the neglect of Somalia. "A Sarajevo-style relief operation," it urged, "would seem the obvious way to help. Indeed it is just the sort of operation that the new, more assertive United Nations should be undertaking."[51] Passivity regarding Somalia was casting multilateralism and the Mulroney government in a bad light. McDougall alluded to the press's impact when she commented that the "world to some extent was driven into Somalia because of the media coverage. At the same time, starvation in the Sudan has been virtually ignored."[52]

Domestically, the issue of the military response to the crisis was connected with criticism of the government's handling of the Somali refugee situation. In July 1992, Ottawa announced special immigration measures to admit 25,000 refugees from the Yugoslav civil war. Discrimination immediately became an issue as Somali refugees began demanding streamlined family unification and immigration procedures. Somalis were concentrated in four suburban cities of Metro Toronto (Etobicoke, North York, Scarborough, and York), where 30,000 resided. From 1989 to September 1993, 14,903 Somalis had claimed asylum in Canada and an additional 6,157 claimants were waiting overseas.[53] Immigration and family reunification was a laboured process because the collapse of the Somali state and mass population displacement made it difficult to locate people and, since documents were outdated or nonexistent, to determine country of origin and familial ties. Immigration policy was also tempered by the government's belief that third-country resettlement could only be a solution for a small number of Somalis.[54] Despite this, the *Toronto Star* stressed on 27 July that Ottawa's Yugoslav initiative was "an example worth remembering when victims of a similarly brutal conflict in Somalia plead their cases for refugee status."[55]

Family reunification was another aspect of Ottawa's detached approach. The government was not helped when, in early August, Employment and Immigration Minister Bernard Valcourt said that "you have to first get the people to want to come. I mean these are nomadic people ... they just don't want to go, they just don't want to leave."[56] This made the government seem unsympathetic, and Valcourt was promptly denounced. The *Toronto Star* editors urged the minister to apologize, and Mohamed Farah of the Somali Islamic Society of Canada wrote to the editor that Valcourt was far off the mark.[57] On 3 August, just days after the Yugoslav refugee announcement, 250 Somalis held a rally on Parliament Hill to publicize their demand for equal treatment. They made emotional appeals, as evidenced by the *Ottawa Citizen* photograph of four-year-old Abdiziz Moalim, who carried a sign during the protest that read *"Please*/Let My Mom Join Me ... Please."[58] Editorial boards believed that the government needed to do more to show it cared. The *Toronto Star*, for example, called for a special reunification program and immigration permits.[59] The national (Somali immigration) and international (peacekeeping/airlift) aspects of this domestic political issue were addressed in late August. The government announced on 21 August that Employment and Immigration officials would present streamlined visa processing plans to Somali-Canadian community leaders in Toronto and that the Canadian Forces would join a UN-led humanitarian airlift.[60]

When, on 23 July, Boutros-Ghali rejected a plan to have the UN Protection Force consolidate artillery in Bosnia under international control because he felt it was beyond the UN's resources, the tension within the organization regarding the reluctance to engage in Somalia erupted. The secretary-general accused the Council of a willingness to spend on "the rich man's war" in Yugoslavia but not on African crises, and he made the pithy comment that the victims from the former looked well fed.[61] On 31 December, he again implied that the Balkans was receiving extra attention. Boutros-Ghali told journalists enduring the Sarajevo siege that "you have a situation which is better than ten other places all over the world. I can give you a list of ten places where you have more problems than in Sarajevo."[62]

The first statement may have influenced Mulroney's decision making. The prime minister believed he had done more for the United Nations than most leaders and resented the secretary-general's July comment. It was never mentioned publicly as a reason to engage in Somalia, but after the outburst Mulroney became much more positive and determined to see Canadian involvement.[63]

The UN's expansion of its Somalia mission, which Boutros-Ghali had called for in his 22 July report to the Council, was more substantive to the government's decision making. The UN had only fifty military observers (the last arrived on the 23rd) and civilians in Mogadishu. Ambassador Mohamed Sahnoun, the special representative of the secretary-general (the head of the mission) was still trying to get Aidid's consent so that the five hundred security troops could deploy. The financing question had not been settled.[64] The UN plan, approved by Council resolution 767 (27 July),[65] was to reduce susceptibility to the lawlessness in the capital and open more access points to rural areas by decentralizing the operation.[66]

The planned expansion of the mission and a multinational airlift into southern Somalia presented the government with fresh options. Mulroney decided that Canada would participate in late July, well before the United Nations informally requested Canadian assets, but the existence of the airlift and peacekeeping plans was important to the context because he never made unsolicited offers.[67] On the 28th, the Privy Council Office asked Chief of the Defence Staff General John de Chastelain to determine if "something significant" could be done relatively quickly to help the United Nations in Somalia.[68] Prime Minister Mulroney did not know what was militarily possible, and he had to rely on de Chastelain's advice. De Chastelain instructed the National Defence Headquarters Joint Staff to do a capability check to determine what Canada could do, at what cost, and for how long (see Chapter 4). Government decision makers believed that multilateralism allowed Canada to differentiate itself from the United States and play a larger world role than it otherwise could. Mulroney acted because he "had a very strong view that Canada is a minor player, of no great compelling consequence, unless its leadership decides to increase its importance by having it involved in the shaping of coalitions and linkages."[69]

The government feared that continued inactivity would negatively affect perceptions of the United Nations. This could diminish the usefulness of Canadian internationalism's most prominent instrument. McDougall and National Defence Minister Marcel Masse wrote a joint memorandum to the prime minister stating that the crisis could be pivotal for the organization. Canada had tried to prepare the United Nations for such situations, they argued, and success in the Horn of Africa could cement support for it. On the other hand, an inadequate reaction, especially if compared with the UN's heavy involvement in the former Yugoslavia, might paralyze the UN and cripple post-Cold War consensus.[70]

Decision makers were most interested in roles involving the protection and escort of relief supplies because Canada had no specific interest in Somalia other than to see multilateralism strengthened and the recourse to multilateral instruments reinforced. As Jeremy Kinsman noted, "we were not intervening to make peace per se, or to work out any particular political solution for the country ... the impulse was humanitarian and the credibility of the United Nations, [and] getting the assistance through."[71] Mulroney informed Boutros-Ghali that humanitarian roles were desired in a 13 August letter. Canada would "provide the use of a military transport aircraft urgently for delivery of humanitarian relief in Somalia." The prime minister supported "proposals for deployment of a larger security force to ensure delivery of humanitarian aid" and said that Canada was "prepared to participate in an operation approved by the Council, in a security or other role."[72]

The first proposal initiated was the contribution of three Canadian Forces Hercules transport aircraft to the UN Children's Fund/World Food Programme airlift being operated from Mombasa and the International Committee of the Red Cross airlift based in Nairobi, Kenya. Shortliffe informed the prime minister on 18 August that a National Defence advance team would visit the Nairobi operating base and the International Committee of the Red Cross headquarters in Geneva later that week to finalize planning for the relief flights.[73] The airlift enabled the government to answer the United Nations quickly and publicly. As the Canadian High Commission in Nairobi noted, this response would catch "the full glare of the global spotlight," since Nairobi was the principal media hub for East Africa.[74] On 21 August, Mulroney made the airlift contribution public, and in doing so he "underlined Canada's support of United Nations efforts to initiate comprehensive security and humanitarian operations throughout Somalia."[75]

When the UN request for peacekeepers was received in late August, the government's answer was a foregone conclusion. The Clerk of the Privy Council convened a meeting of senior officials from National Defence, External Affairs, and the Canadian International Development Agency to discuss Somalia on 17 August. He told the prime minister the next day that the military could respond to all anticipated requirements – whether it be for infantry, engineering, logistics, or medical personnel – and that the "chances are high that Canada will be called upon to participate in this effort."[76] This comment related to the usual bargaining process between the UN and troop-contributing countries. The UN would never formally request assets without being sure that the country in question would agree. Shortliffe was referring to the fact that this dialogue was nearly finished. There had already been discussions "in principle" with Mulroney regarding whether Canada would join the Somalia operation if asked, and the answer had been "yes."[77] On 25 August, the government received the UN informal written request for a 750-person battalion. The northeast zone, centred on the port town of Boosaaso, was the proposed area of operations (see map on p. 10). It was "the most difficult" task.[78] The urgent nature of the crisis caused the United Nations to formalize the request on the 31st, even before Ottawa could agree.[79]

Canada committed itself to the UN peacekeeping mission in Somalia in August, even though financing remained a problem. In late July, the United States continued to resist applying assessment-based funding procedures to the operation, and resolution 767 (approved on the 27th) was almost profoundly altered. The qualifying phrase "in principle" had weakened the operation's founding resolution the previous April, and Washington insisted it be used in the draft resolution 767. It was removed from the final version, but for Ottawa, which was on the verge of engagement, this was a troubling indication of the United States' state of mind.[80]

Decision makers worried that the US attitude, particularly as it related to the financing of the peacekeeping mission, could weaken the collective foundation of multilateral peacekeeping. The government did not want the operation to repeat and entrench the Cyprus precedent that saw contributing nations pay the costs of their contingents.[81] It considered promising troops, even if an assessment-based funding arrangement was lacking, to "shake the Security Council to its senses in this regard."[82] Mulroney used his relationship with US president George H.W. Bush and British prime minister John Major in an attempt to change their minds over funding for peacekeeping in Somalia. He wrote to Bush and Major, saying "that such a major humanitarian disaster calls for a response by the entire world community and warrants being managed and financed accordingly." He argued that although the "cost of a military effort in Somalia will be high, I would hope that possible differences of views concerning the means and sources of funding the United Nations operation can be rapidly reconciled and that the effort to save lives can be accelerated."[83]

Along with domestic US factors, Mulroney's personal diplomacy may have led the Bush administration to relent on the funding issue. At the same time as the letters, Senator Nancy Kassebaum (Republican-Kansas) was discrediting the State Department argument that Congress did not want to pay for another UN mission.[84] After a mid-July visit to Somalia, she said on the *MacNeil-Lehrer NewsHour* that UN security forces were urgently needed and the United States, as a former ally of Somalia, was morally obligated to help. The United States "need[s] to make a larger commitment and to provide a push ... towards ... stepping forward and saying more has to be done and should be done soon."[85]

Bush was considering stronger action, but parts of the US government remained opposed. On 27 July, the administration issued a statement supporting the deployment of security forces; on 14 August, Bush announced a US airlift of food into Somalia.[86] The White House and political divisions of the Pentagon and State Department resisted US involvement because the 1992 election was being fought on domestic issues, and they wanted to protect the president from risky overseas commitments.[87] The prime minister may have helped weaken this opposition. Mulroney had influence with Bush because of their close relationship, and this made it more likely that the president would pay attention to a Canadian issue like peacekeeping financing.[88] Perhaps as a result, when the Council expanded the mission it supported Boutros-Ghali's recommendation that the UN Somalia mission be "considered an expense of the Organization" and that "the assessments to be levied on Member States be credited to the UNOSOM Special Account."[89]

Conclusion

Canada considered supporting peacekeeping in Somalia in April, but it lacked sufficient motivation to do so. The deployment of an inadequate mission (only fifty unarmed observers) showed that the international community was not seized by the Somalia crisis. Not only did the size of the UN Somalia mission mean that there were no opportunities for Canada to play a distinctive role, but it agreed with the powers on the Council that the former Yugoslavia's civil war was more important. Although the government believed that Canada had a responsibility and an interest in strengthening multilateral actions designed to foster peace, it appeared that the Somalia operation would expose the observers to excessive risk and, as a result, decision makers elected not to peacekeep.

The Somalia crisis was neglected until July because Western governments did not see it as a priority. Boutros-Ghali's outburst regarding the amount of attention paid by the Council to Yugoslavia was important because it put the international spotlight on the West's unbalanced approach. The media did the same when they picked up the Somalia story in mid-1992 and contrasted the UN mission in Somalia with the large and robust mission in the former Yugoslavia. The Western media were indispensable in attracting world attention to the civil war and disorder in Somalia, but journalists also tended to depoliticize the crisis and sentimentalize victims in order to make emotional connections with their audiences. This helped ensure that the interest in Somalia did not expand beyond a visceral desire to relieve suffering.

Somalia became a significant issue for the government in late July because the media began to highlight the severity of the crisis and the inadequacy of the UN's activities. Media comparisons of the former Yugoslavia and Somalia efforts troubled government leaders not only because they were interested in maintaining confidence in multilateralism but also because Canada was a prominent participant in the UN Protection Force and had announced special immigration arrangements in July for 25,000 Balkan refugees.

In August, the government accelerated the Somali family reunification and immigration process and contributed to the UN airlift and expanded Somalia peacekeeping mission. This was partly because the international community had assigned a higher priority to the Somalia crisis. In addition, the government was interested in the revised Somalia operation because it appeared credible and it offered Canada opportunities to play a noteworthy role.

The prime minister's main job was to make the decision to engage and to strengthen the multilateral effort by calling for the Somalia peacekeeping mission to be funded collectively by assessment. Mulroney believed in multilateralism because he thought it was a way for Canada to help foster peace and security. He supported the expanded UN operation by offering forces to the UN for Somalia duty even before Boutros-Ghali requested them. The prime minister also wanted assessment-based financing to apply to humanitarian peacekeeping missions like Somalia because this would be an unmistakable sign that this type of operation reflected the will of the international community. He called on states to financially support the UN's efforts in Somalia, and he urged George H.W. Bush and John Major to allow the Somalia operation to be funded collectively.

4
The Humanitarian Airlift Takes Flight

By the late summer of 1992, the United States Cable News Network had brought Somalia's agony sharply into focus for the Department of National Defence.[1] Deputy Minister Robert Fowler later recalled that "something like 300,000 Somalis had been slaughtered in what had become total anarchy." The "people of Somalia were caught in the middle and their suffering was terrible." For Canadian decision makers, the "overarching issue in Somalia was that 1 to 3,000 people were dying a day and it was going to get worse."[2] In response, the United Nations had expanded the United Nations Operation in Somalia I and its airlift. Prime Minister Brian Mulroney wanted to help the United Nations adapt its multilateral tools and procedures to the complex and unfamiliar situation in Somalia. His government contributed to the Somalia peacekeeping mission and airlift because it was concerned for the United Nations, which was being criticized by the media over its ineffectiveness in Somalia. Neither Ottawa nor the United Nations fully appreciated the difficulty that traditional peacekeeping and an airlift would encounter in Somalia. Since the airlift was mounted relatively quickly, this fact was first revealed during the aerial relief efforts in fall 1992.

Like the airlift, the peacekeeping effort, except for its humanitarian mandate, was a traditional operation. The mission was created with well-worn peacekeeping principles in mind: it had to behave nonviolently, be impartial, and not act without the consent of the disputants, regional states, and the major powers on the UN Security Council. In terms of political functions, the operation was to encourage reconciliation and stabilize the ceasefire in Mogadishu. Like most Cold War UN peacekeeping missions, it was overwhelmingly military in composition: Council resolution 751 (24 April 1992) authorized fifty unarmed ceasefire observers, five hundred security troops (delayed, but anticipated), and seventy-nine civilians.[3] The number and roles of nonmilitary peacekeepers multiplied in the early 1990s,[4] but the Somalia mission was not an example of this. Its civilian complement was kept busy by headquarters administration and political functions.

The Somalia mission had to behave in a nonviolent and nonthreatening manner. The avoidance of force except in self-defence had been a basic principle of peacekeeping since the UN Emergency Force I (1956-67), the UN's first large-scale interpositional mission. This tenet was modified for UN Emergency Force II (1973-79) to allow the operation to respond aggressively against those blocking the implementation of its mandate. The revised guidelines shaped all subsequent missions, including Cold War internal operations like the UN Interim Force in Lebanon (1978-present), which had been advised that the "use of armed force is authorised only (a) in self-defence; or (b) in resisting attempts by forceful means to prevent UNIFIL from discharging its duties."[5] The advisability of adopting a firm position was never clear. While passivity could undermine a mission's credibility, presentation of a bold front could lead to a violent encounter.[6]

The Somalia operation was faced with the same sort of dilemma. The mission's numerical inferiority and the pervasive disorder in Mogadishu made it impractical to threaten or use force to safeguard nongovernmental organization (NGO) aid deliveries, even though it was mandated to provide such protection.[7] The Somalia operation was in the middle of an internal conflict in which no government existed to impose order and where factional fighters and unorganized and unaffiliated gangs vastly outnumbered and outgunned the mission. Many gunmen chewed khat leaves, a narcotic that suppressed hunger but also heightened paranoia and aggressiveness. Those who rode in Jeeps or pick-up trucks equipped with heavy machine guns or rockets acquired the nickname "technicals" because the UN was forced to hire some of them as guards, and the item of expenditure used to account for their salaries was called "technical services."[8] In this tense and lawless environment, an attempt by the Somalia mission to escort aid forcibly as mandated by resolution 751 could easily have produced disaster. Canadian Forces Colonel Jim Cox, the deputy force commander of the UN operation as of early October, wrote that if "United Nations soldiers have to fight anyone to protect relief supplies, all United Nations personnel are put at risk that same moment. The sub-clan of looters who may have been thwarted by the force from looting food will strike against the United Nations at another time and place. It will be guerrilla warfare. The United Nations agencies and non-governmental organizations will have to withdraw and the entire relief program will collapse."[9]

Avoiding the use of force suited the UN approach to peacekeeping in Somalia. When Force Commander Brigadier-General Imtiaz Shaheen of Pakistan received the UN Interim Force in Lebanon rules regarding force to guide him in Somalia, his attention was drawn to the "overriding principle": that "force can only be used by a United Nations operation as a last resort and when all peaceful means have failed."[10] The phrase "weapons to be used in self-defence only" was put in a special box on the informal written request for a 750-person infantry battalion that the United Nations sent to Canada on 25 August.[11]

The Somalia mission departed from the precepts of traditional peacekeeping in the significance of its humanitarian assistance mandate. Cold War missions had not been established to perform compassionate acts, though they happened anyway. The UN Peacekeeping Force in Cyprus (1964 to the present) had shown that initiatives could be performed as long as they did not lead to political complications or charges of favouritism.[12] The UN Interim Force in Lebanon, which could not carry out its mandate,[13] instead "used its best efforts to limit the conflict and to shield the inhabitants of the area from the worst effects of the violence."[14] The Somalia mission was more innovative. It linked "the modalities of a cease-fire to the implementation of humanitarian relief operations."[15] For the first time in UN peacekeeping history, the protection of relief supplies and deliveries had been a primary reason for the mounting of a mission.[16]

The prominence of the Somalia mission's mandated responsibility to escort aid prevented it from remaining impartial. This prompted hostility in Somalia because the control of food was vital to the disputants' survival and power. The UN should have anticipated this because some of its leaders were aware that aid protection was antagonistic. UN Under-Secretary-General Marrack Goulding, the head of the Department of Peacekeeping Operations, noted in 1993 that guarding convoys was more akin to peace enforcement (by definition directed against at least one disputant) than peacekeeping.[17] The concept of human rights can breed confrontation because it reaches to the core of the state, to the interface between leaders and their people, and thus to the source and object of state power.[18] Humanitarian assistance deliveries could be perceived as challenges and threats.

Somalia's faction leaders believed that aid had a political impact. They did so despite the statement by Javier Pérez de Cuéllar, the outgoing UN secretary-general, who reminded the factions of the "key principle" surrounding aid deliveries: "namely that such assistance is purely humanitarian in nature and has no political implications."[19] The factional struggle, including the duel between Ali Mahdi Mohamed and Mohamed Farah Aidid, guaranteed that the impartiality of peacekeepers assigned relief protection duties would not be respected. The leaders were fighting for power and privilege, and in such situations humanitarian assistance could easily be viewed as political rather than as a neutral life-saving activity.[20]

The UN recognized that the use of peacekeepers to escort aid was controversial, but the famine was so serious that it had to proceed. The insecurity in Somalia had prevented the UN from delivering food to the starving from November 1991 to June 1992.[21] To improve its response, the UN decided to mix peacekeeping with humanitarian action and to expand its Somalia operation, despite the uncertainty about the practicality of these innovations. Elisabeth Lindenmayer, the political desk officer responsible for the file in the UN Department of Peacekeeping Operations, said a strong desire to help was driving the world institution to experiment in Somalia: "Let me emphasize that none of us is blessed with a gift of prophecy, nor do we have all the answers. But what else can we do but try and do our best to restore and keep the peace and alleviate human suffering ... we have to act before all the evidence is in, since, by the time the evidence is all in, it would be too late."[22]

At the same time, the United Nations was confident, now that the political constraints imposed by the Cold War were gone, that it could handle the situation. The early 1990s were "really very exciting from that point of view," recalled UN Deputy-Secretary-General Louise Fréchette, then Canada's permanent representative to the United Nations in New York. "The atmosphere in the halls of the United Nations was enormously positive and full of energy." A peacekeeping deployment to Somalia would have been out of the question during the Cold War because the Council would not have reached consensus on a mission to such a strategically located country. But in 1992, she commented, the United Nations "could say, 'no, we will not let millions of people starve because warlords want to fight.' This attitude was in the air, and that explains why we got involved in Bosnia as well, it was this notion that everything was now possible."[23] Those at the top of the UN hierarchy were equally optimistic. Maurice Baril, then a Canadian Forces brigadier-general and the military adviser to the secretary-general, recalled being inspired by the enthusiasm of senior Department of Peacekeeping Operations officials Goulding and Kofi Annan, and one of the co-leaders of the Department of Political Affairs, Vladimir Petrovsky.[24]

Progress in Somalia was slow for the United Nations because of the disorder and lack of a central government. The Somalia mission had to deal with a multiplicity of subnational "authorities." Secretary-General Boutros Boutros-Ghali observed that the absence of any administration whatsoever in Somalia was a "completely new" problem for the United Nations, which is essentially an intergovernmental organization, and this made the challenging task of diplomatic peacemaking harder than ever.[25] The UN needed but could not find a trustworthy local leader to present as the Somali face of its peace process. The faction leaders were more interested in seizing power, and they lacked legitimacy since they had gained prominence through violence and conquest and were responsible for prolonging the conflict.

The United Nations had to work with the faction leaders, but it lacked the means to apply pressure on them. The faction heads had no international reputations that could be besmirched if they broke an agreement, impeded peacekeepers, or looted relief supplies, and they had ambiguous chains of command and uncertain control over smaller sub-clans. The problem of how to build peace was further complicated by the fact that of the approximately

20,000 gunmen in Mogadishu, 80 percent were independent bandits who answered to no faction.[26] Only the UN Operation in the Congo (1960-64) and UN Interim Force in Lebanon encountered environments as inhospitable to traditional peacekeeping. Both endeavours were extremely difficult (they each suffered 250 fatalities, the highest peacekeeping totals ever)[27] and they illustrated the unyielding nature of such situations.

Although the Somalia mission had been established after the signing of the 3 March ceasefire, the low level of support received from some factions impaired its diplomatic peacemaking and humanitarian actions. The mission had an especially onerous task because it lacked a firm political basis and the disputants were intermeshed and impossible to separate.[28] By contrast, the UN Transitional Authority in Cambodia (1992-93) rested on the Paris Agreements (23 October 1991) and likely owed its success in organizing and running Cambodia's first democratic election to that foundation.[29] The Somalia mission was based on a shaky ceasefire that the United Nations stopped monitoring after six weeks because threats and mounting violence were being directed toward its unarmed military observers.[30]

Special Representative of the Secretary-General Mohamed Sahnoun, the overall head of the Somalia mission, was nevertheless able to establish influence over Aidid, Ali Mahdi, and some other faction leaders. His efforts lessened the hostility directed toward mission personnel and advanced preparations for reconciliation. Sahnoun relied "to a large degree, on moral suasion to get things done."[31] Sahnoun arrived on 4 May and concentrated on negotiating an end to the conflict and on winning consent from the factions for the deployment of the operation's five-hundred-person security battalion.

His strategy was to put the clan system to work for Somalia. Sahnoun believed that the clans – especially the elders, who were highly respected spiritual leaders within each community – were "politically interesting because they dilute power."[32] The elders were mediators and arbitrators of intra-clan community disputes. While the elders had to stay clear of politics in order to continue in this role, the faction leaders took note because of the psychological authority they wielded over clan opinion. The elders were regarded as the only social group in Somalia who could promote the search for peaceful dialogue within the country.[33] The civil war had marginalized the elders, but as "an indirect way of influencing the warlords" they remained critical of Sahnoun's overall plan for reconciliation. All that the elders required, he argued, "was some leverage, some people to ... convey their views, and so on. And we were happy, because they were beginning to have some effect on the warlords."[34]

Sahnoun made diplomatic inroads, but alleviating the humanitarian crisis in the near or medium term was impossible. Jonathan Stevenson has convincingly argued that "the United Nations' strongest suit is its ability to slog relentlessly ... with gritty diplomacy, without taking sides or parceling out favours."[35] Sahnoun was an example. His patient, personal, consensus-building technique won praise,[36] but his work was not seen as that of an impartial third-party mediator because the UN had become a party to the factions' struggle for power. It was a misconception to believe that the Somalia mission's profession of neutrality would be respected when the parties wished to fight. Sahnoun's difficulty was compounded by the disunity among the factions, their lack of internal cohesion, and the ambiguity of their political programs.[37] The security situation of the UN Somalia operation had improved by August thanks to Sahnoun, but the hijackings and theft of the aid did not significantly decline.[38]

As a result, the secretary-general decided to expand the UN peacekeeping mission and the airlift. These initiatives were first mentioned in Boutros-Ghali's 22 July report to the Council. In it, the secretary-general said "a framework for the security of humanitarian relief operations is the *sine qua non* for effective action." Faced with the mission's difficulties, he concluded that "the United Nations must adapt its involvement in Somalia,"[39] and that operation had to be broadened so that it covered all of Somalia and not just Mogadishu. Through an "innovative and comprehensive approach," the mission would deal with "the cessation of hostilities and security, the peace process and national reconciliation"[40] throughout Somalia.

The second adjustment was the expansion of the UN Children's Fund and World Food Programme airlift, and the parallel International Committee of the Red Cross effort, which were being operated from Mombassa and Nairobi, Kenya. The Somalia mission's inability to defend the food deliveries meant that the aid was leaving the port unprotected and being stolen before reaching the rural areas where the need was greatest. "Many of the most destitute are located in the interior of the country," the secretary-general noted, and "the mounting of an urgent airlift operation may be the only way to reach those areas and should be undertaken as soon as possible."[41] Owing to the delay imposed by the need to determine the specifics of the revised peacekeeping operation, the airlift proposal was implemented first and was the initial activity in which Canada participated.

By late July, decision makers were eager to help because the humanitarian emergency had worsened and assumed a high profile. Interest in multilateralism had become connected with the humanitarian crisis on the ground. Jim Judd, the assistant secretary to Cabinet for foreign and defence policy in the Privy Council Office, said that the television images depicting the famine were compelling and impossible for the government to ignore.[42] Senior officials decided Canada should support the UN's peacekeeping and humanitarian assistance initiatives in Somalia.

The Canadian Forces discussed the peacekeeping mission on 28 July at the morning daily executive meeting, which involved the top leaders in the National Defence Headquarters. Chief of the Defence Staff General John de

Chastelain asked the Joint Staff to conduct an estimate on the deployment of a security battalion to Somalia for six months, noting that his request could become a contingency plan once the costs were known and the operational concept approved by himself. De Chastelain agreed with acting Vice Chief of the Defence Staff Lieutenant-General Kent Foster's suggestion that the Canadian Airborne Regiment, Canada's UN standby battalion, would be well suited for the assignment.[43]

Robert Fowler, the very influential deputy minister, supported the chief. Fowler had a better sense of the political pulse of the government than the Canadian Forces leaders. Fowler was involved in the discussions surrounding a Somalia peacekeeping role because the consideration of new operations was one area where the responsibilities of the chief and deputy minister overlapped. During this period, he offered opinions on humanitarian foreign policy since this was not the National Defence mandate.[44] Fowler had a sense of the domestic and international political climate, and he noted at the daily executive meeting on the 28th that a Canadian Forces deployment would be welcome.[45]

Deputy Chief of the Defence Staff (Intelligence, Security, Operations) Major-General Paul Addy responded to the chief's request for an estimate. It fell to Addy's chief of staff, Commodore David Cogdon, to focus the Joint Staff and actually produce the document. This staff work was done, even though the UN had not informally asked for personnel, because it was considered possible that Pakistan might not supply the five-hundred-person security battalion it had promised, or that other forces would be required in Mogadishu.[46] As a result, Cogdon called a meeting of the Land Force members of Captain (Navy) McMillan's J3 Plans cell to examine whether the Canadian Forces could provide the security force mentioned in resolution 751 (24 April).

The staffing process for Canada's deployment to Mogadishu demonstrated the importance of concurrent activity to operational planning. Among the senior officers, discussions on the UN peacekeeping mission in Somalia continued both informally and formally in daily executive meetings. Below them, the Joint Staff Action Team did the related staff work. Under Cogdon's direction, expertise from all over the Joint Staff was simultaneously tapped and built into the Deputy Chief of the Defence Staff Group estimate. In this case, the assignments were: J1 Co-ordination (the medical support requirement); J2 Intelligence (risk assessment); J3 Plans and J3 Operations (the available Canadian military personnel and impact on air resources); J3 Plans (land forces available and impact on pre-existing Alliance and other commitments); J3 Peacekeeping and J5 Policy Operations (an estimate of the likely tasks); J4 Movement (the air and sealift possibilities and deployment timelines); J4 Logistics (sustainability); J4 Financial Co-ordination (financial issues); and J6 Co-ordination (state of satellite, secure and back-up communications).[47] This division of labour gives a picture of the variety of expertise needed and used by the Joint Staff for operational planning.

Two estimates were prepared, one as requested by the chief, and another done by the Joint Staff that also reached the chief. The estimates reinforced what de Chastelain and Lieutenant-General Jim Gervais, Commander of Force Mobile Command (then the name for the Land Force or army), were thinking: that the Canadian Forces could respond positively to the prime minister's request for a significant contribution to the UN effort in Somalia with a sixty-day self-sufficient battalion, and that the Airborne or one of three other units[48] could be sent to Mogadishu to fulfill the security requirement in resolution 751 (24 April), which was the only clearly defined task in late July. This would cost $58.1 million, of which $23.1 million was nonbudgeted expense incurred because of the mission.[49]

J3 Plans believed that a six-month role was possible despite the Canadian Forces' other tasks (another rotation, a year-long deployment, was also considered feasible).[50] These staff officers anticipated that the support provided would be the same as for the UN Mission for the Referendum in the Western Sahara. Canada would have monitored the Western Saharan ceasefire, protected the smaller contingents, and verified troop withdrawals. The Western Sahara mission had been derailed because Morocco refused to allow its full deployment. While keeping this Canadian Forces mission in mind, J3 Plans assumed that Canada's commitment to it would be withdrawn if the Canadian Forces went to Somalia.[51]

Although J3 Plans and J3 Peacekeeping believed that planning should wait until a second UN Technical Mission (scheduled to visit Somalia on 5-15 August) released its findings, the Joint Staff nevertheless had the impression that time was short and the Canadian Forces might have to deploy to Mogadishu quickly. "If a humanitarian mission is to be mounted at short notice," an aide-mémoire for the chief and deputy minister noted, then "authority should be obtained for a small DND reconnaissance team to proceed to Somalia as soon as possible."[52] The head of J3 Peacekeeping, Colonel Mike Houghton, sounded a note of caution in light of the urgency that he sensed had been attached to the planning and decision making. He commented at the end of July that it "would be a very serious mistake to attempt to pre-empt the United Nations in this matter. They should be allowed to do their job."[53] On 12 August, Aidid finally consented to the deployment of the UN security force after talks with Sahnoun, and the next day the United States offered to fly Pakistan's equipment and soldiers (drawn from its 7th Frontier Force) to Mogadishu. This meant the UN's most pressing requirement, one Canada had hoped to fill, had disappeared.

The new interest in Somalia also influenced airlift planning. With External Affairs and International Trade Canada, National Defence, the Privy Council Office, the Prime Minister's Office, and Canadian special interest groups all involved, with the government conducting public opinion polling and television networks beaming back images of starvation, Somalia had everything necessary to become a high-profile issue. The Joint Staff began to anticipate Canadian Forces involvement. J5 Policy Operations Colonel Bremner said that planning and policy "under such circumstances does not focus very much on whether or not we should participate. You try instead to present the cost of involvement, consequences of involvement, the risks ... You try to present these things rationally."[54] The airlift and ground role (with attention now on the four-zone plan) escalated in significance. The decision making was nonlinear. There was no defining moment. Rather it was characterized by spasmodic bursts of energy, and parallel and concurrent activity, but eventually the government decided to act.[55]

The Joint Staff aide-mémoire invited the government to consider other possible roles in Somalia, in addition to participating in the airlift. Two options that were not selected were sending ceasefire observers and supporting national reconciliation with construction engineering or communications units. Humanitarian assistance efforts could have been bolstered with the provision of medical teams or a field hospital, ground transport to move aid within Somalia, or aircraft to fly in relief supplies.[56] Only the airlift was selected, and this highlighted a key difference between Canada's and the UN's approach to the Somalia crisis. The government strongly desired to join the promising multilateral effort and to help the UN succeed, but it was interested only in a humanitarian contribution. The UN wanted to foster stability and political reconciliation while facilitating emergency food and medicine delivery.

The Joint Staff did not start planning for the UN airlift until Canada was informally asked for a contribution. Sahnoun did so personally on 31 July, when he met staff from the Canadian International Development Agency, Privy Council Office, National Defence, and External Affairs in the Lester B. Pearson building. He admitted that the UN's desire to deploy security personnel would likely not receive the consent of all factions since there were so many of these groups. Airlift support, he argued, was required to evade those who were looting relief supplies before they could be transported out of Mogadishu; as it stood, only 25 percent of requirements were reaching the countryside.[57] Sahnoun pointed to the urgent need to get food to the interior, the reduced security risks in remote rural areas, and the availability of six usable airstrips.[58] This was the third time that an airlift contribution was mentioned as a UN requirement that Canada could potentially fill. The other occasions had been the secretary-general's 22 July report and Council resolution 767 (27 July), which asked the United Nations to "make full use of all available means ... including the mounting of urgent airlift operations" to deliver aid to the needy.[59]

Jeremy Kinsman, the External Affairs assistant deputy minister (Political and International Security), remembered that Sahnoun had a powerful impact with his look of near-desperation and his passionate retelling of the UN's struggling humanitarian effort. "I don't want to say that it was the turning point, but [the meeting] was an important thing," Kinsman said. "At first, the visit was seen as being not a high priority. And then he came, and he kind of got to people somehow."[60] Kinsman pointed to the toll in terms of exhaustion and frustration that the Somalia operation had taken on Sahnoun, who, after three months of effort, had fifty observers on the ground as his only tangible accomplishment. Reid Morden, the under-secretary of state for external affairs, noted that the relevance to decision making of high-level meetings "depends on how strongly held are the views on the agreements which were reached by the political leadership. And when it circled back to the Prime Minister ... he was very anxious that we be seen to be participating in this mission."[61]

Sahnoun's informal request helped military decision makers further isolate the UN's needs and determine what the Canadian Forces could do to fill its requirements. Negotiations between the Canadian Forces and international organizations usually begin vaguely, but gradually the sides move closer together as the players' needs are clarified. "As things get closer to reality," said Larry Murray, then a rear-admiral and associate assistant deputy minister (Policy and Communications), the dialogue "becomes more defined, more specific, as things change. It is a dynamic process. Sometimes this happens over a long time, sometimes over a short period."[62]

By the time of the Sahnoun meeting, the airlift had become a priority for the government because multinational interest in it had become strong and did not diminish. On 12 August, Sahnoun made a public appeal for aerial assistance: "Let us organise a couple of airlift operations as we did for Ethiopia in the 1984-85 famine."[63] A second UN Technical Mission, which was sent to determine the working arrangements of the expanded peace-keeping mission, called for an expansion of the small number of World Food Programme and International Committee of the Red Cross flights, and for examination of airdropping, because this would "bring food right into the villages to keep people from leaving their homes."[64] Boutros-Ghali agreed with this suggestion, stating in his 24 August report that he had "come to the conclusion that the present airlift operation ... need[ed] to be substantially enhanced."[65] The airlift proposal was further supported by Council resolution 775 (28 August), which welcomed the decision to "increase ... the airlift operation to areas of priority attention."[66]

Diplomatic activity took place concurrently with military planning to determine whether Canada's participation in the multinational airlift would be welcome and what form its role would take. The High Commission in Nairobi was asked to recommend potential partners for the Canadian Forces and provide information on the implications of an airlift for peacekeeping in Somalia.[67] Commission personnel consulted with the International Committee of the Red Cross, which suggested that if the Canadian Forces provided a Hercules transport free of charge, it could cancel its existing lease for such an aircraft, thereby saving $1 million a month.[68] The Canadian Embassy in Geneva contacted the International Committee of the Red Cross headquarters, which expressed interest in Canadian Forces' support but wanted "to know who will cover costs of fuel, landing fees, maintenance, and costs related to feeding and shelter of crew."[69]

An air force reconnaissance team visited Geneva to engage in the delicate negotiations regarding these issues. The International Committee of the Red Cross wanted Canada's help but would refuse it if less expensive assistance could be obtained elsewhere. The Canadian Forces' air transport capabilities were limited and expenses had to be kept as low as possible, but the air force wanted the "business" in order to justify itself to the Canadian government and public. It was common for the Hercules fleet to be heavily utilized, and thus the airlift was not the freshest demonstration of the air force's usefulness. Despite this, the air force appreciated the task because it always wanted "to show that we were in demand and doing things out there in the world in support of the country's interests," noted Roy Mould, who in 1992 was a colonel and Air Command Headquarters' deputy G3 (the former deputy chief of staff – operations). "A steady pace of well-managed operations," he added, "justified our share of resources."[70]

Mulroney now decided to write to Boutros-Ghali. The prime minister offered Canadian Forces support to the expanded UN airlift in a 13 August letter. Having been informed by National Defence (via the Privy Council Office) that an aerial role was possible, he wrote that "in response to your recent report and a specific appeal by your Special Representative, Ambassador Sahnoun, Canada will provide the use of a military transport aircraft urgently for delivery of humanitarian relief in Somalia."[71] The political decision had been made. This was confirmed on 21 August, when the prime minister announced the contribution of three aircraft on what the military would nickname Operation Relief. In doing so, he "underlined Canada's support of United Nations efforts to initiate comprehensive security and humanitarian operations throughout Somalia."[72]

In the Canadian Forces, responsibility for the national preparations for Relief fell to the Joint Staff, while the air force worked out the operational details, generated the forces, and provided follow-up support to its deployed personnel. The Canadian Forces decided to send a sixty-five-person Airlift Control Element and three Hercules (one each for the International Committee of the Red Cross and World Food Programme, plus a spare) to Nairobi. J3 Plans conducted a capability check to discover whether the air force could do the job and for how long and, working with J4 Financial, determined the budgetary impact.[73] An estimate prepared on 14 August noted that the expected cost of the three-month deployment was $17.8 million, $6.25 million of which was nonbudgeted "extra" expense.[74] Operation Relief would reduce by 15 percent the resources available for the Quarterly Airlift Plan (which took into account all regular airlift user needs, such as Search and Rescue, resupply of Canadian Forces Station Alert in the Arctic, and training). This meant exercises might have to be reduced and contractors used for some nonoperational transport work.[75]

Relief would be the first mission run out of the Air Command operations centre in Winnipeg. Traditionally, Air Command had delegated its operations to its functional Groups (such as Air Transport Group, Fighter Group, 10 Tactical Air Group, and Maritime Air Group) and had not assumed the responsibilities of commanding its own operations. A Group headquarters was designated as the lead agency in conducting an operation or in co-ordinating the efforts of other Groups where more than one was engaged. The lead Group would then be dealing directly with National Defence Headquarters while keeping Air Command informed. This was part of the legacy of Air Command's establishment in October 1975. In order to create a locus for national air power expertise, senior air force leaders had been compelled to accept a less-than-ideal command and control arrangement in which Air Command owned all air assets but operationally controlled very little.[76] Winnipeg, in pursuit of the principle that air power was indivisible in nature, was able incrementally to strengthen its hold over air resources through the years.[77] In the early 1990s, it became clear to Commander Lieutenant-General David Huddleston that Air Command needed to be in more direct control of all air operations.

The air force undertook a series of restructurings in 1992 in order to prepare for the short-notice, contingency-type taskings like Relief that were expected to predominate in the post-Cold War era. According to then Brigadier-General Gordon Diamond, Huddleston recognized that the air force had to concentrate on the rapid deployment of forces and on improving the planning and management of operations while reducing costs. This resulted in the creation of the Wing structure, which were formations that could be deployed in whole or in part, unlike bases, and the Air Command–driven change to take over Group functions, beginning with airlift in 1992.[78] The role of Air Command had been weakened by the practice of designating a lead Group. For instance, although National Defence Headquarters was not on direct liaison status with Air Transport Group during the Persian Gulf War (1990-91), it could contact the latter directly without going through Winnipeg as long as this was only for information.[79] Huddleston sought to strengthen Air Command's control over air assets and operations. "The Groups," he said, "had their specialized functions to perform, but the air force had to operate as an air force and it had to interface directly with National Defence Headquarters."[80]

Another one of Huddleston's objectives was the creation in Air Command of the same accelerated staffing system for operations that had been established in the national headquarters with the Joint Staff. Deputy Commander Major-General Patrick (Paddy) O'Donnell asked Mould to create such a system for Air Command, initially called the General Staff (now the Air Staff), in the summer of 1992. O'Donnell was promoted and transferred to a new post, and implementation was completed under his successor, Major-General Lou Cuppens. Under the old system, personnel were grouped according to their trade – pilots, finance, maintenance, legal, and so forth – not in relation to what the mission was or the part they played in mission accomplishment.[81] This structure was turned on its side, so with the General Staff everyone was slotted according to what they did: tactical helicopter, maritime air, fighters, and transport. Huddleston knew about joint staffing because as deputy chief of the defence staff during 1989-91 he had overseen the establishment of the Joint Staff, and in Winnipeg he had discussions with O'Donnell and Cuppens about bringing it into Air Command.[82] This change was driven by the primacy of operations and the need to respond swiftly to diverse and unpredictable operational requirements. With the General Staff, said Mould, "You brought the actual maintainer, the actual intelligence or personnel officer, right into the operations centre. That's what made it new. Operations became multi-skilled."[83]

While airlifts are never easy, the Canadian Forces had recent experience in the region that helped it prepare for Relief. Operation Nile (June-September 1988), based in Addis Ababa, had involved two Hercules transports (one was a spare). Nile delivered food, 70 to 75 percent of which was destined for Mek'ele in northern Ethiopia, often having to cope with sharp stones when landing and with airstrips that were indistinguishable from the surrounding countryside.[84] Nile worked for the UN Disaster Relief Co-ordinator and was praised for helping to prevent widespread famine.[85]

Under Operation Preserve (August-December 1991), the Canadian Forces transported grain from Djibouti to Gode, K'ebri Dehar, and other communities in Ethiopia's Ogaden region.[86] Preserve's operational concept – three Hercules flying from one main base for three months – was used in Somalia. Relief experienced many of the same challenges that Nile and Preserve encountered, such as short, unlit, or potholed runways, burst tires, inaccurate or outdated maps, and animals that had to be chased off the runway by a low pass before landing. By 1992, these challenges "had become a pattern," said Huddleston. Air Transport Group, which was responsible for Relief's technical requirements, "had people who had been experienced in the whole routine, and all of the operational aspects of working off these different airstrips."[87]

Air Transport Group's preparations were furthered by the vast body of experience it had with airlift, which enabled it to adjust to the particularities of Relief without much trouble. According to Commander Brigadier-General Jeff Brace on 4 September, eight days before the start of Operation Relief, "Taskings of this nature are never routine; however, such operations are not new to the men and women of ATG ... In many ways this airlift mirrors numerous previous humanitarian undertakings."[88] The steps that planners took when mounting an airlift were in the manual *CF-ACM-2603-Airlift Operations and Planning*, and their preparations were furthered by the April 1992 decision to create a standby Airlift Control Element to speed response times. Lieutenant-Colonel John Jensen noted that 426 (Training) Squadron Trenton had been pre-tasked with providing an Airlift Control Element for six months and had already determined the general requirements for a deployment, including the operations and maintenance personnel required, the mobile air movements teams, and the communicators and administrators, with the specific aircrew being dependent on the tasking.[89] An Airlift Control Element involved creating a temporary base capable of doing most of the repairs that could be done at the aircraft's home base. In this case, the Airlift Control Element included a command and control vehicle (a truck with a high-frequency radio) so that a mobile repair party could be called if necessary.[90]

In mid-August, an Air Transport Group team travelled to Nairobi, site of the World Food Programme airlift, to determine the specific parameters of its assignment. These trips enabled Air Transport Group to establish whom it would be assisting, from where its planes would fly, and under what arrangements. Owing to prior discussions, the Canadian Forces teams left knowing that the air force would likely be delivering food aid and medicines from Nairobi for the World Food Programme and International Committee of the Red Cross, and the visits confirmed this. The Canadian Forces concluded that it should operate from Nairobi and not Mombassa because the latter's airport was full, and that newer Hercules "H"s and not "E"s were needed since the higher altitude at the former would require more powerful engines.[91] Securing good accommodations was a priority for the reconnaissance team. It wanted to avoid the situation encountered on Preserve, when air force members had been forced to double bunk.[92]

Delivery flights in Somalia commenced on 11 September, but complications arose surrounding the need to adhere to special International Committee of the Red Cross rules. To ensure it was never accused of taking sides, the International Committee of the Red Cross strictly barred the transport of anything but its supplies on aircraft bearing its distinctive emblem. Neutrality was a fundamental principle because this normally enabled the organization to gain the confidence of disputants and the freedom of action necessary to carry out its activities.[93] The Canadian Forces had to store any UN insignia behind the bulkhead when on an International Committee of the Red Cross flight.[94] Relief had to configure aircraft for two mission types, which was a unique problem that Air Transport Group had not encountered before.[95]

Poor facilities and the insecure ground situation in Somalia bred uncertainty, adding to the complexity of Operation Relief. The Canadian Forces flew into Somali airfields near Baydhabo (also called Baidoa, and grimly nicknamed the "city of death"), Mogadishu, Kismaayo, Baardheere (also called Bardera), Beledweyne, and elsewhere. The dirt and stone airstrips (except for Mogadishu airport, which was paved) and lack of security made all of them extremely dangerous.[96] Operations were complicated by the fact that the United Nations was unable to provide destinations until the night before or even the day of the flight, and pilots avoided afternoon landings because that was when many Somali men were under the influence of khat.[97] The rapid deterioration of security conditions was always a risk. The need for the hourly monitoring of the situation on the ground was underscored on 19 September, when an offloading at Xuddur had to be abruptly terminated after a skirmish broke out between locals close to the airfield.[98] On 5 October, a Relief crew at Mogadishu International Airport was caught in a firefight between Somalis, but left without casualties or aircraft damage.[99] An engine was often kept running just in case a rapid departure was required. No one, as the Canadian High Commissioner in Nairobi (with accreditation to Somalia) Ambassador Larry Smith discovered when he accompanied a flight to Baydhabo, ever ventured far from the plane.[100]

Airlifting food was only supposed to be a stopgap designed to lessen reliance on the insecure ground routes. By the time of the second Airlift Control Element rotation in late October 1992, it was clear that the international assistance effort was failing. Relief was hampered by ground fire and continued thievery. For example, in October 1992, an assistance flight (not done by Canada) to Baardheere had to be aborted when a few gunmen, disgruntled over having not received airstrip security jobs, fired a rocket-propelled grenade that just missed the aircraft.[101] This highlighted the great difficulty associated with delivering aid without the support of all parties.

The looters soon adjusted to the airlift. Canada and other nations airdropped food to areas made inaccessible because of rain, but these aircraft started to come under fire.[102] Much of what was transferred from the aircraft to the trucks never made it the few kilometres to the warehouses.[103] This did not have a direct impact on the work accomplished by the Operation Relief aircrews. Air Transport Group received reports about the thefts, but its flights continued because no one was actually robbing the aircraft.[104]

Despite these serious problems, Canada and its US, French, Belgian, and German partners obtained important information from their airlifts. It became clear that these operations could not alleviate the suffering because they could not assist the areas of greatest need.[105] This was what happened during Operation Nile, which "in no way ameliorated the intensity of the civil war." As in Somalia, Nile may even "have enhanced the ability of all parties to continue the conflict."[106]

Conclusion

The civil war challenged the United Nations by making the maintenance of consent and impartiality nearly impossible. Although this was not the Somalia mission's intention, some of the leading disputants perceived its attempt to protect humanitarian assistance as a political and potentially threatening act. The economic profit and political power associated with the control of food deliveries made it even more likely that the factions would perceive the mission in partial terms, attempt to undermine it, and refuse to give their consent to anything more than a token, ineffective presence. UN troops were not considered to be impartial nor were they welcomed by Aidid and the unaffiliated bandits. As a result, the Somalia operation was unable to perform its peacekeeping functions: stabilization, diffusion of tension, and the fostering of reconciliation.

It would be an oversimplification to argue that the Somalia mission failed or that peacekeepers cannot operate in civil wars. Humanitarian relief success must await events on the political front, and diplomatic peacemaking progress in such situations will be slow. With the five hundred peacekeepers delayed until 14 September, and with the starvation conditions worsening daily, the United Nations became impatient for results.

Boutros-Ghali's two new assertive initiatives – an airlift to Somalia and an expansion of the peacekeeping effort – were strongly supported by Canada. The former was easier to implement and was Canada's first military role. The government had decided in late July to search for a significant role because it wished to support the UN's faltering multilateral effort. The prime minister's interest in having Canada be a visible actor profoundly influenced the decision-making dynamic and resulted in the commitments being made. The government wanted to be seen alleviating the humanitarian crisis, but was less concerned with the UN's efforts to encourage reconciliation. Consideration of an aid-escort role in Mogadishu and the airlift contribution reflected decision makers' desire to limit Canada's engagement to famine relief. Interest in the crisis did not lead the government to seek a deeper role. It was not clear in mid-1992 that meaningful humanitarian support for Somalia would require much more than an airlift.

The Joint Staff at National Defence Headquarters handled the strategic-level planning and preparations for Operation Relief and worked with Air Command and Air Transport Group to determine that an airlift was a realistic option. The Joint Staff determined the size, cost, and sustainability of the mission and then directed Winnipeg to carry it out. Other than monitoring its progress, the Joint Staff did not concern itself with the daily, routine functioning of the airlift.[107]

Air Command exercised operational command and control of Relief, while Air Transport Group implemented the task and handled the specific requirements. Huddleston believed that for the air force to function properly, it needed to run its own operations, and Air Command must be the body that interacted with National Defence Headquarters on behalf of the air force. In order to prepare the air force to do so, and to enable it to respond to the short-notice missions that were expected to predominate in the 1990s, he implemented a number of changes. Two of them, both crucial, were the establishment of an operations centre and a General Staff in Air Command. Diamond became chief of staff (operations) because his mission orientation and transport experience complemented Huddleston's fighter and Cuppens' helicopter backgrounds, and as a former Air Transport Group commander he was able to ease the transfer, beginning with Relief, of direct management of airlift to Air Command.[108]

Air Transport Group was essential for the formation of the Airlift Control Element and other technical issues. The operations centre at Trenton handled specifics, such as who would lead and make up the Airlift Control Element, the rotations, establishment of the airflow, and the spare parts that should be brought. Airlift was a well-known mission type that could be quickly mounted by Air Transport Group – it conducted its reconnaissance in mid-August and was operational on 12 September – but Relief involved special complications. One related to the rules imposed by the International Committee of the Red Cross on aircraft delivering its supplies. Another was the lawless and disordered operational environment. The constantly shifting ground situation increased the degree of risk and complicated the mission in other ways, such as by preventing the Airlift Control Element from knowing where it would be flying until the night before or day of the tasking.

The greatest problem was that Relief could not sufficiently alleviate the suffering caused by the Somali mass famine. The merits of the airlift were that it could be mounted quickly, relieving some of the pressure on Canada to act, and it did increase the amount of aid reaching the starving, albeit in a manner that was much more expensive than truck convoys. In the end, however, Relief showed that the humanitarian assistance effort remained at the mercy of the factions and bandits who chose to steal the aid. The Canadian Forces and United Nations did not recognize that the local parties would be able to undermine this effort just as easily as they had the land-based assistance efforts. By late November, the UN peacekeeping effort began to crumble in the face of mounting Somali opposition. With the planned expansion of the mission, which was to begin with a Canadian Forces deployment, still more than a month away from implementation, it became clear that more assertive methods would be necessary.

5
Sticking with the (Wrong) Peacekeeping Mission

Brian Mulroney decided to commit to the United Nations Operation in Somalia I in August 1992 to help deliver food to those dying from Somalia's civil war and famine. The government accepted a stability assignment reluctantly, notwithstanding the importance of this task to the UN's conflict resolution strategy. It did not want to become enmeshed in the slow-moving peace process because the opposition parties and nongovernmental organizations (NGOs) were not pushing it to do so, and the domestic media were focused on the famine victims. The Canadian Forces could not sustain a long-term role. Canada's commitment to the UN peacekeeping mission was motivated by media pressure and the prime minister's desire to strengthen and influence multilateral diplomacy, actions, and processes.

The peacekeeping contribution coincided with the UN's adoption of a more determined approach. On 14 August, the Security Council authorized the deployment of a Pakistani battalion to Mogadishu to carry out security and aid escort tasks.[1] UN Secretary-General Boutros Boutros-Ghali later called this "secure humanitarian assistance," which was "something new for United Nations peacekeepers, a form of 'peace enforcement,' as mentioned in *An Agenda for Peace*" (June 1992).[2] Shortly after the Council's decision came the report of the second UN Technical Mission, which had visited Somalia from 6 to 15 August to determine how the operation could be expanded to four zones. The Technical Mission argued that if the factions did not allow the troops to deploy, then "the United Nations should be prepared to do so without the consent of the parties concerned."[3] In his 24 August report to the Council, Boutros-Ghali stressed that the Somalis needed to co-operate "rather than obliging the international community to take initiatives of its own without them."[4]

Canada supported this multilateral effort. Mulroney outlined the government's priorities in his 13 August letter to Boutros-Ghali concerning the Somalia and Yugoslavia crises. He remarked on the "tragic humanitarian situation" and promised that Canada would assist in the relief and recovery.

This was an "appropriately active, co-operative role" that would help the United Nations in the Horn of Africa. The effort to "end the fighting" was not emphasized as it was for the Balkans civil war. The prime minister stressed the need for a "political agreement" and "negotiated solution" to the fighting in Bosnia-Herzegovina in addition to deploring the violence.[5]

The differing approach to diplomatic peacemaking reflected the fact that the Somalia peace process was minuscule compared with that for Yugoslavia. The government's rhetoric regarding peace in Bosnia was louder in large part because there was more dialogue to support. European intergovernmental bodies, beginning with the Conference on Security and Co-operation in Europe, got involved in the Balkans civil war as soon as it started in mid-1991. When the Conference on Security and Co-operation in Europe's consensus-seeking mechanism failed, it delegated responsibility to the European Community.[6] The latter's negotiators were assisted by the United Nations as of fall 1991. The high-profile London Peace Conference (26-28 August 1992) drew up plans for complete sanctions against Serbia/Montenegro but shied away from using force to forge peace.[7] Canada vigorously supported these efforts. During the London talks, for example, Secretary of State for External Affairs Barbara McDougall called for a war crimes tribunal to try military commanders guilty of gross human rights abuses. She offered 1,200 troops for duty in Bosnia on top of the 1,200 in Croatia to help the UN Protection Force become "more active, more dynamic."[8]

The UN Somalia operation, in contrast, received little international diplomatic assistance. Regional bodies – the Organization of African Unity, League of Arab States, and Organization of the Islamic Conference – had helped the UN negotiate the shaky 3 March ceasefire in Mogadishu,[9] but they kept to one side from then on. Special Representatives of the Secretary-General Mohamed Sahnoun (until 26 October) and Ismat Kittani got almost no logistical, communications, or administrative support from the UN Secretariat in New York, which had been overwhelmed by the demands of the UN Protection Force and UN Transitional Authority in Cambodia. The Mogadishu headquarters lacked computers and typewriters and was still sending handwritten faxes in mid-August.[10] Years later Kittani called the mission "more like a parking lot than an operation."[11] The peace process was a one-man show. Aside from the negotiations conducted by Sahnoun and then Kittani personally, nothing was happening.[12]

The passions at play inside Somalia limited what the world community could do. Canada's High Commission in Nairobi noted in September that the disputants' mistrust and hatred were so strong that they would derail any political summit.[13] There was no peace process for Ottawa to push forward, and it had no reason to step out on a limb by itself. Marc Perron, the assistant deputy minister (Africa and Middle East) in the Department of External Affairs and International Trade Canada, wrote that the faction leaders were "not committed to a negotiated settlement to the civil conflict, and an international conference could find itself undermined by lack of local commitment or support."[14] The UN agreed that organizing a Somali peace conference would be dangerous and time-consuming. Its officials believed the threat of intensified fighting and starvation gave the UN no choice but to proceed.[15]

The government's decision was influenced by perceptions of where Canada's interests rested and by the absence of domestic pressure to help. In late October, for example, Under-Secretary of State for External Affairs (Deputy Minister) Reid Morden commented that protecting aid was one thing, but the country should not get involved in diplomatic peacemaking because it had nothing at stake in Somalia.[16] The Permanent Mission to the United Nations in New York saw no reason for Canada to form a contact group.[17] The government lacked the domestic political motivation to press for peace that it had for the Balkans, where the impetus for prompt and forceful intervention came from the New Democrats and Liberals as well as the Government side of the House of Commons.[18] For Somalia, there was no need to pre-empt demands for action from the Official Opposition because they made none. Prior to the deployment of the US-led United Task Force in December, very few questions were asked about Somalia in the House or the Parliamentary committees.[19]

Nongovernmental organizations were not focused on the peace process. Only the largest groups, such as CARE Canada and World Vision Canada, had experience or knowledge of Somalia, and they were preoccupied with the famine. The peacekeeping role, which was made public in September and cancelled in early December, did not exist long enough for serious discontent to emerge among NGOs. Exceptions were the 30 October and 16 November letters by the chair of CARE International, Malcolm Fraser, and the president of CARE Canada, H. John McDonald, urging Mulroney to reconsider his response. McDonald also wanted the deployment location changed. In the northeast, "conditions are relatively stable and the need for assistance much less." If the UN asked to move the Canadian contingent, "I hope you would accede to such a request."[20] CARE Canada was one of the only national NGOs with first-hand knowledge of Somalia's current troubles, but the Prime Minister's Office disregarded its advice and sent a standard "thank you for your concern" reply.[21]

For these domestic and international reasons, the famine loomed largest in the minds of External Affairs bureaucrats. The Somalia operation was seen as a relief task. Assistant Deputy Minister (Political and International Security) Jeremy Kinsman said it "was not a peacekeeping operation. This was an operation to protect the aid corridors to ensure that the humanitarian relief got through. That's all as far as I know that Canada ever signed on for."[22] The troops were needed to stop the factions and bandits from looting supplies brought in by the NGOs and UN aid agencies. National Defence Minister Marcel Masse outlined the government's emergency response on 2 September when he said that the "deployment of the Canadian Airborne Regiment is another example of Canada's ongoing commitment to humanitarian aid by ensuring that supplies will reach those in need." It was "important that we do whatever we can to help the starving people of Somalia."[23]

The government considered engaging even though the Canadian Forces was heavily tasked. The National Defence Headquarters Joint Staff had briefed Chief of the Defence Staff General John de Chastelain on the available capabilities. He had been informed, he later wrote, that the military "could support four simultaneous battalion-sized operations ... only up until September 1993, including the necessary rotations. After that date, and in the absence of receiving additional personnel resources, we would have to cancel at least one of them. I gave that advice to the Government."[24] Not counting Somalia, the Canadian Forces had a battalion-sized contingent in Cyprus and a battlegroup in Croatia and would deploy a battlegroup to Bosnia in the fall. There were 215 people serving with UN Transitional Authority in Cambodia, 180 with the UN Disengagement Force in the Golan Heights, and others in smaller roles. Ottawa was cutting the military's strength as part of a budget deficit–trimming exercise at the same time. The number of combat arms units in Force Mobile Command (later called the Land Force or army), the source of most Canadian Forces peacekeepers, would be reduced from sixteen to thirteen in mid-1993, and after that there would not be enough units to support its four major and three minor commitments without a large 2,608-person-per-year augmentation.[25]

Masse reinforced this message and urged restraint. The Canadian Forces "cannot accept any other mission," he informed the Subcommittee on Security and National Defence of the Standing Senate Committee on Foreign Affairs on 25 November 1992, two weeks before the Airborne was to deploy, "without having some new resources. It is not a question of will. It is a question of dollars ... we cannot be more extended than we are now."[26] Masse's testimony reflected his belief that the government was so determined to play a role on the world stage, and to maintain Canada's nearly unblemished record of participation in UN peacekeeping, that it was putting inordinate pressure on the Canadian Forces. He felt it was irresponsible for the government to push so hard when there was a limited and declining number of soldiers to support its international activism. Masse recalled that in "my speeches, when I talk[ed] about it, I stated that we don't have to be everywhere. But I was the only one who was saying that ... The philosophy was still push, the *Guinness Book of World Records* approach, but at the same time there were budget cuts everywhere."[27]

The defence policy that outlined the reductions fixed the Canadian Forces' expeditionary limit, and with the Somalia assignment the military had reached, but not exceeded, this maximum. In *Challenge and Commitment*, the 1987 White Paper on Defence, the government had reconfirmed the understanding that the Canadian Forces could deploy up to two thousand peacekeepers at one time.[28] This maximum was raised in *Defence Policy 1991* and continued in *Canadian Defence Policy 1992* to permit the Canadian Forces to "maintain a capability for contingency operations anywhere in the world up to and including brigade group level" – or roughly five thousand soldiers.[29] Sustainability was a key issue. De Chastelain informed the Senate Subcommittee that about 4,400 would be deployed worldwide when the Airborne went to Somalia. That was the true limit because 4,500 was all that could be supported overseas for a year, with a six-month rotation.[30] This meant that the Canadian Forces could not handle a Somalia assignment for long. A role in stabilizing Somalia was not desirable because it would be a drawn-out process lacking the same "gift of Canada" media appeal as pictures of Canadian troops escorting bags of grain.

The government discovered its troops would have little aid escort work when they deployed to Boosaaso in northeast Somalia. It had assumed as late as 25 September that the Airborne was needed to protect relief supplies in northeast Somalia,[31] but on the 30th, a team from the Canadian High Commission in Nairobi paid a visit and found that no one in the area was starving. They learned that the Somali Salvation Democratic Front, the region's dominant faction, had consented to the arrival of troops in order to entrench its political legitimacy and for humanitarian reasons.[32] Conversations with the faction revealed that NGO operations were unthreatened and not in need of protection.[33] Government officials nevertheless continued to express interest only in famine relief. Ambassador Gerald Shannon, head of the Canadian delegation to the Co-ordination Meeting on Humanitarian Assistance for Somalia held in Geneva on 12-13 October, said that although reconciliation was vital, "the Canadian military presence will be strictly in support of humanitarian assistance."[34]

Canada equated success with alleviating suffering, and it was concerned that the United Nations had lost sight of this in its rush to get troops deployed. A "strong negative media reaction" was foreseen, External Affairs told Under-Secretaries-General Marrack Goulding of the UN Department of Peacekeeping Operations and James Jonah of the Department of Political Affairs, "if Canadian troops arrived in Boosaaso and then were not involved in activities to secure the delivery of food aid, while at the same time television coverage would continue to show the miserable plight of starving Somalis in other parts of the country."[35] Government leaders informed the UN on 9 October that the mission needed to be successful and be perceived to be successful by the media. For Western publics such as Canada's, this meant getting food to the starving. Canadian officials said if there was anything

Canada could do to get the mission on the right track, the UN need only ask for assistance.[36]

The government did not withdraw to avoid further undermining the operation and to maintain its voice in the Somalia discussions. A peacekeeping success would become less likely if Canada cancelled. Shortliffe noted that the government did not want to complicate matters for the UN by publicizing its grievances. Officials continued to support the mission until they decided to do something else.[37] This was only practical because the operation was Canada's sole means of engagement in the Somalia crisis in the fall. Multilateralism enabled the country to play the roles that decision makers and Canadians wanted and expected Canada to play. Hugh Segal, Chief of Staff in the Prime Minister's Office, commented that "in the sense that we punch above our weight and we have more influence in the world because of our involvement in these things," Canadian officials "would be very reticent to have us be the first to bail out ... and their preference would be that we be the last."[38]

Leaving the mission would have been politically awkward. Government leaders could not forget about the new internationalist foreign policy they had been articulating. Backing out would have gone against the assertive and interventionist principles announced in the policy. The prime minister was concerned about his public image. He might look careless, if he reversed course, for having made the commitment in the first place, and he did not want Canadians to think he lacked direction or determination. "Mulroney would not have wanted to be seen as someone who bailed out on something because it was difficult," said Segal. That "would have been counter-intuitive for him."[39] Peacekeeping's domestic popularity made withdrawing from the operation problematic. Mulroney was doubtless aware that Canadians' approval of the activity could be used to offset his government's unpopularity.[40]

Consequently, the government sought only to change its assignment. External Affairs instructed the Permanent Mission to the United Nations in New York to "ensure that Canadian concerns about the need to have humanitarian relief plans ready for the Boosaaso operation are conveyed to all relevant players."[41] Permanent Representative Ambassador Louise Fréchette arranged meetings with Sahnoun and Under-Secretaries-General Goulding and Jan Eliasson of the Department of Humanitarian Affairs at UN headquarters in mid-October. Fréchette informed Sahnoun that there could be "negative implications for both Canada and the United Nations if troops arrived and found little to do in Boosaaso while to the south the famine continued unabated." She asked Goulding and Eliasson for "assurance that our soldiers would have food to escort once they landed at Boosaaso."[42]

Sahnoun, despite his interest in fostering reconciliation, found himself under pressure from Canada and the United Nations to get troops deployed to escort aid. Sahnoun wanted to stop the over-reliance on Mogadishu's port, which was the civil war's epicentre. His intention was to use UN troops to open other harbours to aid traffic while providing the stability and security that would serve as the foundation for Somalia's reconstruction. Sahnoun therefore curtly rejected, on 16 October, Ottawa's request to include Mogadishu in its reconnaissance.[43] He quieted Canada by authorizing the Canadian reconnaissance and noting that a presence in the northeast was vital because it could be held up as a model, serving as an example of the benefits of co-operation with the United Nations. There remained a kernel of "modern civilisation and stability" in the region that needed to be preserved.[44] Canadian officials were impressed with Sahnoun and willing to continue working with him. The Canadian embassy in Geneva said that he possessed "the intelligence, experience and subtleties that are necessary ... to deal with the Somali factions," and that no one believed "the Secretary-General had chosen the wrong man for this very difficult assignment."[45]

Sahnoun was under pressure to handle the famine quickly, but he was confident that proceeding gradually on reconciliation and not pushing the humanitarian process faster than the factions wanted would bring success. He had been negotiating with the socially influential clan elders and the faction leaders to foster peace and secure consent for the deployments. It took time for the influence of the elders and other grassroots groups (such as local NGOs) to be felt. Sahnoun's approach was reflected in the Somali saying, "If you want to prevent an eagle from flying, take off its feathers one by one," meaning, take time, and eventually it will not be able to fly.[46] Canadian Brigadier-General Maurice Baril, Boutros-Ghali's military adviser, heard the same saying from an elder in spring 1995. The world needed to be patient with Somalia. "The fixing of a country is done at the speed that the country wants to be fixed," said Baril, "I think that was a great lesson."[47]

Although the UN had started to doubt whether Sahnoun was reading the Somalia situation correctly, there did not seem to be any alternative to the tedious soliciting of consent from Mohamed Farah Aidid, Ali Mahdi Mohamed, and the other faction heads. Agreements were reached with local disputants that normally would have implied a degree of co-operation with the UN, but in Somalia deals were often violated.[48] Violence and robbery were so common that UN and NGO workers could not leave their compounds without gunmen.[49] "It was very, very difficult because nobody knew exactly how to handle the situation," Baril recalled, "we didn't really know how to approach it." All that was clear was that it "was a classic Chapter VI approach and we had to convince them."[50]

The political and security situation in Somalia steadily deteriorated. Like the Somali saying, the UN found it was "easy to come, but hard to stay," which was a reference to Somalia's history of gradually undermining its occupiers.[51] Local resentment grew when the UN decided to deploy battalions without the consent of some factions. This was because not all Somalis wanted the civil war to end. Most of the young men who became bandits and faction members used to be nomadic herders, and for them times had never been better.[52] They did not want peacekeepers to arrive and reduce security guard revenues or prevent aid thefts. For Aidid, the assistance effort represented, at best, a brief windfall, and it is unclear how much he and the other faction leaders benefited from the international presence.[53] Disputants did not want to submit to the UN's procedural approach to peace in which negotiation of a deal was followed by implementation.[54] As the UN moved forward with deployment arrangements on 23 October, more violence was directed against it. UN plans were stymied by fighting that closed most airlift landing strips – including those near Kismaayo, Baydhabo (Baidoa), and Baardheere (Bardera) – for days at a time, and interrupted or shut humanitarian relief efforts down.[55]

The United States had, by this point, become impatient with the slow rate of progress and the local actors who were blocking its attempts to help. The start of the American airlift to Somalia in August 1992 had initiated a cycle of escalating US political and media interest in the Horn of Africa. For US journalists, Somalia's appeal was limited until Washington committed military forces.[56] Reporters began to observe that the factions and gunmen were impeding American generosity and to identify them as villains responsible for countless deaths.[57] The factions came to be seen as challengers to US kindness and the international will. Congress was perturbed and President George H.W. Bush came under pressure to do more.[58]

Political recognition of the crisis as an affront accelerated the build-up of the media "pack." The enormous increase in coverage enabled reporters to make Somalia "the" story and influence public opinion.[59] They concentrated on the need for forceful action, citing the horrendous humanitarian situation, UN helplessness, and the moral responsibility of the United States as a former ally of Somalia. The *New York Times* alleged that Bush's neglect was politically driven. His focus on domestic politics during the presidential election year, in the opinion of the *Times*, "clearly played a role in Washington's reluctant, half-hearted response." The editors observed that presidential leadership was urgently needed because it would be "morally intolerable to acquiesce in this preventable tragedy." If the "United Nations intervention means looters risk being shot, that is a risk they bring on themselves."[60]

For weeks, the United States monitored developments at the UN and in Somalia. By late November, the UN mission's position in Mogadishu was so precarious that the deputy force commander, Canadian Forces Colonel Jim Cox, destroyed his confidential papers in the belief that an all-out attack was imminent.[61] The northeast sub-mission was in total disarray. The High Commission in Nairobi had again visited the area, this time with consultant Matthew Bryden, a Somali-speaking Canadian. The team learned that the UN office in Boosaaso did not have a budget or functional communications with its headquarters, had no knowledge of the mission beyond what was outlined in resolution 775 (28 August), and did not know the Canadian advance party's approximate arrival date, even though this was barely a week away.[62] On 24 November, Boutros-Ghali told the Council that the "situation is not improving" and that it was becoming "exceedingly difficult for the United Nations operation to achieve the objectives approved by the Security Council."[63] US acting Secretary of State Lawrence Eagleburger informed Boutros-Ghali the next day that the United States was willing to lead a peace enforcement coalition into Somalia to create a secure environment for humanitarian relief deliverers and recipients.

Conclusion

Canadian decision makers wanted to support multilateralism and humanitarianism in Somalia, and these objectives were supposed to be fulfilled by Canada's UN peacekeeping contribution. The government did not offer deep and intensive support – such as working to construct a democratic system of governance for Somalia – even though this was necessary to achieve self-sustaining peace and security.

The Canadian government was not interested in diplomatic peacemaking roles. It stayed aloof from the UN's Somalia peace process because it was receiving little international or domestic attention. The UN reconciliation effort was weak, poorly supported by the world community, and burdened by the complexity of having to negotiate with numerous subnational parties from all over the country. External Affairs doubted that success could be achieved in the short term because of the mistrust and hatred between the disputants. These difficulties, and the fact that the government was not being pressured by opposition parties or NGOs to do more for peace, ensured that Canada's engagement was centred on humanitarian concerns.

Decision makers concentrated on the famine because this was the main concern in Canada. This was convenient because the Canadian Forces could not have sustained a longer-term role aimed at stabilization. The government contributed to the UN undertaking because it appeared to be a promising operation. Canadian decision makers began to doubt the mission once the true nature of the Canadian Forces' task was revealed. Despite this, the government remained engaged to avoid bringing discredit upon itself for choosing the wrong mission or assignment, and to save the UN embarrassment that would have further undermined its efforts.

The peacekeeping role was maintained until the end of November because it was Canada's only means of involvement, and the prime minister was concerned about improving his public image. The government believed that multilateral activities enabled Canada to play a larger part in the world, and the operation remained the only way to satisfy Canadians' mounting interest in the Somalia famine. In addition, the prime minister did not wish to cancel his offer of troops. He did not want to appear weak, and he was aware that peacekeeping roles were domestically popular and an activist commitment to this activity could help to restore his government's political fortunes.

The government's interest in multilateralism conflicted with its desire to be involved in delivering life-saving food. The government was only satisfied when it learned that there would be some aid to distribute, and that its zone was critical to Sahnoun's overall peacekeeping and peace-building strategy. The pressure on Sahnoun and the United Nations to respond decisively to the food crisis, which was the main concern in the West, undermined the UN peacekeeping mission. Canada added to the pressure on the United Nations that caused it to press forward and lose the consent of Aidid.

Vehicles at Canadian Forces Base Petawawa entrained for shipment
to the Port of Montreal, where they would be loaded on chartered
cargo vessels and sent to Somalia. The vehicles are all painted UN
peacekeeping white, as the Canadian Airborne Regiment was still
expecting to deploy to the northeast port town of Boosaaso for the UN
Operation in Somalia I. November 1992. *Courtesy Jeremy Mansfield.*

Canadian Airborne Regiment Battlegroup Commander Lieutenant-Colonel Carol
Mathieu (centre) and soldiers examine abandoned Soviet bombs and air-to-air
rockets at Baledogle airport, 90 kilometres northwest of Mogadishu. The airport
was the staging area for the deployment to Beledweyne as part of the US-led
Unified Task Force coalition. December 1992. *Courtesy Jeremy Mansfield.*

Hot Christmas dinner for Canadian soldiers at Baledogle airport, prepared by the HMCS *Preserver* galley and delivered by Sea King helicopter. This was one of the Canadian Battlegroup's only hot meals in Somalia; most of the time they relied on hard rations. The Beledweyne deployment commenced three days after Christmas. 25 December 1992. *Courtesy Rod Mackey.*

Canadian Airborne Regiment soldiers dig in to protect themselves from indirect fire at Beledweyne's airstrip. Having just landed, their immediate objective was to secure the airhead and make it defensible. 28 December 1992. *DND 93-016.*

Canadians soldiers drive in Mogadishu in 12½ ton truck on a trip to or from Mogadishu airport and the Canadian Joint Force Somalia Headquarters. Vehicles bearing flags of Italy and France, also major United Task Force contributors, are at left. Spring 1993. *DND ISC93-10106.*

Members of the Defence and Security platoon caught in Mogadishu traffic in a Bison armoured vehicle. They are identifiable as such because they were the first issued the new style helmets seen in the photograph. The D & S platoon was drawn not from the Airborne but from 1 Battalion, Royal Canadian Regiment, and was responsible for protection of the Canadian Joint Force Somalia Headquarters. A soldier readies a C-9 heavy machine gun at the rear of the Bison. Spring 1993. *Courtesy CFB Petawawa Military Museums, DND.*

Aerial view of the Shabeelle River and Beledweyne, the main city of the Beledweyne humanitarian relief sector. The Canadian Airborne Regiment Battlegroup camp was near the upper left corner of the photograph; the airstrip was on the other side of the river off to the right. Spring 1993. *DND 3132-010.*

Somali huts near Beledweyne. Few trees grew in the area and the thick,
metre-high brush was replete with sharp thorns. Such huts and brush were
characteristic of Beledweyne and its vicinity. Spring 1993. *Courtesy Rod Mackey*.

A local Somali clan elder (centre) and interpreter (right) speak to Canadian
Airborne Regiment Battlegroup Commander Lieutenant-Colonel Carol
Mathieu. This was part of the Canadian "hearts and minds" strategy
designed to convince Somalis to work with the Unified Task Force and make
peace. Canadian Joint Force Somalia Commander Colonel Serge Labbé
(background) and Mathieu arrived at this strategy intuitively, with Mathieu
handling day-to-day implementation. January 1993. *Courtesy Rod Mackey*.

A 5/4 ton wheeled ambulance and what would be, after extensive repairs, the Unit Medical Station in Beledweyne. This facility was intended to provide rudimentary first aid to the more than a thousand soldiers located in Beledweyne and Matabaan. Casualties beyond its capabilities would be flown to Mogadishu, a seventy-five-minute trip. The state of the building, with no roof, no windows, and wiring ripped from the walls, was common to Somalia at that time. Eventually US Navy Seabees patched the roof and the Canadians refurbished the inside and installed air conditioning. January 1993. *Courtesy Rod Mackey*

The dismounted 2 Commando, Canadian Airborne Regiment, conducting a foot patrol in Beledweyne. This is the standard kind of patrol for an urban setting and was done many times during the mission. The soldiers look in different directions to cover off angles of approach. It is possible to deduce from the Tilley hats, which were eventually exchanged, that the Canadians had been in Somalia only a short time when this picture was taken. January 1993. *Courtesy Rod Mackey*.

Bison armoured vehicle on patrol in the Beledweyne humanitarian relief sector. The UN markings were removed from the Canadian vehicles once the mission changed and became the US-led Unified Task Force in southern Somalia, but with no time to repaint the vehicles they had to be left white. Spring 1993. *Courtesy Rod Mackey.*

Grizzly armoured vehicles of 1 or 3 Commando, Canadian Airborne Regiment, on patrol in the Beledweyne humanitarian relief sector. The Grizzly performed well in Somalia though there were problems with flat tires caused by sharp stones, spent shell casings, and tough thorns from the local vegetation. It possessed .50 calibre and coaxial 7.62 machine guns. Spring 1993. *Courtesy Rod Mackey.*

Canadian commanders and visiting VIPs meet elders of Beledweyne's sixteen leading clans. Working with the clans, whose positions and representatives were often open to question, was the Canadians' most difficult challenge. Facing the Somalis in the foreground is Colonel Serge Labbé; beside him is Special Service Force Brigade Commander Brigadier-General Ernie Beno; and Lieutenant-Colonel Carol Mathieu is standing. At the head table, right to left, are Maritime Commander Vice-Admiral P.W. Cairns, Deputy Minister of National Defence Robert Fowler, and Land Forces Commander Lieutenant-General Gordon Reay. February 1993. *Courtesy Rod Mackey.*

Life in the Beledweyne camp off-duty. Captain Jeff Wilson, one of the Canadian Airborne Regiment forward observation officers, teaches scuba diving to troops who could get their certification during leave in Mombassa, Kenya. This room was also the sergeants' mess. The television had no broadcast signal but worked with a VCR. February-March 1993. *Courtesy CFB Petawawa Military Museums, DND.*

Master-Corporal Steve Madore (crouched) briefs senior Canadians on the landmine threat. Canadian armoured vehicles struck mines six times, a very high number, but fortunately there were no injuries among the crews. Listening to the brief, right to left, are Colonel Serge Labbé; Lieutenant-Colonel Peter Kenward, who would be the last Airborne Regiment commander; and Admiral John Anderson, Chief of the Defence Staff. March 1993. *Courtesy Jeremy Mansfield.*

Food relief being ladled from a 45-gallon drum. Inside may well have been UNIMIX, a high-protein cereal blend, which was the mainstay of UN and NGO supplementary feeding programs in Somalia. The drum rested on rocks, under which was a log fire that would keep the mixture warm for hours. Spring 1993. *Courtesy Jeremy Mansfield*.

A typical convoy. Service Commando and 3 Commando of the Canadian Airborne Regiment escort supplies and equipment to Beledweyne. A borrowed US Army truck, Canadian Grizzly armoured vehicles, and an ambulance are visible. Spring 1993. *Courtesy CFB Petawawa Military Museums, DND.*

Somalis cluster around Labrador native Private John O'Dell of 1 Section, 6 Platoon, 2 Commando, Canadian Airborne Regiment. This photograph was taken while war artists who painted pictures of the deployed soldiers were being escorted through Beledweyne. Spring 1993. *Courtesy CFB Petawawa Military Museums, DND.*

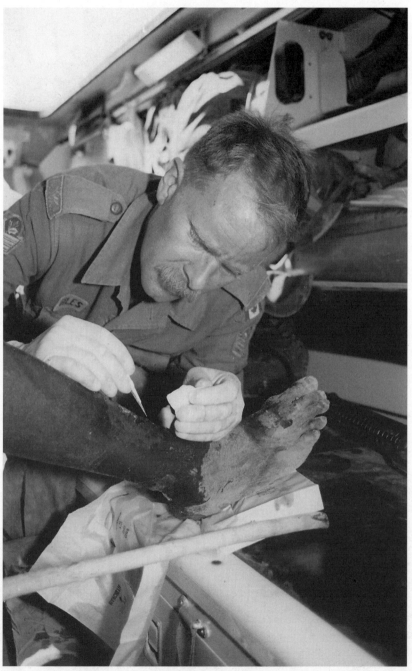

A wounded Somali is tended by medic Sergeant D.W. Giles during a routine humanitarian supply escort mission. The sergeant and the Somali are inside a Bison armoured vehicle, ambulance variant. Spring 1993. *Courtesy Rod Mackey*.

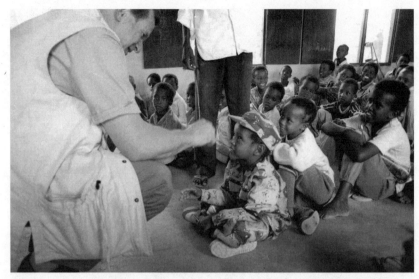

Major-General (ret'd) Lewis MacKenzie greets Somali students in a classroom in Canada's area of operations. MacKenzie, who retired in March 1993, visited Somalia in April as a member of the media shooting a documentary for Baton Broadcasting. Four schools were rebuilt with Canadian assistance. April 1993. *Courtesy CFB Petawawa Military Museums, DND.*

Secretary of State for External Affairs Barbara McDougall addresses members of the Canadian Airborne Regiment Battlegroup in Beledweyne during her May 1993 visit. The troops are presenting a general salute. Having seen schools built with Canadian assistance and a local hospital supported by Canadian medical staff, she began her speech by saying: "I have never been so proud to be a Canadian." May 1993. *Courtesy CFB Petawawa Military Museums, DND.*

UN Operation in Somalia II replacements near the Canadian water point in Beledweyne. These unarmed German logisticians were part of that country's first military deployment outside Europe since the Second World War. Italians and Nigerians would be responsible for UN security in the area. Beside the Germans is the Canadian "silver bullet," a tanker truck that hauled potable water to the encampment after treatment by desalination equipment. May 1993. *Courtesy Jeremy Mansfield.*

Lieutenant-Colonel Carol Mathieu, Canadian Airborne Regiment Commander. He assumed command in October 1992, led the Airborne Regiment Battlegroup in Somalia, and was succeeded by Lieutenant-Colonel Peter Kenward after that operation, in September 1993. *Courtesy CFB Petawawa Military Museums, DND.*

Colonel Serge Labbé, Canadian Joint Force Somalia Commander. This photograph was taken on the HMCS *Preserver* during a meeting with his headquarters staff. *Preserver* served as Labbé's headquarters from mid-December 1992 to January 1993, when a headquarters was formed and co-located with the Unified Task Force's in Mogadishu. *Courtesy CFB Petawawa Military Museums, DND.*

6
Problems with the Expanded UN Operation

As was seen in the last chapter, by contributing troops, Brian Mulroney's government hoped to strengthen United Nations Operation in Somalia I and to show Canadians that their humanitarian values were being acted upon. The UN mission had been expanded to correct certain problems, such as the original operation's over-centralization in Mogadishu, Somalia's capital, and to open new avenues for delivery of relief supplies. Canada accepted a role in the northeast of Somalia, but this presented a problem for the government because no one was starving in that area. The government believed that it would be criticized in the domestic media if the Canadian peacekeepers deployed to Somalia without aid to deliver.

The UN plan also created operational difficulties for the Canadian Forces to grapple with. The strategy did not alter the fact that securing the consent of the leading disputants was extremely difficult in the middle of civil war. The Canadian Forces mission to Boosaaso was nicknamed Operation Cordon. In August, military decision makers determined the shape of the contingent. Canada's military and political leaders shared the UN's determination to press ahead notwithstanding local opposition, but they lacked clear understanding of the tasks the Canadian Forces would perform in Somalia and engaged unaware that the UN plan had been fatally undermined by the overbearing way in which it was implemented. The Mulroney government wanted to strengthen international confidence in UN-led multilateralism, but the operation it supported would have the opposite effect.

Mohamed Sahnoun, the special representative of the secretary-general in Somalia and overall head of the mission, was the inspiration for the enlargement. He believed that Security Council resolution 751 (24 April) could be implemented more easily if the peacekeeping operation were spread out across the country. Sahnoun called for the establishment of UN offices at a major port in four designated areas: the northwest (Berbera), the northeast (Boosaaso), the centre (Mogadishu), and the south (Kismaayo).[1] A zone director reporting directly to the special representative would head each office.

The zone directors would manage the UN peacekeeping, nongovernmental organization (NGO), and UN aid agency operations in their area and co-ordinate with headquarters in Mogadishu.

UN Secretary-General Boutros Boutros-Ghali proposed a fifth zone to be located in Mandera, Kenya, in his 24 August report to the Council. He wanted NGOs and the UN High Commissioner for Refugees to manage the zone and feed the starving Somalis in the adjoining region of Gedo before they were forced to leave home in search of food. The plan called for peacekeepers (at first Nigerians and later Egyptians) to escort food convoys from Mandera to Gedo. Its purpose was also to forestall mass migration into Kenya, thereby decreasing tensions along the volatile Kenya-Somalia border.[2] Boutros-Ghali was optimistic because the second UN Technical Team had visited Gedo in mid-August and found the local people supportive of a UN presence.[3] Without knowing it, UN officials may have made a protocol error. The Kenyan government believed it had not been adequately consulted before the proposal's release.[4] More significant, President Daniel Arap Moi of Kenya was of the view that Somalia's problems should be solved from inside Somalia.[5] Moi was "unusually sensitive to the domestic involvement of foreign countries" since Kenya was in the middle of its first multi-party elections.[6] In early October, he informed the UN that it would not be allowed to establish the zone in Mandera.

The Kenya and Somalia zones were supposed to assist humanitarian relief efforts. NGOs had aid in their "pipelines," but the lack of convoy protection made it almost impossible to deliver food to the capital and the countryside. The International Committee of the Red Cross had been forced to break with tradition and hire 2,600 gunmen to protect its personnel, convoys, and warehouses in Somalia.[7] Red Cross president Cornelio Sommaruga, in the organization's review of 1992, said that "never before had our activities in certain conflicts seemed so fundamentally questioned."[8] Sahnoun expected the presence of peacekeepers in the zone ports to provide delivery options and the security requested by some NGOs. Troops might have "collateral good" for peace and reconciliation, he said, since "because of them we were already working on the idea of having a police. So in a sense all of these things were following each other."[9]

Boutros-Ghali strongly supported this approach, but the UN's objectives may have been too ambitious. He wanted the world body to become more effective in Somalia, and he hoped that the redesigned UN mission would be able to accomplish a broad range of tasks. The secretary-general com-mented that the mission would be responsible for protecting aid deliveries and monitoring ceasefires (peacekeeping), fostering a settlement through "conciliation, mediation and good offices" (diplomatic peacemaking), and demobilizing and disarming the Somali fighters (peace building).[10] The latter related to the construction of self-sustaining peace. The operation's peace-building tasks may seem excessive, but they were consistent with the international community's view at the time that once the UN stopped the fighting and provided stability, the disputants would come to their senses and, with help, sort things out themselves.[11]

The decentralization of the mission created additional problems that should have caused the UN and Canada to reconsider. The zone plan was in response to two problems: security was needed in the countryside and the capital, and the mission's five-hundred-person security force (in place in Mogadishu as of mid-September) was too small and underequipped.[12] The new strategy did not alleviate the second concern. Worse, it sought to avoid the extremely insecure capital even though that city was the heart of the relief effort because it had the country's largest functioning port and was close to the main land routes into the famine-stricken inter-riverine area.[13] This should have made Canada pause since the expanded mission was calling for tasks and deployments that were far removed in some cases from the famine in the south.

The way the mission's strength was increased undercut the entire UN strategy. Sahnoun's negotiations with the factions revolved around five-hundred-person battalions, and the progress he was making is evident from the Council's establishment of the zones in resolution 767 (27 July).[14] Boutros-Ghali's 24 August report to the Council reflected an important shift in attitude, for it recommended 750-person battalions for Mandera and the southern, northwest, and northeast zones, on top of the five hundred approved "in principle" for the central zone under resolution 751 (24 April). In a report addendum, the secretary-general requested another 719 logistics troops, which would increase the operation to 4,219.[15] Boutros-Ghali doubled what Sahnoun had been discussing with the Somalis, and he got Council approval for the plan in resolution 775 (28 August) without pausing to consult the factions about it. The Somalis saw this as an insult and breach of faith. According to Sahnoun, they grumbled, "'These people at the United Nations are double-crossing us. They tell us something, and they are doing something else.' That was the sort of thing people resented ... We were suddenly seen as enemies. They were before more sitting as friends, but suddenly, they became suspicious ... And that is when the problems started."[16]

Council resolution 775 reapproved the zones and by mistake increased the Somalia mission to 3,500. It had overlooked the logistics personnel. The president of the Council rectified this in an 8 September letter (S/24532) to Boutros-Ghali.[17] As Sahnoun indicates, the Somalis greeted the sudden news of the expansion with hostility, and this foreshadowed an important change in how they perceived and responded to the UN operation.

Boutros-Ghali's fait accompli was not a misreading of the Somali political scene, but part of a strategy for dealing with the factions. The UN did not know how to ensure respect of the international community's will in places where no government existed. There was no one who could negotiate a Status of Forces Agreement to confirm what peacekeepers could and could not do (and provide a measure of protection for the mission). Under-Secretary-General Marrack Goulding, head of the UN Department of Peacekeeping Operations, said that the mission's difficulties related directly to the absence of recognized political leaders who could reliably conclude agreements pertaining to mission deployments and activities.[18] The UN thus decided, with Canadian and broad international support, to adhere less rigorously to the peacekeeping principle of consent.

This approach was described in Boutros-Ghali's conflict-resolution blueprint, *An Agenda for Peace* (June 1992). It defined peacekeeping as "the deployment of a UN presence in the field, *hitherto* with the consent of all the parties concerned."[19] This statement did not mean that the UN was prepared to apply force in certain situations, since that would have run against the impartial and nonviolent UN organizational culture.[20] The intention was to give the UN flexibility when it came to coping with less permissive environments like Somalia. In doing so, *An Agenda for Peace* showed that the UN was profoundly naive when it came to trying to control civil violence, in that a decreased reliance on consent could easily, as in Somalia, heighten the resentment local populations felt toward peacekeepers, making avoidance of the use of arms more difficult. This would have negative implications for the UN. While peacekeeping was seen as something the secretary-general managed, the use of force was the purview of powerful states.[21]

UN assertiveness dismayed the Somalia mission officials who had worked hard on its consensual approach. Force Commander Brigadier-General Imtiaz Shaheen, for example, rejected the UN's "boorish attitude," arguing that "we were not there to wage war on the people that we were to save, but arrogance got the better of the powers that be."[22] Sahnoun could not secure agreements for the extra troops announced by Boutros-Ghali, and though he continued as special representative for several months, he believed in late August that he may have to resign.[23]

Sahnoun created tension with Boutros-Ghali by publicly airing his dissatisfaction with the UN aid agency response (especially compared with the International Committee of the Red Cross), but their disagreement was larger than this. Sahnoun "got into a collision course with the Secretary-General," said Maurice Baril, then a Canadian brigadier-general and Boutros-Ghali's military adviser. He "would not agree with the approach we were taking."[24] Boutros-Ghali questioned Sahnoun's efforts to "understand" and establish "warm relations" with Ali Mahdi Mohamed and Mohamed Farah Aidid. He believed that Sahnoun had allowed the operation to succumb to a "protection racket."[25] Sahnoun reportedly told Phillip Johnston, the president of CARE USA, who had taken a leave of absence to serve as director of the UN 100-Day humanitarian relief plan in Somalia, that "For me to do my job, it is essential I have the complete confidence of the Secretary-General."[26] As of October he did not have it.

Boutros-Ghali's preferred course was to deploy a larger force even without the agreement of all factions. This was incompatible with Sahnoun's gradual, consensual, bottom-up diplomatic peacemaking strategy, which involved tapping existing sources of local leadership, such as the clan elders and civil society representatives (intellectuals, local NGOs, and others), to gradually rebuild stability.[27] As Sahnoun noted, "I think there was, on the part of [UN headquarters in] New York, conviction that there was a better fix which will be quicker, and therefore which will be much more visible. And that, in a sense, I was taking a little bit too much time, that I should push things a little bit faster."[28]

The UN's eagerness for more timely results seriously weakened Sahnoun's ability to manage the factions since some of them, Aidid most importantly, refused to permit more blue helmets to deploy. Aidid told *Globe and Mail* reporter John Stackhouse in September that if "the United Nations wants to bring in more troops, it will have to do so by force. It is absolutely illegal and we will not accept it. We are a sovereign state."[29] The UN argued that its peacekeeping operation was impartial and that its "object [was] to save lives, defeat the sceptres of famine and civil strife and pave the way to political reconciliation,"[30] but the secretary-general's fait accompli in August made Aidid unwilling to co-operate with Sahnoun or respect this impartiality. Although Sahnoun continued to make progress in September and October, his last initiative, a cross-clan reconciliation conference held on the Seychelles Islands, took place on 23-26 October without Aidid's support. Sahnoun's resignation on the 26th came after a telex from UN headquarters in New York harshly criticized his decision to hold the conference.

Sahnoun departed as Aidid's mistrust of the UN was on the rise. Osman Hassan Ali "Ato," a chief Aidid financier, told Nairobi High Commission interlocutors in late October that Aidid believed Sahnoun and the UN were playing games with him and wasting time with bureaucratic procedures.[31] On the 28th, Aidid withdrew his consent and promised to oppose the multi-zone plan. The Pakistani battalion "would no longer be tolerated in the streets of Mogadishu," the "deployment of United Nations troops in Kismaayo [the southern zone] and Berbera [the northwest zone] was no longer acceptable," and any other forcible troop deployment "would be met by violence."[32] The operation's position became impossible once Aidid's consent and co-operation had disappeared.[33]

Under the circumstances, Sahnoun likely did as well as anyone could have. However, his gradual reconciliation process meant that millions were being spent to deliver only a trickle of food, and this clashed with the desire in New York, Ottawa, and elsewhere to immediately implement more effective international action. The pressure to act was severe when resolution 775 was approved on 28 August,[34] and as the months passed it became more intense. Few democratic governments did not feel pressed by the clamour to "do something," and UN peacekeeping was "something" that they could "do" in Somalia.[35]

The Joint Staff and Force Mobile Command (later called the Land Force or army) began preparations for the deployment to northeast Somalia in August. National Defence Headquarters' senior operations officers – Chief of the Defence Staff General John de Chastelain, Vice Chief of the Defence Staff Vice-Admiral John Anderson, and Deputy Chief of the Defence Staff (Intelligence, Security, Operations) Major-General Paul Addy – addressed the chief's main challenge regarding Somalia: "assessing our capability for involvement in another battalion-level UN operation – in addition to the ones ongoing at the time – and determining if or how they could all be sustained."[36] Military leaders did not believe the task was a great challenge, but some had difficulty with the UN strategy. The Canadian Forces worried about the lack of a UN evacuation plan, it thought that separating the battalions in Somalia by vast distances was militarily unsound,[37] and, most important, it did not know what its contingent would do upon arrival in Somalia.

Joint Staff preparations had been under way since late July. J3 Plans had found that the Forces could sustain a year-long battalion-sized deployment. J3 Plans had been thinking about Mogadishu, but the estimate remained valid when the mission shifted to Boosaaso. The Joint Staff policy branch was positive about a role in Somalia, in part because it fit the multilateral humanitarian strain in the government's foreign policy. An aide mémoire to National Defence Minister Marcel Masse noted that Council resolution 767 (27 July) had called upon "the international community as a whole to provide urgent humanitarian assistance to Somalia." Canada had "already expressed considerable concern over the situation in Somalia," they wrote, and participation in the Somalia mission was consistent with these statements.[38]

Senior policy officers believed operations like Somalia would be able to protect human rights in war-torn countries. Larry Murray, then a rear admiral and the associate assistant deputy minister (Policy and Communications), has noted that while the Canadian Forces was not euphoric about peacekeeping, "there was a real awareness that the Cold War world was gone, and that the Persian Gulf War had been a successful military intervention." Policy staff in the national headquarters helped determine the UN's needs and what Canada could do. "Somalia caught people's attention" and there was "openness to be as helpful as we could ... that was the mindset."[39]

The mission could easily have remained unattractive in August. The security situation in Somalia was just as bad in August as in May, and the multi-zone plan was militarily questionable and contained few new opportunities for humanitarian relief in the famine area. Mulroney's desire for an engagement, demonstrated by his 13 August letter to Boutros-Ghali, diminished the weight attached to these factors. The expanded mission also seemed more in line with Canada's defence policy as it pertained to peace-keeping, notably regarding the potential for success. J5 Policy Operations Colonel John Bremner said the resolution 751 (24 April) mandate, which was declined, and the resolution 775 (28 August) mandate, which Canada accepted, called for "two different missions ... [with] different force levels, different objectives, different areas, different everything." A second policy analysis had been undertaken, and the Somalia operation was now "assessed as being viable and Canada said yes."[40]

J3 Peacekeeping's Colonel Mike Houghton got to an early start on the mission based on information received informally from Colonel Douglas Fraser, the military representative with Canada's Permanent Mission to the United Nations in New York. For Houghton, the secretary-general's 22 July report was a "major development" that signified the "dropping of the first plan that we had recommended as a result of the technical mission I was on, and a new mission going in, and [the] coming up with an entirely new plan."[41] Canada was neither advised on nor asked to participate in the second UN Technical Mission that developed the second operational plan outlined by the secretary-general in his 24 August report and authorized by resolution 775 (28 August). Had the Canadian Forces been able to place a member (Houghton being the most likely candidate), it would have obtained current and specific information on the peacekeeping operation. These technical reconnaissances could be quite useful. When Canada prepared for its north-east Somalia assignment, it drew on one of the ideas – using HMCS *Preserver* as a floating logistics base and headquarters – that Houghton had developed for the UN while on its March-April reconnaissance.[42]

Part of J3 Peacekeeping's job was monitoring the Canadian Forces' readiness and tracking developments at UN Headquarters. This became relevant when Fraser contacted Houghton informally a second time in mid-August, provid-ing one of the first indications that Canada would be asked for a battalion for Boosaaso and passing on the details of the Technical Mission's plan.[43] Houghton's cell helped J3 Plans determine which battalions could deploy. Commander of Force Mobile Command Lieutenant-General Jim Gervais decided on the unit, but J3 Peacekeeping contributed to the J Staff estimate after consulting with Force Mobile Command. Houghton recommended the Airborne because it had completed desert training in anticipation of the UN Mission for the Referendum in the Western Sahara. He believed it had an edge in the individualist, self-reliant training that would be required in Somalia, which was totally lacking in infrastructure.[44]

Bernd Horn argues that past Airborne commanders like Houghton and Lieutenant-General Kent Foster, who commanded Force Mobile Command until 1991 and briefly was acting vice chief of the defence staff in summer 1992, influenced the selection process for the Somalia mission so that the regiment was chosen. Horn is right that these and other officers pressed for its selection at every opportunity.[45] But Addy and Gervais, the decision makers, were not influenced by them. They had reasons of their own for selecting the unit. Addy has argued that the "Airborne family" was irrelevant and was ignored and that the Airborne was selected for four reasons: it was a well-trained unit whose members had at least one regimental tour with another unit; it had undergone mission-specific training for Western Sahara; they were inoculated; and they were the Forces' designated UN standby unit.[46] These factors made choosing the Airborne a practical decision. Murray, who succeeded Addy as deputy chief of the defence staff in early February 1993, said it was incredibly obvious that the Airborne was the right unit. He could not recall anyone suggesting an alternative.[47]

Of the factors mentioned by Addy, the most decisive one was the Airborne's UN standby status. Considering the operational strain that the Canadian Forces was under, it made sense that the otherwise unoccupied standby unit should take the Somalia assignment. According to de Chastelain, "any suggestion that the Airborne Regiment was recommended for the Somalia operation for a reason other than because it was the standby battalion, is, I believe, incorrect."[48]

Gervais had additional reasons for choosing the Airborne. When it comes to determining the shape of contingents involving their personnel, the Environmental Commanders are extremely important.[49] Although the Joint Staff estimate noted that the Airborne had been recently cut in strength and that it lacked enough qualified armoured vehicle drivers,[50] this was not overly significant to him. Gervais had decided in late July that the Airborne would go because it had recently been on standby for such missions and this suited Force Mobile Command's restructuring program and took into account its heavy operational burden.[51] Brigadier-General Ernest Beno recalled that when he arrived at Canadian Forces Base Petawawa on 7 August to take command of the Special Service Force Brigade, of which the Airborne was one of ten units, the latter's selection for Somalia was a fait accompli.[52]

The restructuring was the key organizational reason behind the assignment of Somalia to the paratroopers. In 1991-92, Force Mobile Command started to regroup its forces into four geographic areas – Land Force Atlantic Area, Secteur Québec des Forces Terrestres, Land Force Central Area (Ontario), and Land Force Western Area – which reported back to the Headquarters. Force Mobile Command itself was renamed Land Force Command in mid-October 1992. Gervais was acting on the principle that the physical occupation of the nation's territory was a unique army responsibility. The new structure was a convenient way to subdivide the growing number of Canadian Forces peacekeeping operations among the Land Force. The idea was to have "at least one major commitment, because there were also others associated with United Nations missions, for each of the three of the areas."[53]

Under the Area structure, the Airborne was the best of the available choices, and this was one reason why it was selected over the three other units in the J3 Plans estimate for Somalia. Force Mobile Command gave Secteur Québec des Forces Terrestres the battlegroup-sized task in Bosnia that the government had accepted in September 1992 called Operation Cavalier (originally Operation Dagger).[54] This meant the armoured units from that Area – 12e Régiment Blindé du Canada and 5e Régiment d'artillerie légère du Canada – were unavailable even though the estimate had counted them as possibilities. Western Area was also "entirely committed." Its responsibilities included Operations Harmony (Croatia) and Snowgoose (Cyprus), a North Atlantic Treaty Organisation role (the Western Area had to be ready to contribute a unit to the Composite Force/Allied Mobile Force [Land] in an emergency), and maintenance of an immediate reaction unit in case of a domestic crisis.[55]

Land Force Central Area and the Special Service Force at Petawawa were consequently named the mounting area and assembly base for Operation Cordon. The Royal Canadian Dragoons, the Special Service Force armoured regiment cited in the J3 Plans estimate, was excluded by Force Mobile Command for three reasons. The Royal Canadian Dragoons was busy because it had to provide up to a squadron (roughly one-third of its strength) to Secteur Québec des Forces Terrestres' Bosnia mission. Somalia was seen as an infantry mission that could be more easily accomplished by mounted soldiers (the Airborne) than dismounted tank drivers (the Royal Canadian Dragoons), and the Royal Canadian Dragoons' main piece of equipment, the Cougar fire support/tank trainer vehicle, was considered overkill for a UN peacekeeping mission.[56] If the Royal Canadian Dragoons was sent to Somalia, Gervais believed, the unit would require cross-training on the Grizzly, which was the less combat-capable general-purpose armoured vehicle used by 1 Battalion, Royal Canadian Regiment. According to Gervais, mounting the Airborne on 1 Royal Canadian Regiment vehicles was better than tying up two armoured battalions (the Royal Canadian Dragoons and 1 Royal Canadian Regiment) for Operation Cordon.[57]

Instead of examining the restructuring plan, the Somalia Inquiry focused on the Airborne. The commissioners concluded that concern for morale within the unit, not its ability to deploy rapidly, was behind its selection. The Inquiry argued that "there was nothing in the designation of the [regiment] as Canada's UN standby unit that uniquely suited it for the Somalia mission," and that, in fact, the Airborne "could not possibly [have] deploy[ed] within seven days for the Somalia operation."[58] The Canadian Forces, as is discussed below, was confident the unit could deploy rapidly.

For the Canadian Forces, morale was only significant in relation to the Airborne's on-call posture. Military decision makers recognized that the Airborne could not always be held back because it was the Canadian Forces' rapid-reaction unit, and thus it was selected for Western Sahara and, when that was cancelled, for Somalia.[59] Morale, de Chastelain noted, was secondary in the case of Operation Cordon, although morale was not a secondary issue in general.[60] While boosting morale was a concern, the Canadian Forces picked the Airborne because the situation was urgent, there were no other appropriate choices, and it was the standby unit. "It would have been unusual," de Chastelain wrote later, "not to select the standby battalion for the task, especially given the number of combat units involved .in other overseas operations."[61]

In addition to the operational pressure being placed on the Canadian Forces in mid-1992, military leaders believed that the Airborne was best because a deployment appeared imminent. Mulroney had indicated that Canada would contribute to the high-profile Somalia mission, the United States had aired the possibility of the Canadian Forces replacing the slow-moving Pakistanis as the lead nation in Mogadishu, and on 31 August, Kofi Annan, then assistant-secretary-general of the UN Department of Peacekeeping Operations, said he hoped the Canada Forces could be deployed to the northeast in two to three weeks.[62] The Airborne had been designated the standby unit to handle contingencies such as this. It could move in a week, assuming that most of its equipment and logistic support was able to follow. De Chastelain wanted to ensure that the UN knew the Forces could move promptly if necessary. At the morning daily executive meeting on 3 September, he asked Assistant Deputy Minister Dr. Kenneth Calder, (Policy and Communications), to remind the UN that the Airborne could be deployed in less than two weeks.[63]

From late August to early September, National Defence Headquarters thought the UN would soon be ready for Canada's contingent. A Department of National Defence press release suggested that the only thing delaying Operation Cordon was the need to finalize agreements with the other troop-contributing counties. "As soon as member states have agreed to the arrangements," the Department noted, "the United Nations will enlarge its present mission in Somalia."[64] The Canadian Forces geared up for a rapid deployment. The Operation Cordon Warning Order issued on 4 September stated that the Airborne reconnaissance and advance party would depart on the 11th and 25th. In the port of Halifax, sailors worked feverishly to prepare HMCS *Preserver* for departure on the 12th. Various equipment had to be installed (such as a worldwide satellite telephone communications system called INMARSAT, a reverse osmosis desalination unit to enhance the ship's capability to make fresh water, and eight .50-calibre heavy machine guns), and it needed to be stocked with supplies.[65]

The contingent's departure was delayed because of disputes with the UN over resources, complications regarding the provision of cargo ships, and the UN's inability to get consent for the operation's establishment. The UN was always under pressure from member states to cut costs, and this could come at the expense of mission effectiveness. The UN, for example, wanted the contingent to deploy with 70 vehicles in total, but in a 4 September briefing in which Force Mobile Command outlined its contingency plan, the chief of the defence staff was urged to ensure that 150 were approved. These would be spread out among the Airborne's three company-sized "commandos," which would each receive 14 armoured Grizzlies owing to the large area of operations (400 × 250 kilometres), the engineer squadron, combat services support company, reconnaissance platoon, and the small reserve.[66] Another issue was the larger-than-normal reconnaissance team Canada wanted to send to their zone because of the uncertainties surrounding the mission. The Canadian Forces did not know what its contingent was supposed to do in northeast Somalia, and it was unsure as to the reception it would receive. To get answers, the Forces wanted to send a sizable group costing $100,000, but the UN refused to pay.[67] Sahnoun's inability to get factional consent for the mission enlargement also delayed the reconnaissance. The military was unable to confirm assumptions built into its plans.

Canadian Forces movement and logistics preparations were complicated by the delays. J4 Logistics had determined that the Canadian Forces contingent could deploy self-contained (with first-, second-, and limited third-line support) by bringing most of its materials, by being resupplied from Canada, and by procurement in theatre.[68] J4 Move calculated that *Preserver* could sail from Montreal to Boosaaso in twenty days and that the UN-chartered cargo ships, the MV *Bassro Star* and MV *Sysette*, could haul the contingent's heavy equipment in a month.[69] *Preserver* had to reach Boosaaso first to support the contingent advance party, which would set up camp and prepare to receive the main body. Before *Preserver* could leave, Addy noted during a daily executive meeting on 11 September, a detailed reconnaissance had to take place to guarantee that the *Preserver* left appropriately loaded and to enable J4 Financial and J1 Personnel to complete their procurement and staffing processes.[70]

The UN's inability to establish the mission or specify what its parts should be doing was another major problem encountered by the Canadian Forces. When the UN introduced more troops (Deputy Force Commander Canadian Forces Colonel Jim Cox and Australian movement and logistics personnel, increasing the mission's military strength from 550 to 564 in October),[71] the factions opposed this, and the UN move only contributed to the dramatic deterioration of the security situation. In the Boosaaso sector, co-operation was more forthcoming, in part because many Somalis from the region had immigrated to Canada and this piqued local interest in hosting the Canadian Forces.[72] According to Cox, the peacekeepers were seen by some Somalis as a humanitarian aid conduit, and in reality they were "after the influx of aid and money, and if it had to be a Canadian battalion to turn on the tap, well, OK."[73] More seriously, Canada's zone did not appear to be starving, and it had been reported that the region was even exporting livestock across the Red Sea to Yemen.[74] This was confirmed by the Canadian Forces' reconnaissance, which Sahnoun authorized on 6 October and took place 14-18 October.[75] It now appeared that the humanitarian role accepted so enthusiastically less than two months ago was not what it seemed and might come to embarrass the government.

The UN defended the zones because it believed they were critical to stability and the national reconciliation process. Shaheen, for example, said Boosaaso was only "seemingly peaceful," and that it "had all of the ingredients of violence on its turf. It just so happened that since warring factions converged onto Mogadishu for control, the far-flung places appeared quiet."[76] The UN intended to use the Canadian presence to show Somalis the benefits of co-operation. Sahnoun explained to Canada's permanent representative to the United Nations, Ambassador Louise Fréchette, that the Canadians would provide security and stability, escort food when necessary, and rebuild sanitation, water, and health services.[77]

Decision makers proceeded with the mission despite Aidid's objections to Canada's role. Sahnoun had authorized Canada's reconnaissance without Aidid's consent, and Aidid responded by asking Mulroney to stop in a 12 October letter. The "deployment of such forces in this manner would promote open conflict in Somalia and thus undermine the peace process we are now engaged in."[78] The government consulted with Sahnoun. On the 16th, Sahnoun informed Fréchette that Aidid's letter could be disregarded since he had no influence in the northeast.[79] The authorization of the Canadian deployment may have heightened the animosity between the UN and Aidid. The latter had a limited area of control, but he had the power to influence outcomes in Mogadishu and the famine-stricken area in the south, and Sahnoun's decision to allow the Canadian Forces reconnaissance team to deploy was another UN action that was against his wishes and interests.

In mid-October, the UN told Canada that its contingent was needed right away. On the 23rd, Boutros-Ghali "suddenly" asked Canada to immediately deploy its advance party, but this posed a problem for the Joint Staff movement and logistics planners, who had been waiting for the arrival dates of the UN-chartered roll-on/roll-off and load-on/load-off cargo ships to be confirmed before making final arrangements.[80] With the Airborne's reconnaissance only just completed, there was not enough time to purchase items like water and fuel storage and distribution systems and get them loaded on the cargo vessels when they docked at the Port of Montreal on 16 November.[81] The J4 Logistics cell advised J3 Peacekeeping that the Canadian Forces could not be ready for the ships. Not surprisingly, Boutros-Ghali was unimpressed when he heard that the Canadian Forces would miss the 16 November deadline and that the Airborne main body would not be fully deployed until early January 1993.

Reportedly, he said that this "would be embarrassing for Canada," since the Canadian Forces had said it could deploy in less then two weeks.[82]

The Joint Staff was able to finish the staff work for the pre-deployment part of Operation Cordon by mid-November and did not miss the rescheduled arrival times for the cargo ships (26 and 29 November). Because of damage to equipment aboard the *Bassro Star* during the Atlantic crossing, a third cargo ship, the MV *Tatarvo,* was scheduled to dock in Montreal on 22 December to carry replacements and supplies. With the reconnaissance analyzed and the Airborne declared operationally ready, J3 Operations Colonel Mike O'Brien issued the Operations Order on 13 November. The national-level military decision making for the Somalia mission was complete. J3 Peacekeeping was expected to monitor developments in Somalia and resolve any problems involving Canada's contingent. Reception of new dates for the cargo ships permitted *Preserver* to set sail on 16 November. It was expected to reach Boosaaso by 6 December. The Airborne advance party was supposed to arrive in several flights, staging through Djibouti, on the 6th to the 16th. The main body was to follow.[83] But shortly before the advance party's departure, the UN Somalia operation collapsed and was replaced by a US coalition, the Unified Task Force (also called Operation Restore Hope).

Conclusion

The Canadian Forces and United Nations planning for the expanded Somalia operation had several characteristics in common. Both were optimistic that peacekeepers could have a positive impact in Somalia despite the difficulties. Each was determined to proceed with significant operations despite a limited understanding of the complexities of the internal war. The Canadian Forces and UN preparations for the multi-zone mission demonstrated a willingness to proceed with deployments and increases in troop strength, although it appeared this would have to be done without Aidid's consent. The UN wanted to go beyond traditional peacekeeping. Canada was a leading sup-porter of the UN peacekeeping mission, but it was subsequently revealed that it contributed without sufficient knowledge of the tasks the Canadian Forces would be asked to perform. The government and Canadian Forces should have asked more questions about the viability of the UN's strategy.

The UN embarked on the multi-zone plan because the Somalia mission as configured by Security Council resolution 751 (24 April) was not succeeding. Sahnoun's objective was to decentralize the operation and deploy battalions to stabilize the four zones (later briefly five), improve the humanitarian situation, and encourage reconciliation. The idea was to avoid the violence in Mogadishu and to encourage uniform, countrywide stability. There was logic to this, but the plan never solved the problem of how peacekeepers were to function in an environment with no peace and no responsible political authorities to deal with.

The UN wanted to act more decisively. Boutros-Ghali increased the mission's strength to 4,219 in late August, which was more than double what Sahnoun had been proposing, without consulting the factions. This was ill conceived because it insulted the Somalis. Even with the higher numbers, the operation would not be able to dominate the country or Mogadishu, and it could not afford to distance itself from the crucial peacekeeping principle of consent. UN–Aidid tensions increased when the UN added personnel to the Somalia mission headquarters and authorized the Canadian Forces reconnaissance and full deployment without his permission. By late October, relations between Aidid and the peacekeeping mission had been poisoned.

Canada welcomed the UN's new approach, as defined by Council resolutions 767 (27 July) and 775 (28 August). Canadian political and military leaders wanted to support UN-led multilateralism and act in a significant way to alleviate the severe humanitarian suffering. The revised mission won the approval of the prime minister because it provided Canada with opportunities for a visible role and appeared to have a reasonable chance at success. From a defence policy point of view, the Somalia operation was now worthy of a Canadian contribution.

The "Airborne family" was not a factor in the regiment's selection for the Somalia mission. Houghton and Addy have argued that the Airborne was the best unit in terms of its training for the mission. Gervais has said that the Airborne was chosen in accordance with Force Mobile Command's policy of assigning operations to specific Areas and brigade groups. The Central Area/Special Service Force had been given Cordon.

The fact that the Airborne was the UN standby battalion was another factor behind its selection. The Airborne was ready to move quickly, but the advance party could not deploy until *Preserver*, the logistics base and headquarters, was on station. Before that could take place, UN approval for a reconnaissance was needed. There were delays because the UN was unwilling to pay for the large group the Forces wanted to send, and Sahnoun needed to conduct further negotiations with the factions in order to authorize all troop-contributing countries' reconnaissances and then their deployments at roughly the same time.

The UN complicated the Canadian Forces' move to northeastern Somalia. The secretary-general decided to go ahead with Canada's deployment, even though Aidid had not agreed to the presence of additional UN troops. This illustrated the UN's impatience with some Somali factions, and especially Aidid's. The Canadian Forces had to scramble to keep up with the UN's determination to press forward and could not be ready for the first cargo ship sent by the UN. New shipping times had to be arranged, and when they were the Canadian Forces deployed *Preserver*, setting its UN peacekeeping commitment in motion.

The UN and Canada encountered difficulty in Somalia because the situation was extremely complex and could not be resolved quickly. Decision makers' problems were worsened because they had energetically committed to the operation without a full understanding of the risks associated with peacekeeping in the midst of civil war, of the Canadian Forces' roles, and of the possible complications arising from the assertive implementation of the UN multi-zone plan. The Canadian Forces had doubts about the appropriateness of its assignment because it learned in October that the northeast was free of famine. Military preparations continued because the Somalia crisis was becoming increasingly dire and there was no alterative to the UN mission until the United States stepped forward in late November.

7
Robust Militarism: Support for the Unified Task Force

The United Nations Operation in Somalia I attempted to take decisive steps to assist the famine-relief effort by occupying the Mogadishu airport. The peacekeeping mission collapsed because a principal faction leader, Mohamed Farah Aidid, did not want UN forces to deploy, and he withdrew his consent completely once the UN changed tactics. Despite these difficulties, Brian Mulroney's government continued to support the blue helmet mission. He held this position until the United States-led Unified Task Force replaced the UN mission in early December 1992, and then he joined the peace enforcement coalition without hesitation. Participation in the coalition allowed Canada to support its interest in robust multilateralism and maintain close ties with the United States, and the Unified Task Force aid protection mandate was what Ottawa wanted to do all along. The government decided to engage in the coalition to serve these national interests and the government's politically motivated desire to be involved in a success and to be seen alleviating the famine. Domestic opposition to the US-commanded mission was muted because of the urgent need to act.

The continuous television reports of the famine shocked Americans as much as Canadians. US president George H.W. Bush decided to mount an intervention to show that he shared this concern and to advance political objectives. The coalition added lustre to the vision of a co-operative and peaceful "new world order" mentioned in his 1991 State of the Union address and appealed to his sense of noblesse oblige.[1] The Unified Task Force addressed the complaints of the Congressional Black Caucus, which, citing the US military actions in Grenada (1983), Panama (1989), and Kuwait (1990-91), had been asking, "Why not Africa?"[2] Ambassador Robert Oakley, special envoy of the president to Somalia from December 1992 to March 1993, noted that while Bush acted for fundamentally humanitarian reasons, the intervention softened criticism of US inaction in Bosnia-Herzegovina, where the Muslim majority population was fighting for survival, and responded to UN

Secretary-General Boutros Boutros-Ghali's charge that the West was helping
Europe but not Africa.[3]

Mulroney decided that Canada would contribute to the Unified Task
Force during a telephone conversation with Bush on 28 November. During
the call, Bush discussed his plans and asked for help. The prime minister
said that Canada would endeavour to do so, implying something would be
done.[4] The specifics were left to the Canadian Forces and the Department of
National Defence to determine (see Chapter 8). To a certain degree, Canada
succumbed to US pressure. The Persian Gulf War had illustrated that the
United States usually got its way with Canada when it focused on any single
issue,[5] and the call to arms was as hard to resist in 1992. And yet both leaders had concluded that something had to be done about Somalia. Jim Judd,
then the assistant secretary to Cabinet for foreign and defence policy in
the Privy Council Office, said the view "was certainly shared between them
that this was a situation that should not be allowed to continue without
intervention."[6]

The prime minister helped Bush because the management of Canada-US
relations through personal diplomacy was his most important priority.
Mulroney developed close ties with presidents Ronald Reagan and Bush
because he believed this influenced the entire relationship, which was absolutely vital to Canada. Mulroney noted after retirement that "the President
energizes the process so when word goes out that the President had a meeting with the Prime Minister of Canada and likes and admires him and wants
a file to be given the highest priority, that goes right through the system
... and things happen."[7] The vastness of the Canada-US link meant that it
did not depend on the leaders getting along. Much bilateral co-operation is
informal and lower-level – ranging from the ad hoc meetings of legislators
to the personal links between US and Canadian officials – and this is one of
the relationship's unique strengths.[8] Yet by developing special bonds with
American leaders, Mulroney sought to ease Canada's pursuit of bilateral and
multilateral concerns.[9]

Mulroney's personal style enhanced Canada's access to Washington's
decision making. The "relationships between the major leaders make a big
difference about what happens in the world and what doesn't," said Paul
Heinbecker.[10] By helping the United States shoulder the risks and burdens
of international problem solving on issues where Canadian and American
interests and values coincided, the prime minister and his senior advisers
believed that Canada could become a larger factor in US thinking. "Burden-
sharing," Mulroney reminded an American audience, "requires decision-
sharing."[11] In the case of the Gulf War, Canada was one of few countries to
receive advance notice of the start of the coalition aerial attacks on Iraq on
16 January 1991. Only the United Kingdom, which was a major contributor
of air forces, was notified significantly earlier.[12] For the Unified Task Force,

Bush called Mulroney the day before UN Secretary-General Boutros Boutros-Ghali brought the initiative to the Security Council's attention.[13]

By contributing forces to US-led initiatives, Canada would find bilateral relations easier to manage. Heinbecker noted that by being helpful, "you also got – and this should not be underplayed – you also got credit from the people who were interested in seeing you participate." There was no *quid pro quo* transference to other issues, but the United States might be more disposed to hearing Canadian leaders out if Canada was well regarded.[14] Washington appreciated Canada's timely contribution to the UN Peacekeeping Force in Cyprus in 1964, for example, and this may have created openness to Canadian positions during talks on the Canada-US Automotive Parts Agreement (1965).[15] By supporting the coalition, Mulroney may have refreshed US goodwill toward Canada.

Mulroney's reaction to the coalition enabled him to support Canada's interest in robust multilateralism. The prime minister was comfortable with the prospect of using force and did not regret the allies' use of its might during the Gulf War.[16] Government leaders believed the time had come to move beyond peacekeeping in Somalia, and they were pleased that the United Nations had sanctioned force. Barbara McDougall told the House of Commons that the "process of achieving an international consensus to act strongly has taken a frustratingly long time, despite the urging of countries like ours. We were indeed among the first."[17] Days later, Mulroney said a Unified Task Force-like mission should be sent to the Balkans.[18]

The government was interested in using international institutions to balance or countervail US influence on Canada, and it thought that the coalition could perform a similar function by preventing the UN from being crowded out by US unilateralism. Since Lester B. Pearson's time as External Affairs minister, decision makers had been of the view that international organizations and activities could diffuse and constrain power and prevent its abuse.[19] By participating in the coalition, Canada could engage but avoid working alone with the United States, could, within the limits of the possible, subject United States power to a collective discipline, and could encourage US recourse to and respect of multilateral instruments. It was in Canada's interests to participate in ad hoc coalitions that served US foreign policy because this could encourage the United States to pursue other security objectives co-operatively.[20] The United States, noted Reid Morden, had been unable or unwilling to contribute many peacekeepers during the Cold War. Now, "we had the Americans and they were prepared to play ... So you had to think very carefully before you say 'no.'"[21]

The political level saw the intervention as an opportunity for co-operation, but External Affairs and International Trade Canada was slightly uncomfortable because it was aggressive and not commanded by the United Nations. The higher level of danger made the mission more controversial.[22] External

Affairs had to talk itself into doing the operation. Ultimately, Morden noted, the feeling was "you would rather do things another way, but if this was the way to get the people with real muscle on the ground which the folks will listen to, and to stop the chaos, then you do it even though it might not be quite what you want."[23] Canada had acted similarly before when circumstances had required, and this had the effect of weakening resistance among most people in government to joining with the United States.[24] Canada had participated in the International Commission of Control and Supervision (1973), which provided the United States with a face-saving means of extricating itself from Vietnam, and Canada had contributed to the US-led coalition in the Gulf War.

But while the Unified Task Force was being discussed and defined, Canada maintained its original UN commitment. Canada was the peacekeeping mission's only supporter by 1 December. Egypt, Belgium, and Pakistan (which had a battalion in Mogadishu serving with the UN operation in Somalia) were joining the enforcement action.[25] The government believed its commitment entitled Canada to play a part in negotiations, but whether this translated into influence over international decision making is questionable. The Permanent Mission reminded the United Nations that "Canada is UNOSOM [and] needs to be consulted."[26]

Government officials asked the United Nations to consider a "Canadian option," in which the coalition would deploy to southern Somalia while Canada operated separately (and distinctly) in the north. It would lead a "UNOSOM pied-à-terre in the northeast."[27] Officials knew Canada had not received a formal written request for a coalition contribution, Boutros-Ghali was not resistant, and the United States thought peacekeepers could succeed in the north.[28] Had the option been selected, troop limitations could have forced Canada to drastically reduce its coalition contribution or make no contribution. Skipping the Unified Task Force does not appear to have been seriously considered, but the idea was looked at. Officials were searching for the best way to further Canadian interests and values. The government could have been put in the uncomfortable position of having to choose either UN multilateralism or a US initiative that was less multilateral but included a vital bilateral dimension. This choice did not have to be made, for on 2 December Boutros-Ghali decided that peacekeeping and peace enforcement should not be permitted to co-exist in the same theatre. The secretary-general suspended the first UN mission until the US-led coalition stabilized the southern half of Somalia.[29] This resulted in cancellation of the option.

With the US intervention about to become a reality and the UN mission receding into the background, Canada did not try to stand behind the world organization any longer. The Gulf War coalition had harnessed the will and military might of like-minded states, while, faced with the Somalia crisis, the UN's consensual approach appeared seriously limited and old-fashioned. Some

Canadian decision makers, such as Judd, believed the "blue helmet concept" had been "called into question big time" by the Iraq-Kuwait conflict. The "United Nations as an institution had not successfully adjusted to the post-Cold War era."[30] The government preferred a broader-based multilateralism centred on the United Nations, but few senior officials in External Affairs and the Privy Council Office were prepared to argue that Canada should stay "true blue" and stick with the UN. National Defence believed that people were starving now, help was needed now, and, since the United Nations could not provide protection, the Canadian Forces should deploy immediately under a non-UN mandate.[31]

Decision makers did not seriously consider waiting for the second UN operation in Somalia, even though the United Nations had thought of asking Canada to lead this mission.[32] Most senior officials did not want Canada to delay. The choice, said Judd, was "between the coalition exercise or waiting around God knows how long for the United Nations to finally get its act together."[33] Privy Council Office, External Affairs, and National Defence officials met to discuss whether Canada should join the United States or second UN operation in late November or early December. Mark Moher, the director-general of the International Security Bureau in External Affairs, was the only strong supporter of the United Nations. His position was that the coalition mandate and command arrangements were flawed, Canada was being rushed, and the military did not seem totally confident it had the right force to deploy. "Instead of being there with all the primaries," Moher suggested, "we would be the heart of the follow-up." Delay would be consistent with past policy and would have positioned Canada to make a more significant contribution later.[34]

Moher did not win support for the second UN operation, but the United Nations was still an important factor in Canadian decision making. UN approval remained vital so that the US-led coalition could intervene gleaming with international legitimacy. Canada "will be there in one form or another," McDougall told reporters on 3 December. It was "very difficult to say what form that will be until we know what the position of the United Nations is going to be."[35] Boutros-Ghali freed the government to act by removing the lingering concern that the United Nations wanted to save Canada for its mission. McDougall and senior officials from External Affairs and National Defence met the morning after approval of Council resolution 794 (on 3 December), which officially authorized the ad hoc humanitarian intervention soon to be named Unified Task Force, to discuss what the government should do. Shortly before the start of the meeting, she was called out to take a telephone call from Boutros-Ghali, who said that Canada's peacekeeping credibility was needed immediately even if this meant it could not contribute to the UN's second operation.[36] At that point, everyone assembled knew Canada would join the enforcement mission.[37]

Mulroney made the decision to engage after receiving a written request from Bush on the 3rd. The prime minister regularly consulted and discussed foreign policy options with McDougall, but she was cautiously pragmatic and publicly she generally stayed close to his positions.[38] Mulroney was devoting a considerable amount of time to foreign affairs. McDougall's special policy adviser, Gerry Wright, was surprised at the many minor issues – such as the appointment of Canadians to multilateral bodies – that went straight to the Prime Minister's Office.[39] The prime minister had already agreed in principle to a contribution, and as a result, Bush's official written call for troops was anti-climatic and not pivotal. Hours before the Council voted on resolution 794, the president expressed his desire that "the Canadian troops designated for UNOSOM quickly join the coalition forces in the area of operation in the south where the need is greatest." He added, "I ask you to join me in the necessary commitment at the United Nations and militarily that will allow humanitarian relief efforts in Somalia to go forward."[40] The president's letter in hand, the prime minister decided, likely on the 4th after learning of the McDougall–Boutros-Ghali telephone call, to contribute a 1,300-person joint force comprising the Operation Relief airlift, HMCS *Preserver*, and the Canadian Airborne Regiment Battlegroup to the Unified Task Force.

The government had to convince Canadians that contributing to the US peace enforcement coalition was not a break from Canadian tradition and was the right thing to do under the circumstances. The perception among some members of the media was that the coalition was another example of Canada following the United States' lead. The *Calgary Herald* editorialized that "Canada is once again obediently tagging behind," its foreign policy "in lock-step with the United States."[41] During the Mulroney era, there had been serious disagreements on major issues like South Africa, arctic sovereignty, and UN financing,[42] but the impression of subservience to the United States was prevalent. Historian J.L. Granatstein said in 1992 that the Mulroney government had "followed American policy on most world issues and [this] disturbed a lot of Canadians." He later added that Canadians were deeply suspicious of the United States and frightened by its global dominance.[43]

Government ministers stressed that the commitment was in step with Canada's multilateral tradition. This was important because peacekeeping was one of the main expressions of Canadian nationalism, and participation in US-commanded peace operations posed a major problem for Canadians.[44] Associate National Defence Minister Mary Collins reminded Canadians that the United States was acting in support of the United Nations. Collins told the House of Commons on 7 December that "the willingness of the United States to exercise its power through the United Nations ... should be welcomed. For years middle powers like Canada have sought to engage the United States in multilateral endeavours of just this sort."[45]

The government made the point that the coalition was part of peacekeeping's adjustment to the more complex and dangerous challenges of the 1990s. It believed that the distinction being made by the media between peacekeeping and peace enforcement was artificial and that the choice between the two was more a function of the crisis. The "evolution of the Somali situation," said McDougall, "may change a word to another word, but the danger is the same with one word or another."[46] The application of force was seen as a necessary extension of peacekeeping. McDougall commented that Canada was "helping to develop, as we said we would, the capacity of the United Nations to meet threats to international peace and security in new ways."[47]

Domestic opposition to the intervention was muted primarily because of the belief that Canada had a moral duty to act to help Somalia. The *Ottawa Citizen*, for example, editorialized that a Canadian Forces role was "necessary because we cannot demand that 'something' be done about the tragedy in Somalia and then expect others to take the risks."[48] Shortliffe informed Mulroney that media reports about Canada's role in the coalition were "with very few exceptions, positive" and that editorials, which more directly targeted public opinion, were "overwhelmingly positive." His memorandum added, "those with serious objections concede that there is little choice but to mount such a mission."[49]

Some journalists wrote that Canadian participation was needed so the Unified Task Force did not appear excessively dominated by the United States. The *Ottawa Citizen* said the operation "must be seen to be multinational" because the world community has "legitimate fears about the United Nations continually being high-jacked by trigger-happy Americans."[50] Even though it was critical of Mulroney's decision to engage, the *Calgary Herald* appreciated the importance of involvement. "There must be some counter-balance to United States interests in United Nations operations," the newspaper opined. "The more nations that participate, the more difficult it will be for the United States to unilaterally set the agenda."[51]

Canada was encouraged to perform a bridge-building function by drawing international support to the intervention. The secretary-general believed Canadian engagement would improve the coalition's political credibility, and when he spoke with McDougall, he said Canada was needed so the force would not be seen as a unilateral US action.[52] This was consistent with what John Holmes, a noted Canadian diplomat and scholar, said could be a Canadian post-Cold War role. He suggested Canada should not behave like a US agent but rather should aim to preserve the multilateral structures that would make it easier for the United States to reassume its traditional position of leadership.[53] President Bush was thinking along the same lines. "It is vital," he wrote to Mulroney on 3 December, "that there be international contributions to make this a sound effort under United Nations auspices."[54]

The intervention allowed the government to present the humanitarian profile it wanted Canadians to see, and it saw no reason to get embroiled in the arduous reconciliation and reconstruction activities that would fall to the second UN operation in Somalia. In a memorandum to the prime minister, Shortliffe commented, "We would not foresee a significant role for Canada in the longer term in Somalia (given the absence of any significant bilateral interests)." Although Canada's interest lay elsewhere, "it is incumbent on us, to some extent, to ensure that the United Nations and its members are seized of these issues."[55] When publicly announcing Canada's contribution on 4 December, McDougall said Canada "will participate in the enforcement action only. We do not plan to participate in any subsequent peacekeeping operation."[56] The government re-emphasized this in the House on the 7th, when it defeated a Liberal motion (140 to 91) to have the military stay behind and assist the UN mission.[57]

One concern the government sought to pass on was that the Unified Task Force ought to disarm the factions. External Affairs sided with the United Nations in its public debate with the United States over the mandate. Boutros-Ghali contended that without full occupation and disarmament of Somalia, "I do not believe that it will be possible to establish the secure environment called for by the Security Council resolution" (794 of 3 December).[58] The *New York Times* questioned his call for forceful arms seizures but agreed that the coalition goals needed definition. Aid protection "leads inescapably to a wider goal of disarming the warring factions, so that, even after foreign forces depart, food can be distributed."[59] Yet the Bush administration refused to broaden the coalition beyond its humanitarian parameters. Deploying to the north did not appeal to Washington since the famine was confined to the south, and systematically confiscating weapons would be extremely time-consuming and dangerous. Somalia was saturated with arms and was such a harsh environment that a gun was often the difference between life and death. Oakley, the senior US diplomat in Somalia for most of the Unified Task Force, said full disarmament was "absolutely impossible," and, if attempted, "we could have a very messy situation."[60]

UN and US military leaders made diverging arguments regarding the risks and likelihood of successful arms removal. The deputy commander of the first UN operation in Somalia, Canadian Forces Colonel Jim Cox, believed factional disarmament was possible and that the Unified Task Force could contribute immensely to its achievement. It would be possible to have "the degree of security that all of us expect at home," he reasoned. Coalition forces were expected to number 35,000 troops (10,000 non-United States). This was enough to make progress. "We could have a pretty healthy crack at it with that amount."[61]

American and Canadian military commanders, on the other hand, were wary about moving beyond the role of providing a safe environment for humanitarian aid deliveries. The coalition wanted to have control over heavy weapons, including the armed Jeeps and trucks nicknamed "technicals," but not to strip weapons away from average Somalis. A total arms seizure, said Unified Task Force Commander Marine Corps Lieutenant-General Robert Johnston, "would have been mission impossible, and we would have been there for a year trying even to get a handle on it."[62] The Canadian Forces had a similar view. On 18 December, Shortliffe indicated to the prime minister that the Canadian Forces considered full-scale, methodical disarmament to be physically impossible.[63]

External Affairs and the Canadian media agreed with the United Nations because of the fear that Somalia would descend once again into chaos without disarmament. The *Toronto Star* editorialized that while the United States was "understandably reluctant," the weapons had to be taken to give the UN's second Somalia operation the best possible start. "The job won't be easy," it wrote, but "disarming at least the clan-based militias is crucial to creating the security needed to mount a peacekeeping operation."[64] These statements reflected the widely held view that the UN's force would not be as militarily strong as the coalition's and that therefore as much as possible should be done while southern Somalia was still under coalition authority. But when the Washington embassy spoke with the US State Department on 23 December, they found that the "assumption appears to be that UNOSOM II will be able to solve many problems after most United States forces leave."[65] The next day, McDougall said that seizing arms was necessary because it "will not be good enough to feed the starving populations if armed groups are in a position to move back in, immediately after the task force has departed."[66] Washington refused to reconsider, and the UN-US debate was not resolved during the Unified Task Force's existence.

Conclusion

For Canada, the collapse of the first UN operation in Somalia in the face of mounting resistance on the ground was not a major setback because its main interest was not a strong United Nations but rather effective and credible multinational action. The Unified Task Force was focused on the aid delivery effort in Somalia, which was what Canada had wanted all along. Canadians did not strongly object to working with the United States in the peace operation because it was felt that Canada had a moral duty to act due to the suffering in Somalia and because the government stressed that the commitment was not a break from Canada's peacekeeping tradition.

The US coalition was relevant to Canadian bilateral interests. Mulroney decided that Canada should contribute after receiving a request from Bush. The personal link between these two leaders was important because it made it more likely that Mulroney would be approached for a contribution and that the prime minister, with an eye toward opportunities for smoothing

Canada's pursuit of its bilateral concerns, would agree to a role. Mulroney was likely attuned to the possible benefits that Canada could derive from being there to help its ally. As a result, and in light of the successful Gulf War precedent and the failure of the first UN mission to cope in Somalia, the government was not seriously concerned by the fact that the intervention was an aggressive non-UN peace enforcement coalition.

The coalition was directly related to the government's long-held goal of deepening US involvement in world institutions. US power could immensely improve the effectiveness of such bodies, and Ottawa preferred to work with the United States in conjunction with other like-minded states. The debate over disarmament, however, demonstrated that even in a co-operative setting the government's ability to influence decision making in Washington remained limited.

Ottawa nevertheless believed it should engage to demonstrate that non-UN coalitions would be used for humanitarian causes like mass famine as well as to secure strategic interests like oil. In doing so, Canada could play its traditional bridge-building role. Its contribution would draw support to the mission by making it less likely that it would be perceived as a unilateral US initiative.

8
Unified Task Force: Canada's First Post-Cold War Enforcement Coalition

In November 1992, the United Nations Operation in Somalia I attempted to be more assertive in its dealings with the Somali factions. For the Canadian Forces, Somalia became a high priority for the first time when the United Nations admitted in late November that the peacekeeping effort had failed and Prime Minister Brian Mulroney decided to join the US-led Unified Task Force formed in December to establish a safe and secure environment for relief deliveries. The US coalition was a challenging mission for the Canadian Forces because it did not have much time to adjust to the unfamiliar and more aggressive task, and it had questions about the role and the coalition's rules of engagement. And yet, the Canadian Forces had no reason to expect that operations on the ground would not go well.

Following the resignation of Mohamed Sahnoun, Ismat Kittani was named special representative of the secretary-general and given responsibility for implementing the firmer UN approach. Sahnoun had worked hard building consensus, but he could not significantly improve security conditions for the relief deliverers and recipients. Likely because Sahnoun felt there was no other option, he had acquiesced in the theft of roughly 60 percent of aid shipments.[1] Kittani had a more formal and terse diplomatic style and a different mandate. "Kittani's mission," said Boutros Boutros-Ghali, then UN secretary-general, "was to stop the factions from getting the humanitarian assistance. The difference was in methodology. Naturally, if you decide to not allow this, you will be less popular."[2]

The United Nations believed that it needed to move past peacekeeping's traditional limits in order to make progress in crises like Somalia. Boutros-Ghali argued in the fall of 1992 that in cases where humanitarian supplies were being robbed, missions might have to use force more often than in the past to complete their mandates.[3] One of Kittani's main conclusions from his experience as special representative was that the United Nations needed to develop much more forceful techniques to deal with Somalia-like situations. He called attention to the "category of conflict where something less than full-scale enforcement is called for, but which nevertheless requires something more than traditional peacekeeping treatment ... to protect humanitarian relief, for example."[4]

Kittani set to work as soon as he arrived in Mogadishu on 8 November. One of his first actions was to meet Mohamed Farah Aidid and Ali Mahdi Mohamed and to express UN dissatisfaction with progress up to that point.[5] The peacekeeping mission's occupation of the Mogadishu airport on the 10th, which was in the Aidid-controlled southern part of the city, was another of the steps planned to facilitate the relief effort. Kittani made a deal with the Hawadle, the faction that controlled the airport and the lucrative extraction of landing fees, in which the UN occupied the airfield while the former provided perimeter security. "Keeping the airport closed is what some factions wanted," Kittani said. "I think what you needed was to be more decisive with some of the factions."[6] The initiative soon stalled. Aidid claimed that the UN's agreement with the Hawadle was invalid because he had not been involved in the negotiations,[7] and he demanded that the UN withdraw from the airport. The UN stayed put, and on the 13th its five-hundred-person Pakistani battalion stationed on the beach in front of Mogadishu was shelled by Aidid's forces, starkly revealing the risks associated with determined actions.

The occupation of the airport was the only act carried out, but other measures were planned. Force Commander Brigadier-General Imtiaz Shaheen announced in mid-November that the first UN mission to Somalia would soon move from its beach and airport base into the capital and would do so without factional concurrence if necessary. The escorting of food convoys into the northern (Ali Mahdi) and southern (Aidid) parts of the city was to be started and the seaport reopened.[8] Kittani delivered a tough message on 17 November to the factions in the northwest, which had declared independence for their area, naming it Somaliland. These leaders did not want to host Egypt, which had been assigned to the area following Austria's withdrawal from the UN operation, because Boutros-Ghali had once been Egypt's foreign minister and during that time Egypt had been a supporter of Mohamed Said Barre, Somalia's former dictator. "President" Abdirahman Tuur was inclined to accept Egypt, but among those who disapproved was Colonel Ibrahim Abdullahi "Degaweyne," who controlled the port city of Berbera, the planned Egyptian base of operations. Kittani told them that the UN decided which units were placed where, and that further delay might result in no UN presence at all.[9]

The United Nations found it could not cope with the number and inconsistent behaviour of the factions. Kittani could not build on the airport initiative because the Hawadle reneged on the original deal. A day after the airport deal went into effect, the Hawadle returned, denied that they had made a deal, and presented exorbitant new demands.[10] Another dispute arose during a meeting with the northwest faction. Kittani reported that Tuur had refused to sign a prenegotiated agreement to permit Egypt's deployment. Tuur, by contrast, said that Kittani had rudely demanded a signature and left immediately when asked for time to read the document.[11] These difficulties arose because of the large number of factions, whose positions were constantly evolving in response to local conditions. By 20 November, Kittani seemed overburdened by the complexity of the Somalia crisis.[12] The mission, having sought to move beyond peacekeeping in order to satisfy the international demands for progress, had been knocked back again. "When things go wrong on the ground, there's always a tendency to go in for a lot of finger-pointing," said Sir David Hannay, the United Kingdom's permanent representative to the United Nations, but "I think you have to attribute a good deal of the responsibility simply to the inherent difficulty of the conditions on the ground."[13]

The international community decided to press forward and, with Canada's support, create a peace enforcement mission. On 24 November, Boutros-Ghali wrote to the Security Council about the need to "review the basic premises and principles of the United Nations effort."[14] The international community was no longer willing to tolerate the frustration of its humanitarian relief efforts. Peacekeeping had proven inadequate, but leading Western countries were willing to raise the stakes and deploy a force strong enough to ensure that the aid got through. On the 29th, he informed the Council that it "now has no alternative but to decide to adopt more forceful measures ... Experience has shown that this cannot be achieved by a United Nations operation based on the accepted principles of peacekeeping."[15] Five new options were outlined. The fourth one, "a country-wide enforcement operation undertaken by a group of Member States,"[16] was selected, although the United States, which offered to lead the force, would focus the resulting coalition on famine-ravaged southern Somalia.

The Unified Task Force was a humanitarian intervention. The United States engaged because the severity of the mass starvation was so troubling and international assistance continued to be frustrated. The intervention was authorized by UN Security Council resolution 794 (3 December 1992). On 4 December, when President George H.W. Bush announced that he would deploy a peace enforcement coalition to Somalia, he noted that it was "now clear that military support is necessary to ensure the safe delivery of the food Somalis need to survive ... We're able to ease their suffering. We must help them live. We must give them hope."[17]

Canadian leaders voiced approval. The prime minister had indicated in May that he supported a more interventionist United Nations and greater US participation in multilateral actions.[18] "We support strong action," Barbara McDougall said on 4 December. "We are not in a position as an international community to deal with this in traditional ways."[19] Clearly something needed to be done about Somalia. As Bush noted, when "we see Somalia's children starving, all of America hurts ... Now we and our allies will ensure that aid gets through."[20]

Chief of the Defence Staff General John de Chastelain believed that the Unified Task Force was another indication that Canada was in the midst of a new generation of multilateral peace operations. A prominent feature of these conflict environments and missions was the need for increased military robustness. On 27 November, he noted that Canada was "going into these operations ... with forces that are much more heavily armed than they have been in the past ... with the idea that should somebody at a low level try to impede us, we can do something about it."[21] The coalition mission seemed especially dangerous before deployment since it was not clear if the factions and bandits would offer resistance. But it was not unprecedented. "I would say it is a risky operation," the chief noted at a press conference on 4 December, the day Ottawa's decision to commit 1,300 land, sea, and air forces was taken and made public, but "I would say it is not any more risky than Lebanon is for UNIFIL [United Nations Interim Force in Lebanon] today, I would say it is not any more risky than Bosnia is today."[22]

This comparison is useful because it highlights how the Canadian Forces perceived the intervention. The coalition was different from traditional peacekeeping because it was intended to *impose* peace temporarily,[23] but peace enforcement was far from fighting war. Despite the name, the "force" in peace enforcement related only to the potential use of arms. The Unified Task Force was in between peacekeeping and war fighting because it was constrained in how it could apply military power since it had not been created to subdue an enemy under the laws of war. It could use force only in response to a violent action and its response had to be proportionate to that action.[24] Heavy weapons were brought to intimidate and impress the Somalis, but securing the co-operation of the faction leaders remained highly desirable because, otherwise, conflict – and casualties – could result.

American and Canadian military leaders shared this view. General Colin Powell, chairman of the Joint Chiefs of Staff (the highest post in the US military), explained during a 2 December telephone call with de Chastelain that the intervention would be able to return fire against anyone attempting to impede aid deliveries and to pursue those parties. Powell doubted that a heavy force would be required since the factions "seem to have been bending over backwards to be accommodating over the past few days, once they heard we might be coming."[25] On the 4th, Powell added that he had stopped using the term "enforcement" because he doubted its appropriateness.[26]

Colonel Serge Labbé, the commander of the Canadian Joint Force Somalia, understood that the Unified Task Force was chiefly a show of military power, but he knew the situation was unpredictable and could require the use of arms. "We were not going off to war, we recognize[d] that," he said, "but we also recognize[d] that in the snap of a finger we could be in a situation where we were amongst warring belligerents in a very hostile scenario."[27] Labbé's view is similar to that of Andrew Leslie, who in 2003 was a major-general and commander of the Canadian contingent deployed to Kabul in 2003 to help create a peaceful and secure environment in Afghanistan. Leslie also deputy commanded the International Stabilization Assistance Force, the North Atlantic Treaty Organisation ad hoc peace enforcement coalition. Leslie noted that training "focussed on war fighting" because the estimate showed "if the situation became thoroughly unpleasant – and it was on a knife edge – that the greatest concern we had was not necessarily the terrorist be it Al-Qaeda or Taliban, but ... the warlords."[28]

It is clear from the Council's hopeful deliberations that peace enforcement was more robust than peacekeeping but was still a restrained activity. Ambassador Edward Perkins, the permanent representative of the United States to the United Nations, commented that "one point should be clear: our mission is essentially a peaceful one, and we will endorse the use of force only if and when we decide it is necessary to accomplish our objective."[29] The permanent representative of France, Ambassador Jean-Bernard Mérimée, underlined the United Nations' desire to rely on consent rather than arms. "We hope that the Somali parties," he said, "will take due note of the international community's determination and that they will choose to co-operate in ensuring that the humanitarian goal of our action may be achieved without resort to force."[30]

Although the Unified Task Force had similarities with previous missions in terms of the operational environment and the constraint on the use of force, the Canadian Forces still found it difficult to develop rules of engagement. This was a challenge because assisting assertive multilateral humanitarianism was an unfamiliar assignment and because a visible role had to be secured under significant time constraints. Aside from the Persian Gulf War (1990-91), coalition rules of engagement were not something with which the Canadian Forces had much recent experience. Larry Murray, a rear-admiral and the associate assistant deputy minister (Policy and Communications) in 1992, later noted that "this was not something we had done 23 times ... formulating the ROE for an operation like that in a coalition sense was quite unique and precedent setting."[31]

For the Unified Task Force, the Canadian rules of engagement were only issued to soldiers as they were deploying. Once it became clear on 5 December that Canadian rules would be needed, the J3 Plans joint cell asked the coalition leader, the US Central Command in Tampa Bay, Florida, for a copy of its rules to ensure the Forces' were compatible. National Defence Headquarters was responsible for writing the Canadian rules. Operational commanders normally interpreted the rules for their troops and prepared the aide-mémoire (soldier field cards containing distillations of the rules) issued to each contingent member. The lack of familiarity with peace enforcement and time pressures involved made this difficult for Canadian Airborne Commander Lieutenant-Colonel Carol Mathieu.

Captain (navy) Ken McMillan's J3 Plans cell wrote the rules of engagement for the Airborne because the unit had to start training, and by the time the Airborne received direction from National Defence Headquarters on the nature of the mission and the type of rules to be employed, time would have grown short.[32] J3 Plans did the work so that the Airborne would have an approved set of rules before deploying. The J3 Plans rules were sent up the National Defence Headquarters operational chain and approved by the chief of the defence staff on the 11th. McMillan's staff then faxed the rules to Labbé. On the 16th, McMillan offered to prepare the Airborne aide-mémoire to bring it more in line with the rules.[33] National Defence Headquarters put its rules on soldier cards and delivered them to the contingent on 22 or 23 December.

This was done because the cards written by the Airborne were more aggressive than National Defence Headquarters' rules. Mathieu's staff had tried to imagine what peace enforcement would be like. According to McMillan, the Airborne trained on a combination of traditional peacekeeping and something thought to be more aggressive and suited to the peace enforcement aspect.[34] The Airborne deployed with the approved rules of engagement (received 11 December), but the J3 Plans soldier cards could not be completed before the departure. Labbé decided go ahead with the Airborne cards and adopt the J3 Plans version in the theatre as soon as it was available.[35] This is significant because Labbé's and Mathieu's comfort with the stronger Airborne card may have led or enabled members of the regiment to interpret the strictures governing the use of force too liberally. It is because of the Somalia mission that the aide-mémoire/soldier cards are no longer the responsibility of field commanders and now fall under the mandate of the chief of the defence staff.[36]

Another reason for the inconsistencies in the Airborne's application of the rules concerning force was insufficient training time.[37] The deployment schedule was tight, with Labbé and his twelve-person headquarters advance team departing for Somalia on 13 December (after a two-day delay caused by a snowstorm and then by an aircraft equipment failure), and the Canadian Airborne Regiment Battlegroup advance party leaving three days later. The rules of engagement were discussed in Somalia, however, and Mathieu repeatedly assured Labbé that his unit knew them.[38]

In fact, uncertainty persisted about using arms in a peace enforcement context. When Airborne personnel shot and killed a Somali camp raider (see Chapter 10) on 4 March 1993, Labbé had to admit that in "hindsight, it is conceivable some confusion existed in the minds of a few as a result of transition" from peacekeeping.[39] To Labbé, 4 March suggested "that inexperience with Chapter VII ROE and last minute mission changes resulted in a requirement for a level of training which was perhaps not fully achieved uniformly in all sub-units of the Cdn AB Regt BG prior [to] deployment."[40] Since Somalia, mission-specific training on the rules and cards has become an integral part of pre-deployment preparations for all contingents.[41]

Vice-Admiral Murray, deputy chief of the defence staff as of February 1993, has made a similar point. On 4 March, Murray was the senior officer responsible for operations in National Defence Headquarters. He argued that while there was no criminal intent, the incident demonstrated a systemic problem within the Airborne regarding the understanding of rules.[42] The problem, he told the Somalia Inquiry, revolved around "a misinterpretation of hostile intent and a misinterpretation potentially of the use of deadly force after hostile intent had ceased and to people [who] are fleeing [and] ... no longer constitute a threat."[43] It has been suggested that a lack of training in military law directly contributed to the 4 March and more serious 16 March incidents, but it is doubtful that the soldiers needed legal guidance to understand that torturing and killing prisoners were unlawful under any circumstances.[44] Rather, there was simply no way of knowing at the time about the rules misunderstanding that Murray and Labbé described. Military decision makers did not believe that the Airborne should not have deployed or that the 4 March incident should have been anticipated. Despite the tight timetable, the Joint Staff did not believe that the Canadian Forces contingent had been inadequately prepared.

The struggle to accommodate the land contingent personnel cap of 900 was a further complication. The Somalia Inquiry took the addition of 185 personnel six weeks after deployment as proof that the Canadian Forces rushed to engage while remaining under the assigned limit.[45] The commissioners state in their report that had military police been deployed, the 4 March incident could have been quickly investigated, and this, they speculate, might have disrupted the atmosphere that allowed the 16 March incident to happen.[46] This is questionable because it implies military police held the balance between legal and illegal behaviour.[47] In any case, at the time, while the personnel cap complicated preparations to augment the battlegroup and Labbé's headquarters for the enforcement mission, it was not a serious problem. Labbé has said that commanders always want as many people as they can get – double and triple redundancies if possible – and that, despite his and Mathieu's requests for more, the total received in December 1992 was sufficient.[48] Land Force Commander Lieutenant-General Jim Gervais, who was responsible for generating the ground portion of the Canadian Joint Force Somalia and who approved all augmentations, decided 900 was "about right," although he had not ruled out the need for adjustments.[49]

Despite the complications regarding the rules of engagement and the cap, the Airborne was considered operationally ready in early December. When the secretary-general suspended the first UN operation on the 2nd, the unit's deployment had been only four days away. The Inquiry has pointed to the high rate of personnel turnover in the Airborne in the summer of 1992 and to the missed training opportunities in late October and November.[50] Based on this, it has questioned whether the unit was ready for the UN or US missions.

Brigadier-General Ernest Beno, on the other hand, has stressed that the Airborne was adequately trained and prepared for its Somalia missions. The regiment, he noted, had been trained for the UN Mission for the Referendum in the Western Sahara (another desert peacekeeping mission that had been cancelled in February 1992). The Airborne had worked with the US Marine Corps at Camp Lejeune, North Carolina, in the spring and had participated in a brigade concentration in the spring and in regimental exercises in the spring and fall.[51] Combat arms units, Beno says, do not need more training than this.[52] He has argued that training opportunities were not missed and that the training in the lead-up to the deployment was appropriate to peacekeeping. The initial burst of mission-specific training in September was curtailed because it appeared the Airborne would deploy immediately, but then it was continued until the vehicles had to be quarantined and the arrival of winter weather and snow made field preparations for the African desert impractical and counterproductive.[53]

It seems that these senior officers did not know about problems with the Airborne's internal culture that contributed to the much more disturbing 16 March incident. The Somalia Inquiry argues that the Airborne's suitability "ought to have been an issue," but that "commanders and staff officers at all levels never questioned their assumption that the Airborne was trained, disciplined, and fit for deployment ... [but it was] not what it was assumed to be."[54] There is evidence that supports this. While the Land Force was focused on fulfilling the government's desire to support multilateral peacekeeping, it does not seem to have been aware that there was an unprofessional culture in the unit. This culture was a reflection of the regiments' habit of sending their troublemakers to the Airborne. A "hidden cancer" existed in the unit that was not evident to Gervais.[55] Although he and Beno, who commanded the Special Service Force Brigade, of which the Airborne was a part, had three conversations about the unit, they believed that the main problem was its senior leadership.[56] Paul Addy, then a major-general and the deputy chief of the defence staff (intelligence, security, operations), has noted that the leadership problems were deeper than this and should have been better known but were not.[57] Gervais, with a whole army to command, trusted his subordinates to inform him of serious problems. This did not occur because his subordinates, in their professional judgment, believed that the discipline issues were not that serious.

Major-General Lewis MacKenzie, the commander of Land Force Central Area (the level in between Gervais and Beno), is an example. He recalls that one of the disciplinary incidents the Inquiry examined – the discharging of pyrotechnics at a junior ranks mess party and of pyrotechnics and ammunition in Algonquin Park near Canadian Forces Base Petawawa during the night of 2-3 October 1992 – he had taken part in when he was a young officer.[58] The Airborne did not stand out within the Land Force with respect to such infractions. The number of disciplinary cases in the unit was not out of proportion with similar-sized units.[59] While the Airborne had internal problems, no one imagined that some of its members would kill a civilian under highly questionable circumstances. In December 1992, MacKenzie said, the concerns did not seem bad enough "for anyone, including me, to stand up and say to the government of Canada, 'Sorry, we can't fulfill this mission.' They were absolutely the best prepared that we had. And good enough, I hasten to add, and good enough."[60]

In contrast with its inadequate understanding of the Airborne, the Canadian Forces was very much focused in December 1992 on whether it had sufficient time to deploy to Somalia. Canada's commitment was made public on the 4th, and the US plan was to intervene on the 9th. This was a major concern, because if the Canadian Forces was to serve the nation's interests by co-operating in a visible way with the United States, it needed to deploy before all the desirable roles were assigned. The Somalia Inquiry has argued that the Canadian Forces should have resisted the political pressure to get involved, and, considering the discipline issues and time pressures, should have set aside its "can-do" attitude and questioned the Airborne's suitability.[61] In the event, the Canadian Airborne Regiment Battlegroup advance party arrived at its staging area, Baledogle airfield, during the period 15-23 December. They were among the first elements of the Canadian Joint Force Somalia, which would include the large land component (845), the HMCS *Preserver* (319), the previously separate Operation Relief airlift (65), and the joint headquarters (55).

Joint Staff members have rejected the view that the Canadian Forces pressed forward even though it might have been unprofessional to do so. Commodore David Cogdon, the chief of staff to the deputy chief of the defence staff, has stressed that while the Airborne was the only unit that was available for deployment, it was still considered a good unit by the Land Force, and the mission was viewed as being within the Canadian Forces' capability or else it would not have been accepted in the first place.[62] The "can-do" approach, he argues, never got in the way of professionalism; it reflected the Canadian Forces' willingness to cope with manageable challenges. "All that was required was building-in the additional sub-units," to make the battlegroup, said Cogdon. "If you mean 'rushed' in terms of 'happening quickly,' then yes, the Somalia deployment was certainly rushed. But I cringe at the negative connotation of 'rushed.'"[63] Most of the land contingent had been ready for the UN peacekeeping mission in Somalia, and it was not difficult to augment it for the Unified Task Force. For Land Force Command (Gervais), Land Force Central Area (MacKenzie), and the Special Service Force Brigade (Beno), adding robustness – a Royal Canadian Dragoon squadron for direct fire support and a Royal Canadian Regiment mortar platoon for indirect fire support – was straightforward and routine.[64]

Joint- and national-level planning and preparations were not undermined by the rapid switch to peace enforcement. Indeed, the Joint Staff had been created precisely to make this sort of quick response possible (see Chapter 2). J3 Plans, for example, had a capability-based plan already prepared (with input from the Environmental Commands) that outlined the land, air, maritime, and joint possibilities for a coalition contingency. It had the deployment-related timelines.[65] This enabled strategic-level military decision makers to determine before the Cabinet meeting on the 4th what sort of joint force the Canadian Forces could generate. Shortly after the commitment to the Unified Task Force had been approved, this option rose to the fore as the most likely Canadian response. It was essential when proposing options involving the use of force, as was the case here, that the government be provided with sufficient detail to permit an informed decision on whether it wished to proceed.[66]

The decision to deploy was made by the prime minister, but by the start of December it was obvious to the Canadian Forces that it would be a part of the Unified Task Force. National Defence and External Affairs policy analyses reinforced the general sense, emanating from the prime minister, ministers, and other government sources, that national-level decision making was moving in this direction.[67] Shortly before the decision to engage was made, the Canadian Forces had already anticipated that the UN peacekeeping mission was not going to happen. For the J5 policy staff, the concern was whether the Canadian Forces could adapt its UN commitment in time to secure an appropriate mission in the US-led force.[68] Yet the Joint Staff could not commence formal preparations until Cabinet gave its approval. This had to wait, as was noted at a special meeting chaired by the chief of the defence staff and Deputy Minister Robert Fowler on 3 December, because UN sanction was essential and Cabinet would not meet to discuss the issue until the Council had authorized the Unified Task Force (it did so that evening with resolution 794).[69] The Chief, J3 Peacekeeping Colonel Mike Houghton, and another officer briefed an ad hoc Cabinet committee the next day. They offered a concept of operations and outlined the two options but did not recommend either since this had not been requested.[70] The "military's advice was that the risks were reasonable."[71]

The Joint Staff had to proceed rapidly once Cabinet approval had been obtained on the 4th to win the visible role desired by the government. On the 4th, de Chastelain learned from Powell that the United States had not even thought about the Canadian Forces since it assumed Canada would remain with the UN operation, and that at best the Canadian Forces might receive a secondary role along with various other militaries "in due course."[72] A seven-member coalition had initially been planned, but Canada would have been not the first but the fourth or fifth country that the field commander, Marine Corps Lieutenant-General Robert Johnston, would have looked to for a contingent.[73] This became a major issue shortly after the Canadian commitment was decided upon. Part of the motivation for a commitment had been to receive a meaningful role that enabled the Canadian Forces to contribute according to the capabilities it could bring to the table. The government wanted a high-profile assignment in order to sustain public support for the initiative and to justify its military spending, while the military needed to show that Canadians were getting value for their tax dollars.[74] The Chief reflected this when he said "further delay, or a role that was seen to be secondary, would not sit well with the troops, with me, with the Government or with Canadians."[75]

The most pressing problem was to find a way to fit the Canadian Forces into the US plans. If the Canadian Forces was to be a player, liaison needed to take place immediately with Central Command and with Johnston, who was based at Camp Pendleton, California. On 5 December, Murray visited Central Command for strategic-level discussions to see whether an adequate Canadian Forces role was possible. This meeting went well, and it opened the way for negotiations for a task with Johnston. Canada was the only country granted direct access to the commanding general.[76] Labbé had few details about the mission, but he knew that he had a highly motivated force with considerable organic capabilities (experienced paratroopers, a ship with helicopters, and transport aircraft). Labbé impressed Johnston. He said that Labbé's message was, "I'll go anywhere, you give me a mission and frankly give me one that's not very easy. I'm not going to sit on an airstrip, I have paratroopers here, they are very capable."[77] Labbé left Camp Pendleton with an agreement in principle that the Canadian Forces would have a visible mission and strategic airlift support (the entire US Army 10th Mountain Division was delayed to move the Royal Canadian Dragoons' Cougar armoured vehicles)[78] to get to Somalia more rapidly.

Despite this success, the complications presented by the lack of a precedent for peace enforcement remained. Labbé returned to Canada on the 8th, only three days before his planned deployment, and he was still struggling with the nature of his task. Commanding a Canadian Forces joint operation with the authority to use arms to protect aid was a challenging task. A humanitarian peace enforcement mission, Labbé noted, was difficult to conceptualize because there "hadn't been too many of those in the history of the United Nations."[79] The specific tasks remained unclear. Johnston and Labbé agreed that the Baledogle airport about 90 kilometres northwest of Mogadishu would be the Canadians' staging area, and the interior towns of Beledweyne,

Baardheere, and Baydhabo to be secured in the operation's second phase were mentioned as possible areas of operation. The US Marines Corps had been assigned responsibility for the initial lodgement, the seizing of Mogadishu port and its airstrip on 9 December. It was not until the 19th that the Canadian Joint Force Somalia was assigned Beledweyne. By that time, the Unified Task Force had deployed and the mission picture was clear.

Conclusion

Sahnoun's replacement with Kittani marked the beginning of the UN's attempt to move beyond peacekeeping to a state where the consent of all disputants would not be a precondition for action. Kittani's mandate was to prevent the factions from stealing food aid and to be more decisive when dealing with them. The only assertive initiative carried out under Kittani, the arrangement with a faction that opened the way for the UN occupation of the airport, produced a violent backlash from Aidid and was undermined by the faction's subsequent disavowal of the agreement.

The UN operation's collapse in fall 1992 illustrated that violating the traditional principles of peacekeeping was not possible. Although the first edition of *An Agenda for Peace* (June 1992) and some of Boutros-Ghali's and Kittani's statements indicated they believed that the factions could be pushed to go along with the UN if it was insistent, this was erroneous. The UN did not comprehend the diversity of positions and the rapidity with which the Somali faction leaders changed them in response to local pressures. UN officials underestimated the faction's ability to frustrate the world organization's intentions. When the UN went beyond peacekeeping – by remaining impartial to the conflict while it sought to alleviate the humanitarian crisis even without full consent – it soon found itself caught. Consent was so essential that the peacekeeping mission could not function without it.

Although Canadian leaders supported the Council's authorization of the Unified Task Force peace enforcement operation on 3 December, some only partially understood this tool. Enthusiasm was expressed in Canada regarding the use of force, but the coalition involved the show of force and only potentially its application. If the US-led coalition did use arms, it had to ensure that this was proportionate to the threat to which it was responding. While the Unified Task Force reserved the right to do what it felt was necessary to fulfill its mission, it sought to remain impartial to the conflict and to rely whenever possible on consent.

The government responded enthusiastically when the coalition was created in part because it did not see peace enforcement as a dramatic shift in peace operations practice. The Unified Task Force furthered the government's desire to bolster assertive multilateral actions and to alleviate humanitarian suffering in Somalia. Once the government committed, a major concern became finding a visible role. Decision makers wanted to contribute sizable resources to co-operative initiatives that reflected the sort of interventionist multilateralism they hoped to develop.

Writing national rules of engagement for a peace enforcement coalition was a challenge given the time constraints and need to train, and as a result the Joint Staff stepped forward and offered some assistance. As with preparations for the mission in general, the writing of the rules and soldier cards was complicated by the brief time between the announcement of the Canadian Forces' role and the deployment of the Canadian Joint Force Somalia. Rules/ soldier cards deal with the essential questions of when force can be used and how, but the rapid transition from peacekeeping to peace enforcement prevented a thorough training of all battle group personnel and led to confusion about the use of arms.

Uncertainty regarding the Canadian role had an impact on the way the Canadian Forces dealt with the personnel cap assigned by the chief of the defence staff. National Defence Headquarters understood that the Unified Task Force was a humanitarian mission and not a combat operation, but it was not clear whether the intervention would be opposed during the initial landings. The Land Force struggled to fit its augmentations to its original UN peacekeeping contingent under the 900-person cap. The perceived need for armed strength resulted in certain specialists being cut and additional personnel being added later in order to deploy as many fighting soldiers as possible. At the time, the Airborne's disciplinary problems were not seen as major concerns, and no one imagined that unit members would be capable of beating a civilian to death on 16 March.

Once the ad hoc Cabinet committee decided on a Unified Task Force role, the Canadian Forces' most pressing concern was to find a visible task. An identifiably Canadian role was one that fully tested Canadian Forces capabilities and attracted media attention so that the government received benefit from the expense it was incurring. Securing a "good" role was part of the incentive when such tasks are assumed. By sending senior teams down to Central Command and Camp Pendleton, the Canadian Forces was able to involve itself in the high-profile mission. Otherwise, it might have received only a secondary role.

9
Stay or Go? Weighing a Role in the Second UN Mission

Having engaged in the US peace enforcement coalition, the government had to decide what to do next concerning Somalia. Canada's troops could depart with the Unified Task Force or stay to assist the succeeding UN mission. Prime Minister Brian Mulroney's government knew that the Unified Task Force, which started to arrive in Somalia on 9 December 1992, was to last a few short months and that command would be passed to a UN force whose assignment would be sustained stabilization and peace building. When Canada committed to the Unified Task Force, it was with the understanding that it would not join the United Nations Operation in Somalia II, the first peace enforcement mission in UN history. But as the handover date, 4 May 1993, drew near, the government was asked repeatedly by the United States and the United Nations to assist with the mission. The prime minister decided against a role because the conflict was intractable and of almost no relevance to Canadian interests, the Canadian public had lost interest in Somalia, and higher priorities for Canada's scarce military resources existed elsewhere. Mulroney's decision was not influenced by the scandal that related to the conduct of some Canadian troops in Somalia.

The Unified Task Force was shaped to serve US interests as understood in the White House, State Department, and Pentagon. President George H.W. Bush wanted neither to appear paralyzed during his last months in power (he had lost the November 1992 presidential election to Bill Clinton) nor to leave an unfinished military commitment to his successor. Bush wanted the coalition and most US forces out of Somalia by inauguration day, 20 January 1993. He reconsidered after a meeting attended by National Security Advisor Brent Scowcroft, Secretary of Defense Dick Cheney, and Chairman of the Joint Chiefs of Staff General Colin Powell. They advised him that the mission could not be finished by then and that withdrawing might be harder than he had envisioned.[1] Before leaving office, the Bush administration often reminded the United Nations – in staff-level consultations and formal reports to the UN Security Council – of the need for prompt transition to UN-commanded operations.[2] The Clinton administration maintained that approach. The US permanent representative to the United Nations, Ambassador Madeline Albright, told the Security Council in March 1993 that it was "time for the United Nations to reassume its rightful leadership role in restoring peace to Somalia."[3]

The Pentagon agreed that the United States had to avoid getting mired in Somalia, and it crafted the intervention to suit this policy. The Pentagon long resisted getting involved in the humanitarian effort in Somalia because it was a potential quagmire, and the United States, like Canada, had no national interest to advance there. By fall 1992, Department of Defense and military leaders in the Pentagon had changed their position to one of support for the president's venture. They had correctly concluded that the mission could be tailored to suit the military's preference for a quick and "doable" engagement and that Somalia would not present any significant military challenges, and they wanted to support President Bush, knowing how much he had done to bring the US armed forces victories, low casualty lists, and warm public support during his time as president (1989-1993).[4]

The Pentagon's design for the Unified Task Force reflected US priorities. Planners intended to send enough troops to guarantee success while ensuring that the coalition was not stuck in Somalia keeping the peace or turned into a political force charged with the creation of a new government.[5] Council resolution 794 (3 December 1992) founded the coalition along these lines. Invoking the enforcement provisions contained in Chapter VII of the UN Charter, the resolution authorized the use of "all necessary means" to establish a secure environment for aid workers, deliveries, and recipients.[6] The coalition would inch past its mandate after deploying. It attempted arms control, partially reconstructed the police, and facilitated community-level reconciliation (see Chapter 10).[7] But the resolution committed the United States to brief humanitarian operations, not a long-term solution in Somalia.

The United States split the Somalia mission into two parts. The Unified Task Force's establishment of a secure environment would be pointless if fighting resumed after its sophisticated combat troops left, and so the second UN operation had to maintain stability and conduct peace building in order to succeed. To ensure that the United Nations could successfully take over, the United States believed that it needed a mandate, a concept of operations, a level of armament, and rules of engagement that were little different from the coalition.[8] The Security Council agreed, and with resolution 814 (26 March 1993) gave the United Nations Operation in Somalia II enforcement powers to consolidate the coalition's achievements and pursue national reconciliation, reconstruction, and full disarmament throughout Somalia.[9] The second UN mission had fewer troops at its disposal than the Unified Task Force, but this did not trouble the United Nations, which believed that the smaller number would be sufficient because US-led forces had broken down resistance and taken control of the situation.[10] However, the UN mission was more comprehensive, dangerous, and costly than the coalition's. As Albright observed, the UN's task was "an unprecedented enterprise aimed at nothing less than the restoration of an entire country" and "probably the toughest co-ordination challenge of its history."[11]

US and Canadian media representatives questioned the international community's split approach and particularly the strictly humanitarian mission assigned the coalition. Charles Krauthammer, writing in *Time,* identified one inconsistency. There was "no such thing as pure humanitarianism" and "no such thing as just feeding the hungry, if what's keeping them from eating is not crop failure but vandalism and thuggery."[12] Canadian papers were of two minds in their praise for the Unified Task Force and Canada's role. The *Ottawa Citizen* said the coalition was "in the vital interest of international decency and humanity," but the editors expressed "great uncertainty about how long the international forces will be required. And nobody knows how or when civilian society can be re-established."[13] The *Globe and Mail* voiced what many were thinking but apparently unable to do much about – that the coalition was not enough. "Almost everyone agrees," the editors wrote, "that the country will not truly be safe until it has a functioning government that can rebuild the pillars of civil society." The *Globe and Mail* noted that a political settlement was essential even though it would be extremely difficult and require time, patience, and considerable foreign help.[14] This was what the Unified Task Force had been designed to avoid and was one reason why it had appeal for the Canadian government.

Canada's political leaders wanted to know whether their contribution to the United Task Force was still popular. The government learned that the humanitarian mission continued to "play positively" in the national media.[15] Not only was the coverage supportive, notwithstanding the nagging questions relating to what came next, but also the strong sense of confidence and optimism that was expressed regarding the coalition surely gratified and reassured the government. The Clerk of the Privy Council, Glen Shortliffe, noted some criticism over the Unified Task Force's delay in escorting aid supplies beyond Mogadishu, Somalia's capital, and "a growing sense of optimism about the success of this mission."[16]

As officials in Ottawa monitored the Canadian Joint Force Somalia operations, they received requests from the United Nations and United States to participate in the second UN mission. The government's position was that Canada would stay until the end of the enforcement action.[17] For Colonel Serge Labbé, the commander of the Canadian Joint Force Somalia, that position was unclear because the second UN mission would be an enforcement action too.[18] Ottawa knew that the UN operation would have enforcement powers by 9 February 1993, if not earlier,[19] but stayed silent, likely in order to protect its position on that operation. The government was willing to consider participating in the UN's second Somalia mission. Canadian officials listened patiently to the United States and United Nations but did not let them determine their decision making.

The United Nations pressed Canada extremely hard. It pushed "as much as we could, short of embarrassing Canada and calling them a coward and everything," said Maurice Baril, then a brigadier-general and military adviser to the UN secretary-general.[20] The United Nations already had enough infantry for its second operation; what it needed were specialists (like aircraft controllers, military engineers, or a tactical helicopter detachment). Canada received a formal request for such personnel in February 1993. This would be to a maximum of 150 troops and was in addition to an earlier request, already accepted, for up to fifteen mission headquarters staff officers.[21] Special Representative of the Secretary-General Ambassador Jonathan Howe, head of the UN mission, met with Canadian diplomats. He spoke several times with Ambassador Lucie Edwards, the High Commissioner to Nairobi (with accreditation to Somalia);[22] Ambassador Louise Fréchette, the permanent representative to the United Nations;[23] and, during her Somalia visit in May 1993, Secretary of State for External Affairs Barbara McDougall.[24] He wanted Canada to make a new contribution or extend its existing contingent for at least thirty days and hopefully longer. The United Nations might have been more insistent, but it knew Canada was significantly engaged in Cyprus (since 1964), the Golan Heights (since 1974), and the former Yugoslavia (since 1992) and had agreed to a new Haiti mission.[25]

The United States, too, repeatedly requested Canadian participation in the UN operation. United States Ambassador to Canada Edward Ney told Canadian officials in December 1992 that if Canada agreed in principle it would be invited to Washington for mission planning with US and UN officials.[26] US embassy representatives asked Canada to reconsider during a démarche on 13 January 1993 and on other occasions.[27] The Department of National Defence cited "considerable pressure" from the United Nations, United States, and other allies as its reason for recommending that a small contribution would be in the national interest.[28] The Privy Council Office anticipated that President Clinton would "press the Prime Minister to commit forces" for UN use in Somalia and for post-settlement operations in the former Yugoslavia at the Vancouver Summit between Clinton and Russian president Boris Yeltsin on 3-4 April.[29]

The government resisted these entreaties largely because the international effort was not succeeding. The challenges to peace and reconstruction, despite the Unified Task Force's presence, remained immense. UN Secretary-General Boutros Boutros-Ghali reported on 3 March that security conditions fluctuated from region to region and week to week and were especially unstable in the countryside. The Unified Task Force was subject to sniper fire, and recent major incidents of fighting or rioting had occurred at Kismaayo and Mogadishu.[30] The faction leaders appeared unwilling to reconcile. This was troubling because peace is not something that can be imposed. Boutros-Ghali wrote "the experience thus far has shown" the need for UN involvement "not only in organizing, but also in promoting and advancing, the cause of national reconciliation."[31]

UN diplomatic peacemakers were also encountering problems. At the Conference on National Reconciliation in Addis Ababa (15-27 March 1993) convened by the United Nations, the fifteen major factions and a cross-section of Somali civil society and women's groups reached agreement on the establishment of regional councils for each of Somalia's eighteen regions and a Transitional National Council that would serve as the central political authority and repository of Somali sovereignty.[32] Aidid signed the agreement, but he preferred a governance structure that gave the five strongest factions (including his own) most of the power. He did not see the deal as binding and planned to change it during implementation.[33] Aidid and the other faction leaders continued talking after the conference adjourned. On 30 March, they adopted an accord that violated the spirit and letter of the conference agreement by excluding women and stipulating that the factions would choose most of the Transitional National Council members. Aidid and the other leaders demonstrated that despite the Unified Task Force's successful "freezing" of the military situation, factional manoeuvring and power plays continued unabated on the political level. The United Nations refused to embrace the 30 March document but in doing so may have "set the stage for clashes" between some factions and its anticipated second Somalia operation.[34]

Canadian government officials were justifiably concerned about the approaching UN-commanded phase. They were mindful that no one knew how to disarm the factions and gunmen, for example, which was essential to the rebuilding of Somalia. Shortliffe noted in a memorandum to the prime minister that "the logic of disarmament is compelling, but the operational challenges in succeeding are enormous."[35] Perhaps as a result, the government publicly stressed the importance of effective disarmament of the Somali factions but stopped short of specific action.[36] Officials probably took note of Boutros-Ghali's report, which said the "cost of restoring Somalia as a nation and society will be enormous" and "take many years."[37]

Senior bureaucrats were openly questioning the usefulness of a Canadian role in the second UN operation by February 1993. Somalia's problems were such that the modest specialist contribution, which would have been manageable without too much difficulty, seemed pointless. Although External Affairs and International Trade Canada initially supported the UN request, Under-Secretary of State Reid Morden expressed misgivings. "The option recommended is ok," he wrote in February, "but is really rather simplistic, given the overall magnitude of the task of reinventing Somalia ... it seems to ignore the civil, social and political issues unresolved – many still even unaddressed."[38] National Defence and the Canadian Forces favoured the first choice on the government option paper – departure after an orderly transition to UN command.[39] Defence decision makers observed that the UN was trying to restore viability to a state that arguably had never been viable and that the "presence of a Canadian unit for a further forty, sixty, or ninety days is not going to make the slightest difference in the long run."[40]

No final judgment had been made to decline a role in the second UN mission. The decision was subject to "continuing review" in March, as requested by Prime Minister Mulroney, and was still being justified and explained to him in April.[41] The onus fell on those senior bureaucrats who felt strongly enough to argue why Canada should not engage.[42] One of their main points was that the international effort was not achieving the desired result. "Was it possible to bring peace to Somalia?" asked Shortliffe. "At the end of the day, the answer was no."[43] It would have been counterintuitive for the government to accept a commitment that did not bring credit to the country and itself. As Morden said, why should Canadians be "tying ourselves down to something that ... isn't working" and, "as far as we can make out, can't work?"[44] It was incumbent on these advisers to ensure that Mulroney, the decision maker, had access to this advice.

The other point made by officials was that operational demands had exhausted the Canadian Forces.[45] In March, National Defence Minister Kim Campbell asked Mulroney to support her department's plan to withdraw during June because the current operational tempo was unsustainable beyond November 1993. With this "adjustment," Canada would only be doing what it said before deploying, and it would not be leaving the United Nations in the lurch because other countries had stepped forward to take the place of the Canadian Joint Force Somalia.[46] It seemed reasonable to argue that Canada had done its share and should leave. John Anderson, then an admiral and chief of the defence staff, has said that the military and government as a whole had to take a balance sheet approach to some extent and determine whether Somalia was worth more scarce Canadian resources.[47]

Decision makers had to consider how available resources could be used most effectively to advance the national interest. This had to be done in the context of a massive expansion in UN peacekeeping worldwide[48] and budgetary and personnel reductions to the already modestly sized Canadian Forces. Canada was becoming a smaller player on the global peacekeeping stage and therefore had to be selective in choosing its missions. Officials concluded that Canada's national interest would be better served somewhere other than Somalia.[49] Anderson recalled it was clear that Canada had a much greater interest, though still a limited one, in the Balkans conflict. This made questions about allocating Canada's finite military forces straightforward and simple to answer.[50]

The military and bureaucratic advice was easier for the government to accept because it mirrored the domestic political climate, which was now less inclined to see resources devoted to Somalia. The government noticed that it was not long before the US-led coalition lost salience as an issue in Canada. Media coverage quickly declined from the peak level of early December. On the 18th and 22nd, Shortliffe informed the prime minister that "at this point, with the operation continuing to unfold relatively smoothly, media attention is shifting" and "the focus of interest is ... Bosnia."[51] External Affairs found the public ambivalent to remaining in Somalia. They would support a withdrawal as long as it did not appear precipitous.[52] The Unified Task Force acted like a safety valve in that public and media concern for Somalia dissipated once the itch to act was scratched. The government understood that it would receive little credit from the electorate for deciding in favour of a UN contribution and suffer little or no political damage for deciding against one. Canada withdrew from Somalia when the crisis faded from the headlines and lost its power over domestic politics.[53]

Prime Minister Mulroney nevertheless considered a new Somalia commitment. He enjoyed the prestige of being part of initiatives like the UN operation and was concerned about the withdrawal because Canada was being asked to stay. Mulroney strongly supported multilateralism and he knew the stakes for the United Nations were high. The prime minister's special representative to Somalia, David MacDonald, MP, reported after a fact-finding trip that disorder was "a very real possibility, and would involve substantial loss of credibility for the United Nations."[54] Mulroney asked the government to think about contributing to the second UN operation,[55] but eventually he heeded the bureaucracy's and military's advice on the need to withdraw. One of his later discussions was with Jim Judd, the assistant secretary to Cabinet for foreign and defence policy in the Privy Council Office. Judd explained why Canada should not contribute during the Russia-United States Summit in Vancouver in early April 1993. National Defence learned of the prime minister's decision on 7 April; the Canadian Joint Force Somalia heard about ten days later. In the end, Canada assigned four to five officers to the headquarters of the second UN mission on what the Canadian Forces would call Operation Consort.

The prime minister was not influenced by the controversy over the torture and beating death, on 16 March, of a Somali teenager in custody of the Canadian Airborne Regiment Battlegroup (the largest unit of the Canadian Joint Force Somalia).[56] While government decision making was not altered or accelerated, Shortliffe noted that 16 March "certainly complicated the decision ... and made the issue of 'what are we doing here' more focussed."[57] Senior bureaucrats looked on 16 March as an anomaly. "The incident indicates a continued concern for the safety and security of our troops," wrote Shortliffe in a memorandum to the prime minister dated 17 March. "They have been relatively minor in nature however, and sporadic in their overall effect on an otherwise calm situation."[58] The furor the incident raised in

Canada did not dampen Mulroney's desire to help the United Nations. On 4 May, for example, Judd asked National Defence to explain why the Canadian troops in Somalia could not be extended for a month or more to fill personnel gaps in the second UN effort.[59]

The Somali death in detention did not command media attention until the end of March because limited information could be released and other subjects were of interest. Labbé provided details to the Canadian Press and either CBC Newsworld or Standard Broadcast News on the 18th and issued short press releases on 17 and 19 March.[60] National Defence was immediately aware of the gravity of what had occurred, but in terms of further public announcements the government was constrained by intense concern to protect the legal rights of those who might be charged with a crime.[61] The department's policy was not to publicize soldier charges and serious field incidents,[62] though details could be released when (and if) the media specifically requested them. Governments never want to call attention to incidents occurring on their watch, and discretion was especially prudent on this occasion since ministers did not wish to mar National Defence Minister Campbell's campaign to succeed the retiring Mulroney as leader of the Progressive Conservative Party (and as prime minister).

Yet the absence of coverage was surprising. Senior bureaucrats had advised the government to expect media attention and more information, including the details of the investigation results, when known.[63] There had been reports to the press; news releases had been issued, though initially they were quite terse because of the time required to isolate precisely what happened and weigh what could be said; and Canadian journalists had come in and out of the area of operations. Instead of the 16 March incident, media were drawn to another story that broke the next day. The story concerned a Somali guard working for the International Committee of the Red Cross who had been killed during a violent riot by Battlegroup soldiers acting in self-defence.[64]

Campbell officially announced her intentions to run for the Progressive Conservative leadership during an address televised from Vancouver on 25 March. Six days later, *Pembroke Observer* reporter Jim Day published an account of the 16 March incident and of seeing first-hand the soldier responsible for the killing being carried away on a stretcher after a suicide attempt.[65] His article raised awkward, troubling questions that reporters wanted the government to answer. Day had witnessed the procession by accident, and this gave the media reason to suspect that something unusual had happened in Somalia that the government was not admitting. The Liberal Party saw what a wonderful opportunity this was, and they capitalized on it to gain the maximum political advantage. The Liberals worked to scandalize the Progressive Conservatives, cloud the Conservative leadership transition, seize the political spotlight, and put what they claimed were Campbell's failings on public display.

The scandal (as opposed to the incident) focused on what Campbell knew and when she knew it. Campbell was fairly caught. As a lawyer and former justice minister, she understood the imperative not to disclose information that could deprive individuals of the due process of law, but her leadership campaign objectives were being damaged by the Liberal and media allegations that her department covered up the questionable killing.[66] The National Defence minister might have declined comment except to explain and reaffirm the government position respecting the ongoing investigations. Instead, Campbell sought to convince Canadians that she had acted in good faith and to deflect responsibility for the lack of disclosure to her military and public service advisers. No suggestion of criminal intent had been made, she stressed, during a crucial briefing by Deputy Minister Robert Fowler and Anderson on 18 March. Once Campbell became aware of the incident's criminal dimension, she had instructed the department to release everything it could. However, her credibility was undermined by Anderson, who publicly disputed her statements about the briefing,[67] and by opposition politicians and sceptical journalists.[68]

For National Defence and the Canadian Forces, the scandal was another reason to bring the contingent home. Canada's "strongest images of itself" had been violated.[69] A harsh media climate developed in which reporters were "capitalizing on any blemish the Airborne may have had over the years."[70] Military leaders and bureaucrats, who rarely had to contend with media scrutiny of their performance during the Cold War, found it extremely difficult to quickly and adequately respond to the criticism.[71] Anderson and Fowler were also worried about how the Canadian Joint Force Somalia would handle the possibility of charges being laid in at least one of the military police investigations (into the 4 and 16 March incidents) and the accidental death in early May of an Airborne Regiment soldier. "This," they emphasized, "combined with the highly politicized debate back home, has placed untold stress on the members of the unit [the Canadian Airborne Regiment Battlegroup] and their families, and in our professional judgment the troops must be brought out now."[72]

The government had to seek protection from the partisan and media attacks. It shielded Campbell from the opposition in the House, who were claiming she had hidden evidence relating to the 16 March incident and neglected her responsibilities as National Defence minister while campaigning for her party's leadership.[73] The government could have dealt with the scandal honestly by recognizing that soldiers had been sent to Somalia who should not have been there and promising that those who failed to see what was happening and prevent it would be censured in accordance with military procedures, while also standing up for the positive work accomplished by the rest of the contingent under very difficult circumstances. To the politicians caught up in the passions of the time, an inquiry appeared to be the best way to tack to calmer political waters. This would allow the government to show it was responding to the public's concerns about the incidents and cover-up allegations while delaying a final and definitive accounting until a more convenient future time. Government leaders could gain a measure of control over the highly explosive debate, assuming the inquiry call produced a more manageable domestic political environment. An inquiry would also focus attention on and position the Canadian Forces to receive the brunt of the criticism.

Campbell moved to set up an inquiry in April, but there were two problems. One was that Canadian courts had ruled that inquiries could not deal with ongoing criminal proceedings or police investigations.[74] Campbell was also concerned about a possible conflict between her ministerial responsibility to govern the Forces and her quasi-judicial role within the military justice system. She turned to the Office of the Judge Advocate General and asked how she should proceed, and when its assistance proved insufficient, to Deputy Attorney General John Tait.[75] Campbell concluded an inquiry could be convened so long as its terms of reference were carefully defined and it adjourned at some point to allow the criminal trial and appeal processes associated with the incidents to complete.[76] On 26 April, Campbell informed the House that a board of inquiry mandated to examine all Battlegroup pre-deployment and employment matters, excluding those relating to any investigations, would be formed and begin hearings behind closed doors as soon as possible.[77] As prime minister in mid-June, she presided over the Canadian Joint Force Somalia withdrawal. The contingent's operations and that withdrawal are the matter of the following chapter.

After mid-1993, Canada largely turned from Somalia, though the inquiries into the deployment, launched by the Conservatives and then the Liberals, continued until spring 1997. Some Somalis have argued that the disengagement was an opportunity missed for Canada. One commented that Canada was impartial to the factional conflict and was therefore well positioned to help Somalia achieve a government committed to peace, sustainable democracy, and justice.[78] The bureaucracy believed Canada should avoid further involvement in the troubled African country. The Canadian International Development Agency (CIDA), for example, objected to development help for the same reason that National Defence and External Affairs had opposed additional military aid. A day after the United Nations reassumed command in Somalia, CIDA officials asked the government to think twice about new initiatives since the "reconstruction of Somalia will be a complex, long-term and costly task, [and] the situation remains volatile and sustainable results are uncertain."[79]

Conclusion

The United States government organized and led the Unified Task Force in order to create a secure environment in Somalia for humanitarian relief deliveries. The United States, like Canada, had no desire to get bogged down in the Somali civil war or UN-led reconciliation effort. The United States designed the Unified Task Force to be a short-term mission that would seize control in southern Somalia and hand over command to a UN force after a brief interval for sustained peace building, full disarmament, and national reconstruction.

The United States, Canada, and other allies brought enough forces to ensure the success of the Unified Task Force. Although the Canadian government was pleased to note that its engagement had been well received in Canada, questions were raised in the media about the direction being taken. Journalists and newspaper editors noted that the Unified Task Force was only half the answer and that at some point the world community must disarm the factions and build peace or everything would be for nought. The media speculated about what it would take to rebuild Somalia, but the Canadian government was largely silent because its intention since the Unified Task Force was first created was to withdraw with the coalition to give the Canadian Forces the opportunity to recover and retrain.

The government had stated publicly that it would stay in Somalia until the end of the enforcement action. However, the enforcement phase did not and arguably could not have ended with the Unified Task Force. The United States had split the one true Somalia mission into two halves, and both required enforcement powers if they were to have a hope of success in Somalia. This was borne out when the second UN mission received a mandate as robust as that given to the Unified Task Force. The significance of this is that the government's principal rationale for departing need not have precluded a role in the UN's second operation.

Canada decided not to participate in the UN mission, despite pressure, because it believed the international effort in its totality was not working, media and public interest and support were weak, and the Canadian Forces could not sustain the commitment beyond November 1993. The United States and the United Nations urged Canada to reconsider. The government could not see how Canada or itself would benefit from participation or how a Canadian contribution could make a difference to the multilateral effort. The government wanted to maximize the benefit to the national interest derived from available military resources, and the bureaucracy appears to have believed that there were higher priorities in the world than Somalia.

The prime minister was the decision maker, and he was strongly inclined to support the United Nations or allies when asked for help. He does not appear to have been seized with the Somalia crisis after December 1992, but he had a latent interest in supporting UN-led multilateralism in Somalia. It was not until early April – based on advice from senior officials that the Canadian Forces was exhausted and anything Canada could contribute would not noticeably enhance the doubtful UN undertaking – that the prime minister agreed Canada should withdraw as it had stated in December 1992.

The scandal that emerged because of the incidents in Somalia did not materially affect the course of government decision making. The government and the military did not try to conceal that a Somali had been beaten to death by Canadian troops in Canadian custody on 16 March. This controversial and specific point did not emerge immediately because the facts took time to isolate and verify, there was concern not to violate the legal rights of those who might be accused of a crime, and media attention initially was directed elsewhere. A scandal erupted once the incident's criminal dimension became public. Campbell said she had not been adequately briefed and that this prevented her from disclosing the incident's disturbing nature sooner. Challenged by Liberal and media criticism, the government tried to protect her and itself and to regain control over the debate by calling a board of inquiry.

10
The Canadian Joint Force Somalia: In the Field

The Unified Task Force landed in Somalia on 9 December 1992. The United States had decided to lead the multinational peace enforcement coalition to create a secure environment that would enable humanitarian relief deliveries to proceed in famine-stricken southern Somalia. The Unified Task Force's mandate avoided contentious tasks that could have prompted opposition, such as the promotion of full disarmament and political reconciliation. These were assigned to the successor mission, the United Nations Operation in Somalia II. But even without such assignments, many Somalis refused to support the US intervention.

Canada's contingent, the Canadian Joint Force Somalia, encountered some of this resentment when it deployed to the Beledweyne humanitarian relief sector in late December on what the Canadian Forces nicknamed Operation Deliverance. The Canadian Joint Force Somalia secured its area, built relationships with local people, and encouraged peace. Its work was marred by incidents in which Somalis were killed under questionable circumstances, one while in custody of the Canadian Airborne Regiment Battlegroup (the largest unit of the Canadian Joint Force Somalia). These incidents revealed leadership and discipline problems at the Battlegroup unit and subunit level but should not obscure the fact that the Canadians accomplished their mission. The Canadian Joint Force Somalia and other national contingents achieved much, and the Unified Task Force was making progress toward ending the civil war, but the coalition did not stay long enough to provide Somalia with peace and stability.

The Unified Task Force sought to create a benign environment for aid deliveries through a strategy combining dialogue and co-optation. Using the implied threat of overwhelming force, the coalition tried to encourage the faction heads to gain prestige by showing leadership and co-operating with the international community.[1] Before the landing in Somalia's capital, Mogadishu, US Ambassador Robert Oakley, the president's special envoy and the Unified Task Force's political contact point with the Somalis, met powerful faction leaders Mohamed Farah Aidid and Ali Mahdi Mohamed to explain the coalition's mandate. The Unified Task Force participated in the joint security committee they formed to reduce tension in Mogadishu and set up a Civilian-Military Operations Centre for Unified Task Force and nongovernmental organization (NGO) co-ordination. The success of these bodies and the Somali tradition of relying on committee leadership to achieve consensus decisions gave Oakley the idea of working through broad-based committees. Before each humanitarian relief sector was occupied, he met local community leaders and representatives of all major factions (not just Aidid's and Ali Mahdi's). Once the sector was secured, the Unified Task Force sponsored the formation of local committees; by using these committees as a forum for explaining their plans and learning from Somalis, coalition and NGO personnel could maximize humanitarian and military success while minimizing friction and tension.[2]

The coalition forces (initially American, although significant numbers of French and Canadian troops arrived in the first week) swiftly occupied and divided the area of operations in southern Somalia into eight (later nine) humanitarian relief sectors. The Unified Task Force's strength peaked in January 1993 at 38,300, of which 25,400 were US forces. Rapid progress was possible because of Oakley's advance political preparations, good tactical intelligence, slight resistance, and the coalition's formidable military reputation.[3] The coalition developed according to the four-phase concept of operations devised by Commanding General Lieutenant-General (US Marine Corps) Robert Johnston. The first phase was complete as of 16 December, by which time Mogadishu port and airport, Baledogle airport (later the Canadian Airborne Regiment Battlegroup staging area), and Baydhabo (also known as Baidoa) had been seized. The occupation of all sectors, phase two's objective, was achieved on 28 December after a combined Canada–United States aerial movement secured Beledweyne. Phase three, controlling and protecting land routes to interior relief areas, was underway by mid-January 1993. The US government was by then signalling to the United Nations that the coalition was almost ready for the last phase, the transition to the second UN mission.[4]

Although the coalition operation was initially mocked as a walkover, the closer one looked, the more intractable Somalia's problems appeared. When the Unified Task Force landed on the beach at dawn, the troops had to pass through the camera floodlights of the international media determined to film the event "live." The humour this provoked – one cartoon pictured a rotund soldier with campaign medals for "Best makeup in a combat situation" and "Most graceful photo-op in a land invasion"[5] – belied the chaos and violence in Mogadishu. The Unified Task Force was such a capable and confident force that it was able to intervene decisively even though the US Marine Corps and Army knew little about Somalia.[6] But it soon became clear that maintaining order would be challenging. The coalition gradually came to terms with the fact that their potential adversaries were tough and skilful manipulators, waist-deep in a war of attrition. "We have a simple desire for simple solutions," a US Army captain said two months into the deployment, "and all of a sudden we're playing chess with Boris Spassky ... this is the big leagues."[7] According to Major-General S.L. Arnold, US Army Force Commander in Somalia, as Unified Task Force learned more about the conflict it "became apparent that history was not on our side."[8]

The Western view of the civil war appears to have been influenced by a well-meaning but patronizing attitude regarding Somalia. Journalist John Stackhouse noted that the Western media helped create the perception that Somalia was sick and unable to care for itself. "The Somalia we created in the world's mind was an invalid. The real country was not." He said there were "food crops, rivers, oceans and human talent in Somalia that almost none of us ever reported."[9] The invalid image served the purposes of Western governments, militaries, and relief organizations. Aware that the suffering on television had drawn public sympathy and concern, Western governments engaged in Somalia because they were confident their forces could end the suffering. To a certain degree, the Unified Task Force showed that the West was still seduced by modern colonial stories of white knights sorting out black threats. The mission was not free of Western ideologies of superiority over the largely nonwhite developing world.[10]

To Oakley, the coalition's strictly humanitarian mission was prudent. On one occasion, he appeared relieved that national reconciliation was not his responsibility because this activity was overly complex and likely not achievable in the short term. "There's an awful lot of negotiating going on amongst every possible faction and all of the clans," he commented. "It's something I don't understand. It's something that I think is almost impossible for a foreigner to understand ... I don't envy [head of the first UN mission] Ambassador Kittani his job."[11] Oakley and his deputy, John Hirsch, wanted local political institutions with which the Unified Task Force could work. Somali community and civil society leaders were invited to pick any structure they wanted any way they wanted, as long as it was not through the barrel of a gun. A few, such as Baydhabo's "governor," a representative of Aidid's faction, resisted this. The coalition removed him and repulsed his attempts to regain authority over the region.[12]

Oakley and Hirsch had no preconceived ideas of how to encourage reconciliation. Before long it became evident to them that the committees should be used to organize local grassroots leaders. As Hirsch noted, "we quickly identified the existence of local community leaders, and the willingness on the part of a lot of people to try to restore a modicum of normal life at the town and village levels. So we worked in that direction."[13] Another positive result of the committee process was the after-the-fact hope that it might make the UN's diplomatic peacemaking easier.[14] Otherwise, the Unified Task Force did not intervene in Somali politics. Long-term reconciliation was left to the Somalis and the second UN operation because the United States wanted to avoid entanglements and antagonisms that could complicate the Unified Task Force's humanitarian mission.

Despite the care that was taken, the coalition proved to be provocative. The Unified Task Force went to great lengths to appear sensitive. For example, Johnston decided that US Marine and Army forces would eat field rations while in Somalia and not have hot food and turkey for Christmas. He believed that since Somalia was an austere environment, his troops should live austerely.[15] Social and cultural issues were still sharp because the West was forcing help on Somalis and dictating the contact with local people. Somalis who expected the United States to bring prosperity and shut down the factions were seriously disappointed when the coalition showed no interest in doing so.[16] Those who had occupied responsible positions in the former Somali state found it humiliating taking orders from foreign expatriates, many of whom were young and inclined to act as if they were indispensable to success.[17] The coalition even had implications for gender relations. On 15 December, a mob attacked and disrobed a Somali woman suspected of consorting with French Foreign Legionnaires. The mob accused coalition forces of spreading HIV/AIDS.[18] Before long, youth groups were distributing leaflets deploring the West's loose and corrupting ways.[19]

Commander of the Canadian Joint Force Somalia Colonel Serge Labbé noted that Somalis in Mogadishu were beginning to resent the coalition. He observed on 15 December, his second day, that "many [are] neutral, many visibly happy with our presence but some, particularly the young men, [are] scowling with disdain."[20] It was not long before the Canadian Airborne Regiment Battlegroup encountered the same in Beledweyne. In his situation report for 9 January 1993, Labbé commented that "the mood in Belet Uen [Beledweyne] has changed. In essence, the honeymoon is over. Although there have been no overt demonstrations of hostility, there are more and more young men glaring disparagingly at Canadian troops in much the same way as those of Mogadishu do."[21] This was evidence of the resentment that had emerged because of the Unified Task Force, despite its carefully scripted humanitarian image.

Labbé and Canadian Airborne Regiment Battlegroup Commander Lieutenant-Colonel Carol Mathieu responded with a campaign of "hearts and minds," similar to what the British had used to defeat a communist resistance in Malaya in the 1950s. This involved earning the respect of the local people and convincing them to align themselves with the security forces, winning their hearts and minds in other words, and marginalizing troublemakers. Labbé and Mathieu settled on the British model intuitively as the only way to achieve both tracks of their two-track strategy. They wanted to establish short-term security and the conditions for self-sustaining peace. Most of the humanitarian relief sector would be under control in seven weeks. The Canadian Joint Force Somalia spent about 70 percent of its time working on track two, encouraging Somalis to reject violence as a political tool.[22] Labbé believed that the Unified Task Force would not leave a lasting legacy of peace unless the Somalis came to see the foreign troops as genuine guarantors of their livelihood and not as fly-by-night opportunists.[23]

The Battlegroup would be responsible for winning Somali hearts and minds, but moving its personnel and equipment 290 kilometres inland to Beledweyne was a joint and combined effort that involved the other two Canadian Forces environments and US troops, respectively.[24] Somalia was the first time in many years that units from all three Canadian Forces Environmental Commands were placed under a joint task force commander (Labbé) to achieve one mission in one Canadian area of operations.[25] The multi-environment or "joint" co-operation was closest during the Canadian Forces arrival in the theatre. HMCS *Preserver*, for example, assisted with watercraft and Sea King helicopters that unloaded and transported tons of contingent supplies ashore. The ship served as Labbé's headquarters for a month until a joint headquarters was formed and co-located with the coalition's in Mogadishu.[26]

The Unified Task Force advised the Somalis in Beledweyne that the Canadians were coming and then sent the Canadian Airborne Regiment Battlegroup to secure the area. The coalition airdropped psychological warfare leaflets explaining its friendly intentions on 26 December. James Kunder, the country director of the US government Office of Foreign Disaster Assistance, reinforced the message in meetings with community and faction leaders a day later on behalf of Oakley (who was in the United States at the time).[27] On 28 December, the members of the Battlegroup advance party, who had gathered at Baledogle airport, their staging area, in anticipation of the move, marched into Canadian air force Hercules transports and flew to Beledweyne. Unsure about what to expect upon arrival and unwilling to take chances, they moved quickly to seize control of the airstrip and town and establish a commanding presence through determined day and night patrolling.

Coalition forces actively assisted the Canadians. On the 28th, F-18 fighters were launched from the aircraft carrier USS *Kitty Hawk* to conduct patrols above Beledweyne and give Somalis a tangible demonstration of the Unified Task Force's power, and a US Army 10th Mountain Division battalion accompanied the advance party on Marine Corps and Army helicopters.[28] As the Battlegroup main body arrived in waves over the next three days, the US soldiers simultaneously redeployed south of Mogadishu. Arnold, commander of US Army forces in Somalia, called this a flawlessly executed example of combined operations and coalition co-operation.[29] During five days of surge operations, eight Canadian air force Hercules transported 1,125 people and 480 tons of supplies

In the Field 151

in 56 flights. By 1 January 1993, the entire Canadian Airborne Regiment Battlegroup was in the humanitarian relief sector, though its vehicles did not arrive by contracted sealift and complete the two-day journey down the Imperial Highway, an Italian-built colonial era road, until 15 January.[30]

Labbé's concept of security operations was to divide the 30,000-kilometre-square Beledweyne humanitarian relief sector into four zones. Mathieu allocated these zones to his Battlegroup. Mathieu assigned the southwest, nearest the humanitarian relief sector commanded by the French Foreign Legion, to the Airborne Regiment's 1 Commando (which comprised members of the French-speaking Royal 22nd Regiment). The footborne 2 Commando (Princess Patricia Canadian Light Infantry) and 3 Commando (Royal Canadian Regiment) received Beledweyne and the southeast zone, respectively. The Royal Canadian Dragoon's A Squadron, whose Cougar armoured vehicles came equipped with the strongest weapons (76-mm guns) in the Battlegroup, was sent to the northeast. This zone was the most unstable because of the presence of two opposing factions, Aidid's branch of the United Somali Congress and the Somali National Front under General Omar Hagi Mohamed Hersi.[31] The Airborne Commandos operated from Beledweyne and the Dragoons from Matabaan, which was approximately 90 kilometres northeast of Beledweyne.

The Canadian Airborne Regiment Battlegroup took control despite the harsh conditions. The day and night patrolling continued, and its armoured vehicles – Cougars, Bisons, and Grizzlies – were rumbling along the roads soon after they arrived. The Canadians were soon referred to by the Somalis "as the white technicals who never sleep."[32] The regular patrols were meant to create an impression and gain the people's respect, and they had the desired effect. The Airborne had secured its zones by the third week of February. The northeast was more difficult because it was so volatile and the Canadians had too few troops to cover the zone.[33] The whole humanitarian relief sector was declared "secure" by 27 March.

This was achieved in "the worst environmental conditions experienced by the Canadian Forces in many years." Simple day-to-day survival was a constant challenge. Cleanliness was next to impossible because fine, flour-like sand blew around incessantly and covered everything. Normal daytime temperatures were a punishing 35-45 degrees Celsius with 60-80 percent humidity.[34] Soldiers used bottled water for drinking and washing because local sources were unsafe, and the decision not to bring cooks required the Canadians to choose from a limited selection of prepackaged dinners for almost all meals during their entire tour (except for periods of leave). No indigenous support was available, the indigenous infrastructure had been completely destroyed, and there was a constant risk of disease, scorpion and snakebites, and armed Somali attacks.

Labbé and Mathieu reduced the risk of destabilizing violence several ways, but most important was the pursuit of arms control rather than disarmament.

The US position was that the coalition should not forcibly seize Somali weapons (see Chapters 7 and 9). Johnston therefore left this to the discretion of humanitarian relief sector commanders. The Canadian Joint Force Somalia dealt with weapons and most mission challenges in the same general way. This involved a "complete immersion into the communities of the humanitarian relief sector, which led to the confidence-building first between Canadians and Somalis, and then between the clans themselves."[35] The intelligence gained helped the Canadian Joint Force Somalia analyze the political-military weapons issue and to convince faction leaders to keep heavy weapons out of circulation and most light weapons identified, tagged, and removed from view.[36] Local leaders were urged to store heavy and crew-served weapons (those requiring more than one person to operate) in one of three cantonment sites. Ammunition and arms caches were seized. Personal weapons were tolerated but had to be pointed at the ground in Beledweyne, and armed vehicles, including "technicals," were banned. "I will not tolerate any armed vehicles on the roads," Mathieu said. "I have been repeating that every day."[37]

Arms control, patrols, and unceasing vigilance yielded security sufficient for humanitarian operations and the winning of hearts and minds. The Canadian Joint Force Somalia did not have preconceived ideas about relations with NGOs, but the coalition provided a model. The Unified Task Force was holding daily meetings to determine what the aid groups needed. Labbé and Mathieu adopted a similar policy. A group of soldiers was assigned to meet local NGOs regularly and arrange assistance as required. The group's senior officer had Mathieu's complete support and was the sole contact with the NGOs.[38] The Battlegroup escorted NGOs such as the International Committee of the Red Cross, Save the Children, and International Medical Corps, while OXFAM-Quebec relied on the Somalis to protect them and their animal vaccination program.[39] The soldiers impressed some NGOs. "They came, they listened," Michelle Kelly, the International Medical Corps program director in Beledweyne, observed. As a result, "the situation has really improved." She was encouraged by the initiative they had shown. The Canadians were "innovative and forward-looking. They don't want to just sit on a few food trucks."[40]

These extra efforts won the appreciation of Somalis. Although not obligated to do so, the Canadian Airborne Regiment Battlegroup helped the Somalis recruit teachers and rebuild schools, roads, and bridges; they ran a hospital that cared for the Battlegroup and provided medical training and aids to the Somalis; and they re-established and obtained uniforms for the police force.[41] Guy Naud, co-ordinator of the OXFAM-Quebec program coincidentally located in Canada's sector, wrote that the Battlegroup won the community's admiration through their gentlemanly behaviour and by working side by side with the people. Local authorities "deplore the imminent departure of the Canadians and wish that the Canadian Army would continue working here instead of being replaced by military forces from other countries."[42] Didier Roguet of the International Committee of the Red Cross delegation in Beledweyne recalled that after departing "the Canadians were quickly regretted" by Somalis and NGOs.[43]

Good works were used to draw attention to the benefits arising from nonviolent methods of dispute resolution. The Canadian Joint Force Somalia followed Oakley's lead and, with some coalition assistance,[44] created broad-based grassroots committees on relief, reconstruction, security, and reconciliation. "We always recognized," Labbé said, that "you must get the local people to make the decisions."[45] Committees were the Canadian Joint Force Somalia's most challenging task because it was an unfamiliar role, adjusting to local nuances of deal making and bargaining was difficult, and there were sixteen clans that appeared to have multiple representatives and sometimes presented conflicting claims that were virtually impossible to verify. The Canadians had to be patient and use the relationships they had developed to further the consensus building among Somalis that was essential for collective action. Labbé believed longer-term security depended on the committees achieving some form of success before the Unified Task Force departed.[46] But he and Mathieu, in the pursuit of timely results, may have inadvertently caused offence by neglecting existing alliances, favouring some leaders over others, and short-circuiting the way that Somali clan elders painstakingly forge binding contracts.[47]

The Canadian Joint Force Somalia found working with Somalis difficult. Labbé noted that the Unified Task Force came as "guests in Somalia, not as an occupation force or a colonial power to govern, but as part of a coalition committed to providing this country with a secure environment so the Somalis can re-establish and govern themselves."[48] From the intervention's first days, many Somalis appeared unwilling to welcome the Unified Task Force on that account. Somalis expressed disdain for the aid effort by looting and selling food on the black market. They taunted, stoned, swarmed, and sniped at NGO and coalition personnel, including Canadian Joint Force Somalia sailors and soldiers. Night and day thieves raided the Battlegroup base in Beledweyne, called Camp Pegasus. Airborne patrols, including the "heart patrols" sent to encourage community members to work with the coalition, could be met with smiles – or stones.[49] According to one Canadian, "many soldiers were intensely frustrated to realize that not all Somalis (like the bandits put out of a job) welcomed help."[50]

Animosity did not escalate dramatically, notwithstanding the disturbing incidents that involved the Canadian Airborne Regiment Battlegroup. On 17 February, Airborne paratroopers shot and killed a Somali while repulsing a violent anti–Unified Task Force demonstration that included an attack on Camp Pegasus. David Bercuson has argued that this was a sign of rising tension between Canadians and Somalis,[51] but this is doubtful. The Canadian

Forces determined that the riot did not represent a groundswell of local dissatisfaction with the Canadian presence and that the townspeople were satisfied with the Battlegroup. The agitators responsible had been paid by Aidid.[52] Oakley said the incident was related to certain Canadian Joint Force Somalia and coalition actions that were against Aidid's interests. The Canadians were marginalizing his local "governor" by supporting community leaders with genuine popular support and, in conjunction with US Special Forces, were interdicting the communication and supply lines of Aidid forces to the northeast and the southwest of their humanitarian relief sector. This was valuable to the coalition because it helped stifle his faction and allies and prevent fresh conflict. The coalition wanted to keep everything bottled up since fighting in one part of Somalia automatically resulted in difficulties elsewhere. Aidid had arranged for the riot to show he disapproved of these efforts.[53]

Problems emerged in March because some Battlegroup leaders could not completely control themselves or their men. The Somali response to the Unified Task Force may have affected the contingent in a way a straightforward military attack would not. Canadians prefer to believe that their military commitments (short of war) are shaped by values such as human rights and noble instincts like helpfulness and compassion, but Canadians have never been inherently good, and this virtuous self-perception did not shape the clay of the mission for every Canadian soldier. Paradoxically, some Canadian soldiers reacted by caring less about the human rights of Somalis while the rest of the Canadian Joint Force Somalia asserted its special responsibilities toward them.[54] The government and military leaders in Ottawa did not have solutions to recommend when those the Battlegroup had come to assist acted like enemies. In frustration, like some Belgians in Somalia and US soldiers in Kosovo in 1999, several Canadians turned their anger inward and closer to home.[55]

Labbé was a professional commander, but the command climate in the Canadian Airborne Regiment Battlegroup was unable to handle these strains. Commanders, through their leadership style, attitude, self-discipline, and drive create a climate or environment around themselves. Informal and formal factors (such as orders and standard operating procedures) help shape the climate, but personal example is the key. Subordinates read and adopt the attributes of the commander when setting the environment at their level.[56] Labbé's charisma and professionalism as a commander have been recognized. Johnston awarded him the United States Legion of Merit in May 1993, and Oakley, Hirsch, and Johnston praised Labbé in letters to Canadian government leaders. Vice-Admiral Larry Murray, the deputy chief of the defence staff in National Defence Headquarters as of February 1993, never lost confidence in Labbé as a commander.[57] Steve McCluskey, who served in Canadian Joint Force Somalia headquarters in Mogadishu, said he has rarely met a more capable officer and "would go to war with the man in a heartbeat."[58] Lucie

Edwards, Canadian High Commissioner to Nairobi (with accreditation to Somalia), has called Labbé "a hero," an honour she rarely bestows.[59]

As Canada's man on the spot in the Somalia theatre, Labbé represented the country operationally. His main responsibility as Canadian contingent commander was the management of command and control arrangements between Canadian Forces units and coalition headquarters. Labbé received strict instructions from the chief of the defence staff that defined when and under what conditions operational or the more restrictive tactical control could be transferred to allied commanders.[60] Initially, given the urgent need to stabilize the area of operations under an existing coalition chain of command, Labbé placed the Battlegroup under the operational control of the Unified Task Force. (The latter delegated control to 10th Mountain Division, the coalition land component, for about three weeks until the division redeployed. Thereafter the Airborne returned to the direct control of the Unified Task Force.) Later, at Johnston's behest, Labbé placed the HMCS *Preserver* under tactical control of the coalition's multinational maritime component, called Naval Force, for specific missions limited in time and place. One such mission was the provision of the *Preserver,* with its three forward infrared radar-equipped Sea King helicopters, in support of US and Belgian combat operations in the Kismaayo area (18 February-2 March).

The reality, however, was that Unified Task Force headquarters did not like dealing directly with individual units. The coalition gave direction to the Canadian Airborne Regiment Battlegroup via Labbé's headquarters. In light of this, with the departure of *Preserver* on 6 March and arrival of Canadian Forces Twin Huey utility helicopters to replace the Sea Kings, Labbé seized the opportunity to restructure the Canadian contingent. He decided to put his headquarters, and hence his entire newly reorganized seven-unit force, under coalition operational control.[61] This brought him formally into the operational chain (between the Unified Task Force headquarters and the Battlegroup), while keeping the contingent intact as a joint force under his command.[62]

Normally it is axiomatic to say that national commanders are responsible for their entire contingent. Scholars have argued that the principle of command responsibility and personal liability is fully recognized by national and international law. Officers who order, collude in, or fail to prevent abuses by subordinates may be held accountable for those actions.[63] Yet, in the Somalia case, it was not realistic to hold Labbé responsible for the climate or actions by members of Battlegroup subunits. Labbé regularly visited the Battlegroup and could monitor its activities by scanning its situation reports, but he was headquartered in Mogadishu and removed from day-to-day operations until 7 March. Though he informally conferred with Labbé, operational taskings were Johnston's responsibility until that time, when as noted the Canadian Joint Force Somalia headquarters shifted into the operational chain.

In this context, what command responsibility means is thrown into question. Andrew Leslie, a major-general and the Canadian Forces contingent commander in Afghanistan in 2003, has observed that as the commander Labbé was responsible, but he could not exercise operational oversight or possess full situational awareness of Battlegroup subunits when that was two rank levels below and in a different chain.[64] Even with frequent visits, it was entirely possible that a commander would not pick up all the issues, especially if there were people who did not tell him about certain things he should know. Labbé, then, was not responsible for the incidents, but he was responsible in the sense that the troops who committed those actions were under his command. Labbé did not order or collude in any abuses and could not have prevented incidents he did not know were about to occur. He trusted Mathieu to set the Battlegroup climate and expected that the Canadian rules of engagement would be strictly followed.

Labbé made the second change to the contingent structure when the operation was winding down. It was not because the 4 March incident occurred shortly before. Though Labbé did not lose confidence in Mathieu, this incident revealed that Mathieu was having trouble adopting Labbé's command presence with the necessary fidelity. Mathieu had unintentionally undermined the Battlegroup command climate when he told his officers on 28 January 1993 that Somali thieves raiding Camp Pegasus could be shot. Everyone present "understood they could use deadly force against someone, armed or not, who fled after stealing Canadian equipment." Some of Mathieu's officers believed the instruction, which was later clarified to mean shooting at the legs (to maim), to be immoral, if not illegal, and they refused to repeat it to their soldiers. The instruction was not rescinded until 8 March.[65]

Mathieu was responsible for the command climate of the Battlegroup and its subunits, and his comment about shooting intruders may have resulted in the national rules of engagement not being followed by members of his command.[66] On 4 March, Captain Michel Rainville, the officer commanding the Airborne Reconnaissance Platoon, was ordered to provide Camp Pegasus' engineering compound with extra night-time security. The platoon took up various positions and monitored the compound perimeter. It also laid out bait to draw would-be-thieves to a specific area. Before the night was over one Somali would be wounded and another killed. Service Commando Surgeon Major Barry Armstrong, MD, believed that the Somali had been executed at close range. This allegation was refuted by the pathologist's autopsy and the Royal Canadian Mounted Police ballistics report included in the ensuing National Defence Headquarters military police investigation.[67] The Somalia Inquiry, after very careful examination, was "not able to endorse or rule out" his hypothesis.[68]

The Inquiry determined that Rainville had erred. It argued that the incident was a clear violation of the rules of engagement resulting from "an abhorrent failure of leadership."[69] Labbé's testimony partly reflects this. He said Rainville exercised bad judgment when he placed bait (rations and water) to entice Somalis into the camp, and the wounding may have been an excessive use of force in contravention of the rules of engagement (see also Chapter 8).[70] Labbé also defended Rainville. He argued that the killing was within the rules of engagement because the platoon had cause to fear for its safety given that shots had been fired (they did not know for certain by whom), it was dark, and a Somali was running toward them ignoring orders to halt. They had to react instinctively in seconds.[71] Labbé added that Rainville had tried to respect the rules of engagement and honestly believed that he had done so.[72] Rainville appears to have acted within his authority, but he did not act wisely or humanely.[73] On 4 March, he fell short of the professional standard expected of him. Rainville did not display a most important attribute of professionalism, expertise, which for the military profession is defined as the ordered management of violence.[74]

Mathieu's instruction also appears to have confused Major Anthony Seward, who was having trouble restraining 2 Commando. A 2 Commando patrol entered a mined area that Mathieu had declared off limits on 7 January. This was only one of the signs that Seward was not in total control.[75] On the 16th, Mathieu had issued Seward a reproof (nonjudicial reprimand) for ignoring directives to reduce aggressiveness in accordance with the hearts and minds campaign. Seward was fined for accidentally discharging his weapon, one of a large number of misfires (five) by 2 Commando.[76] Mathieu believed a lack of command and control was involved,[77] but his attempt to give Seward direction was undermined by the "shoot intruders" instruction. This comment "bewildered" Seward because it seemed to contradict a restrained approach.[78] The aggressive patrolling and actions in contravention of Mathieu's orders continued. In early February, 2 Commando was again criticized for behaving too forcefully toward the Somalis.[79]

On or about 14 March, Seward ordered that intruders infiltrating the Commando compound should be "abused." Seward wanted these Somalis run down and physically apprehended, if necessary abused, but not killed. He did not ensure this nuance was communicated to his soldiers[80] prior to the 16th, when sixteen-year-old Shidane Arone was brought to the Commando holding area (a bunker) for the night to await transfer to local authorities. Master-Corporal Clayton Matchee, with Private E. Kyle Brown's active assistance, tortured and beat Arone to death while he was in Canadian custody. Seward's order was interpreted as being authority to abuse prisoners, and this directly influenced the treatment Arone received. Matchee told observers of the torture that his officer had approved the abuse.[81] This may explain why, as sounds came out of the bunker, no one tried to stop Matchee. The incident was attributable to Seward's abuse order, and as the officer commanding 2 Commando, Seward was responsible for the climate in which the killing occurred. Whether Matchee and Brown killed Arone accidentally or by design, they were responsible for their actions. Their lapse in discipline was egregious. On 19 March, Matchee, now under arrest, attempted to hang himself. The suicide attempt left him seriously brain-damaged and unable to explain his actions.

The 16 March incident can be compared to the Abu Ghraib prison abuse scandal involving US troops in Iraq in 2003. According to Johnston, the Unified Task Force commander, both episodes demonstrate that when soldiers are given power over others, personal character flaws can come to the fore that open the door to unethical and immoral behaviour.[82] Just as the US prison guards' actions did not reflect the attitudes or behaviour of all American forces in Iraq,[83] so too Matchee's and Brown's actions were not representative of the Canadian Airborne Regiment Battlegroup or Canadian Joint Force Somalia. Most of the Battlegroup's members remained disciplined despite the camp intrusions and provocations. For example, the Dragoons and a US Special Forces Detachment that was working closely with them received mortar, 106-mm recoilless rifle, and M-47 tank fire at Balanbale on 10 February 1993, but they did not shoot back because of the risk to noncombatants.[84] Speaking privately to reporters, some Airborne soldiers confessed feeling the urge to lash out, but overall their record was one of restraint in the face of hostility.[85]

In Canada, the incidents were soon overshadowing the Canadian Joint Force Somalia's accomplishments and the changes to the international effort in Somalia. Labbé urged Canadians to be balanced when assessing the Canadian Joint Force Somalia, noting that the work completed was "something all Canadians should be proud of" and "we should not let an incident that might be an aberration cloud that."[86] It was to no avail. National Defence Minister Kim Campbell told the House of Commons that the 16 March incident, which had triggered a massive political scandal and a second military police investigation, "casts a shadow on the fine reputation of the Canadian Forces."[87] The new chief of the defence staff, Admiral John Anderson, admitted that 16 March was a "black mark" on the mission's leadership aspects.[88] *Maclean's* editor Robert Lewis said that the Canadian Joint Force Somalia had "besmirch[ed] the peacekeeping tradition that has become ... a major source of this country's positive self-image in the world."[89] Allegations of widespread racism and neo-Nazi connections began to be made about the Airborne.[90] As fresh revelations emerged and the momentum grew, sharply critical stories became commonplace. Labbé wrote that he found April and the succeeding months among the most difficult of his life because he had to reconcile the impressive work he saw being achieved with the negative press coverage in Canada.[91]

The Canadians continued to provide security and rebuild the Somali community in their humanitarian relief sector, but flagging morale complicated matters. The 16th of March was not the final incident. On the 17th, an Airborne patrol shot and killed a Somali guard working for the International Committee of the Red Cross while trying to control rioting Beledweyne citizens who were unhappy because the humanitarians had not used locally hired truck drivers. The De Faye Board of Inquiry determined this use of deadly force was in accordance with the rules of engagement.[92] These disruptions did not deflect the Canadian Joint Force Somalia from its pursuit of short-term security and peaceful long-term stability. They were first in the coalition to re-establish schools.[93] Retired US Navy admiral Jonathan Howe, the new special representative of the secretary-general for Somalia who arrived in March, officially opened the first school on 8 April in Matabaan (three others were opened in Beledweyne before the end of May). Canada's High Commission in Nairobi provided $25,000 to build the last two schools from the mission-administered Canadian International Development Agency Canada Fund and $50,000 to the restoration of a Mogadishu orphanage by sailors from *Preserver* and NGOs.[94] Good works were largely overshadowed by the 4 and 16 March incidents in Canadian news coverage of Operation Deliverance. This became a morale issue for the Canadian Joint Force Somalia. Labbé observed that many of his soldiers looked dejected, depressed, and stunned by the news depictions, and he tried buttressing spirits by keeping them active.[95]

In addition to the storm brewing in Canada, the lack of a clear withdrawal date hampered morale.[96] Labbé knew that the decision to send a second rotation should have been taken in January, because months were needed to select, train, and deploy troops for missions. In February, when Deputy Minister of National Defence Robert Fowler toured Canada's area of operations, and in mid-March, when Admiral Anderson did so, Labbé reminded his guests of the closing window of opportunity (leaving with the coalition) and of the morale and logistical reasons for not prolonging the rotation.[97] Military personnel work hard when they know why and for how long, and Canadian Joint Force Somalia soldiers and air/ground crew (*Preserver* had departed for home on 6 March) knew the government had stated that Canada would depart when the Unified Task Force did.[98] Not only would an extension be disappointing, but also the harsh conditions and negative media coverage had made the mission especially taxing.

The timing of the withdrawal grew more pressing as United Nations Operation in Somalia II took shape and the transition to UN command neared. On 26 March, the UN Security Council created the second Somalia operation by approving resolution 814. The blue helmets did not take charge until 4 May, but the United Nations and United States could finally conduct detailed transition planning.[99] Like Ambassador Howe, UN military commanders wanted the Canadian Forces to stay for another six-month rotation or at least delay its departure (see Chapter 9). This was raised, for example, during a briefing following the Canadian-initiated mission (13-22 March) to the city of Gaalkacyo (also known as Galcaio) north of the Unified Task Force area of operations, to deter aggression and defuse tension between Aidid and other factions. US Army Major-General Thomas Montgomery, the deputy force commander of the second UN mission, observed that the Canadians should be kept on and their area expanded to include the Gaalkacyo district.[100] But Labbé, in his dealings with Somalis in Beledweyne, refused to compromise on the principle that the Canadians were short-term guests. He resisted the Somalis who wanted Canadian Joint Force Somalia personnel to make decisions for them because he believed lasting peace could only come from the people.[101]

The push toward peace was frustrated by the short-term nature of the Unified Task Force's deployment, which did not allow the Somalis enough opportunity for nonviolent dialogue through the committee system. The United States and its allies like Canada were not willing to provide the long-term political and military commitment required to achieve sustainable and measurable peace.[102] The international community's success in Somalia depended on whether pressure was maintained on the faction leaders to keep them talking and moving toward peace.[103] The promise of state offices or shares of state resources might have facilitated co-optation of some faction heads. The US desire to leave quickly heightened the chances that the international effort would encounter turbulence. It introduced the possibility, which in fact came to pass, that the Unified Task Force's approach to fostering dialogue backed by superior force would not be continued by the second UN operation, that the United Nations would not have an effective alternate strategy, and that the United Nations would not be ready for the magnitude of the task being thrust upon it.

As of April 1993, Labbé still did not know whether the Canadian Joint Force Somalia would be assisting the UN's second mission or when the Canadians would be departing. The Canadian Joint Force Somalia was pleased to learn on 17 April that National Defence Headquarters finally approved its redeployment plan. Approval meant that if all went well, Canadians could start going home on 15 May. At the start of May, 1 Commando was redeployed to Mogadishu to provide security at the Old Port, where vehicle washing and sea container packing would take place. The UN flag was raised above Canadian Airborne Regiment Battlegroup headquarters on 4 May to signify that the Unified Task Force had left Somalia and the second UN operation was the new headquarters, but the Battlegroup never donned UN accoutrements even though it would operate under UN command for over three weeks.[104] Complications arose when the UN's second Somalia mission had trouble finding a successor to the Canadians in Beledweyne, and this delayed the redeployment.[105] Not long after the 15th, a German logistics formation was confirmed, and the Germans agreed to maintain the hearts and minds approach. An Italian force, along with a Nigerian force of which it would have operational control, would provide security. The change of command ceremony took place in Beledweyne on 31 May, and afterwards the remaining Canadians redeployed to Mogadishu.

The Canadian Joint Force Somalia had ceased operations, and 550 Canadians left the theatre on 3 June. As the rest of the contingent waited their turn to go, the security situation in the capital deteriorated dramatically. On 5 June, in the early morning, Aidid's fighters ambushed Pakistani forces with the second UN mission during an inspection of five weapons-collection points, including four in Mogadishu. Near two of the Mogadishu sites, twenty-four Pakistanis were killed, many brutally, six Pakistanis declared missing (one later died and five were returned), and sixty-one UN troops were wounded.[106] Ferocious firefights between gunmen and UN rescue forces continued until the afternoon.

The Canadians were spread out at three locations – the Old Port (vehicle/equipment washing), the New Port (where the supplies would be loaded on ships), and the airport (flights to Canada) – and no longer privy to intelligence from the second UN mission. Labbé did not know how the United Nations would react to the 5 June attacks. He learned from Canadian Brigadier-General Jim Cox, then chief of staff of the UN's second operation, that the United Nations would start attacking Aidid's infrastructure on 12 June.[107] Labbé decided to consolidate at the New Port and airport by the 10th. This would make force protection easier while waiting for sealift to arrive. This was accomplished without incident, and, a week later, Labbé and most Canadians left Somalia by air, bound initially for Nairobi, Kenya. On the 18th, two chartered container ships – the MV *Anderma* and MV *Guber* – sailed out of Mogadishu port with the Canadian Joint Force Somalia equipment in their holds, and the last members of the Canadian Joint Force Somalia flew out of Somalia.

Conclusion

The Unified Task Force deployed to Somalia to create security for aid deliveries. The coalition had a strategy of dialogue and co-optation, through which it hoped to encourage the factions to co-operate with the intervention. Oakley understood the local dynamics and was able to quickly begin working with faction leaders on resolving their differences. The troops occupied southern Somalia swiftly because the force was so confident and capable and resistance was slight. However, Unified Task Force had much to learn about the civil war in which it had intervened. To a certain degree, the West was still under the influence of ideologies of superiority over the largely nonwhite developing world. Ending Somalia's suffering and disorder proved to be difficult.

Oakley and Hirsch did not have a mandate to rebuild Somali political society. They wanted political structures with which Unified Task Force could partner, and they decided to create committees to work and share information with Somalis in hopes of avoiding misunderstanding and confrontation. Oakley and Hirsch thought the committee system could be an asset to the second UN mission, which had been assigned comprehensive national reconstruction and peace-building tasks. The committees provided Somalis with an opportunity to reconcile and build a peaceful future. With a longer commitment, the committees might have brought lasting stability to Somalia.

The US-led coalition took care to avoid antagonizing the Somalis, but the presence of foreign troops was still provocative. The factions co-operated minimally because the Unified Task Force was so militarily powerful. But many Somalis wanted the coalition to provide more help than its leaders were authorized to deliver. Somalis who were educated professionals or intellectuals saw the Unified Task Force as a visible reminder of their country's humiliatingly weak position. The prospect of unmediated close contact between Somali women and coalition troops was an immediate source of cultural and gender-related tensions.

Labbé detected these feelings in the Beledweyne humanitarian relief sector. He and Mathieu responded with a "hearts and minds" campaign that encouraged Somalis to align themselves with the security forces and with peace while marginalizing fighters and malcontents. The hearts and minds campaign dovetailed with the Canadian Joint Force Somalia two-track approach to their assignment. The first track was establishing a secure environment in the humanitarian relief sector so that relief deliveries could proceed. Though not easy, especially in the harsh Somali environment, this was largely achieved in roughly seven weeks. Contributing to this success was the Canadian Joint Force Somalia decision to conduct arms control and eschew disarmament, which could have turned local Somalis against the Canadians.

The second, more difficult, track was building local capacities for longer-term, self-sustaining peace. Through voluntarily performed good works, the Canadians sought to draw Somali attention to the benefits obtainable with peace. This included re-establishing schools and the police in Beledweyne. Another important track two element was the committee system that Oakley and Hirsch developed and Labbé and Mathieu adopted for use by the Battlegroup. The Canadians worked hard at this because Labbé believed that the committees would not survive unless Somalis saw achievements from the nonviolent instrument before the Canadian Joint Force Somalia left. The Canadians found understanding the local nuances of deal making and bargaining difficult to master, and they may have been forced to rush this delicate process.

The Canadian Joint Force Somalia found that working with the Somalis could be a major challenge. Many Somalis were resentful of the coalition and unwilling to appreciate or even tolerate what the international troops were trying to do for them. It was simply unacceptable that the Western-led coalition had forced help on them and strictly delineated how much help would be provided. As a result, many Somalis appear to have had no difficulty stealing from the aid effort and lashing out at coalition troops. Some Canadians found this situation extremely frustrating.

The four incidents that resulted in Somali deaths were not signs of escalating animosities. The 17 February and 17 March incidents are not controversial because they occurred during the normal performance of duties. The 4 and 16 March incidents, and particularly the latter, have been held up as proof that the Airborne was almost out of control and that the entire military was in crisis. Both incidents can be attributed to the flawed command climate at the Airborne unit and subunit level. Mathieu's comment about shooting intruders may have contributed to the national rules of engagement not being followed on 4 March. Rainville appears to have believed that what he was doing was right, but on this occasion he exercised flawed judgment by leaving out bait and using excessive force contrary to the rules of engagement. Seward could not maintain an appropriate command climate in 2 Commando. By ordering the abuse of prisoners and not ensuring his full meaning was understood down the chain of command, Seward diminished the subunit command climate to the point where some undisciplined soldiers imagined torturing prisoners was permissible.

The 4 and 16 March incidents and the Armstrong allegation quickly came to dominate Canadian media coverage of Operation Deliverance. This was a heavy blow to the Canadian Joint Force Somalia, which had to keep going even though conditions and tensions were as severe as before. The final months of the mission were doubly difficult because the Canadian Joint Force Somalia did not know until mid-April – four months after arrival – when they would be coming home.

It must have seemed ironic to Labbé that while the Canadian Joint Force Somalia was being denounced in Canada, officials with the second UN operation were asking Canada for a second rotation and an extension of its current contingent. The Canadian Joint Force Somalia had deployed expecting that it would withdraw roughly when the Unified Task Force did. An extension would have been a blow to morale. In the event, the Canadian Joint Force Somalia served under the second UN mission for over three weeks before being relieved by UN forces. The fighting that flared up in June was in part an indication that many Somalis were prepared to rise up against foreign troops and were not committed to peace.

Conclusion

Ottawa decided to participate in the United Nations Operation in Somalia I in August 1992 when several factors converged for the first time. Prime Minister Brian Mulroney was being pressured to act by the media, which had made Somalia's famine and civil war a major domestic issue, and he wanted to support Canada's interest in multilateralism. The prime minister was a Pearsonian internationalist who believed in multilateralism, and he used peacekeeping as a political tactic to support his unpopular government. In December 1992, Mulroney contributed troops to the US-led Unified Task Force for the same reasons, as well as to maintain warm ties with the United States. The decision-making context was shaped by the government's optimism for the United Nations in the post-Cold War era and Canada's multilateral and peacekeeping traditions.

The main drivers behind the decisions – Mulroney, the media, and multilateralism – were interlinked, but the prime minister was pre-eminent among them. In April-May 1992, his first impulse was to help and he expressed interest in a role with the United Nations Operation in Somalia I but did not insist that Canada participate. Mulroney likely changed his mind because of advice received from the bureaucracy, and he was influenced by the fact that the crisis was not well known to Canadians and that the UN's peacekeeping and diplomatic peacemaking efforts in Somalia were just getting under way and had yet to be discredited. Canada declined a role in Somalia in April-May 1992, officially because the first UN mission was too unsafe.

But by July, the media had brought the Somali famine to the public's attention and Mulroney was feeling pressure to do something about it. Mulroney's vigorous contribution to the UN effort in the former Yugoslavia contrasted with his inattention to Somalia, and this suggested to some that the United Nations and the Mulroney government were ignoring Africa. Mulroney was susceptible to these criticisms, and he was doubtless aware that he could enhance the unpopularity of his government by participating in an activity with a wide appeal. He was optimistic about peacekeeping's potential and thought that the expanded UN mission in Somalia would be able to ease the suffering. Although the situation in Somalia in late July and early August was as dangerous as before, Mulroney decided that Canada should contribute to the first UN Somalia operation. Military planners and bureaucrats stopped wondering whether Canada should get involved in the crisis and implemented this decision.

In late November and early December, Mulroney decided that Canada would join the Unified Task Force. The prime minister attached great importance to maintaining smooth relations with the United States through personal diplomacy. As a result, he agreed to assist when President George H.W. Bush requested that Canada support his coalition and help make it appear less dominated by the United States. Although the Mulroney government had been criticized for being too pro-American, its decision met with little public opposition. Most Canadians agreed that something drastic had to be done about Somalia.

The Mulroney government saw the Unified Task Force as a continuation of Canada's multilateralist and peacekeeping traditions. Government leaders believed the Unified Task Force was necessary because the post-Cold War era was awash with vicious internal wars traditional peacekeepers could not tame. They noted that Canada had been urging the United States to get more heavily involved in peace operations because this would strengthen multilateralism. The government engaged in support of multilateralism when the crisis became a major international issue, when the UN and US efforts in Somalia seemed likely to succeed, and, in the case of the Unified Task Force, because the United States wanted Canada to do so.

The Canadian media, which in the main supported the government's decision, agreed that Canada's participation was necessary so that there was a counterbalance to US interests in the multilateral agenda. Media pressure played an important role in prompting government action. Senior leaders became strongly interested in the possibility of involvement when rising media and public interest made it politically advisable to do so.

In spring 1993, Ottawa had to decide whether to withdraw from Somalia or contribute to the second UN operation in Somalia. The prime minister was receiving requests to engage, he wanted to support multilateralism, and he enjoyed the prestige associated with participating in coalitions. Mulroney seriously considered but decided against contributing because it appeared that the international effort in Somalia was not succeeding. Bureaucrats assumed that the second UN mission would be long, dangerous, and extremely costly, and military leaders insisted that nothing the Canadian Forces could do would measurably improve the second UN mission's prospects. The government was aware that the public no longer supported a role in Somalia as vigorously as before. And other conflicts, such as the civil war in the Balkans, had a stronger claim on resources because Canada had a greater national interest at stake there.

The foregoing discussion has significance that extends beyond the Somalia case. Our understanding of Canadian foreign policy, for example, is enhanced by examination of power and the state system, Canada-US relations, and Pearsonian multilateralism. Specific issues and developments such as prime ministerial leadership, the co-operation between the political and military sides of the government, and the error that resulted because decision makers did not have complete information also have wider ramifications. The importance of the Somalia case to security and defence studies is evident from the path-breaking work of the Canadian Joint Force Somalia and the lessons learned during that operation.

Mulroney's foreign policy during the Somalia crisis showed his mature attitude toward Canada-US relations and his understanding of the need to court and respect power in the state system. Like Lester B. Pearson, Mulroney believed Canada would not be a world player unless it maintained warm ties with the United States and other powerful countries that shared its interests and values. He had a more "adult" view of Canada-US relations than the Liberals who succeeded Pearson as prime minister. Mulroney believed that Canada would not further its national interests unless leaders in Ottawa and Washington could get beyond minor disagreements and not let disputes disrupt their ability to address issues of common concern. On peace operations in Somalia and many other files, Mulroney's foreign policy showed that he did not fear Canada's national identity would be assimilated or diminished through close co-operation with the United States.

Mulroney's approach to Somalia showed that he shared the traditional Pearsonian concern for maintaining effective multilateral institutions and processes. He understood that credible multilateralism was in Canadian interests because they were predictable, rule-bound, and co-operative, and could present opportunities for meaningful decision making and power sharing. The Canadian preoccupation with process has been criticized. This approach is not focused on substance, it has been argued, or on definable, practical results; it would be better if Canadians decided and acted on where they stand and what values they hold dear.[1] But what was important to Mulroney was getting the process right because this would serve Canada's national interests and the common good of the international community. The prime minister contributed to the United Nations Operation in Somalia I when he saw that the operation was losing credibility. He agreed to a Unified Task Force role partly because Canada's participation made it less US-dominated and more legitimate to the world.

The importance of what Mulroney was trying to do is evident when one looks beyond the Somalia crisis to the acrimonious spring 2003 debate between the United States and other Western powers over war in Iraq. The resulting process breakdown created the worst diplomatic rift in the history of the North Atlantic Alliance and had other consequences just as grave. The North Atlantic Treaty Organization (NATO) ceased to be the point of contact for strategic transatlantic security dialogue.[2] The United States had to lead a coalition into Iraq with a pale legitimacy in the eyes of much of the world, and the coalition's operational effectiveness was probably reduced by the absence of many allied militaries, including Canada's, that have worked to remain interoperable with the US armed forces.

Mulroney did not view the world through a Canadian prism or indulge in national narcissism and self-flattery as did some Liberal government leaders. He thought the most constructive and authentic way to express and stimulate Canadian nationalism was not by lathering up with the notion that the world needed Canada but by galvanizing and inspiring Canadians with a foreign policy that was influence seeking and activist and that took a broader view of the national interest. In the case of Somalia, this involved projecting and protecting values such as respect for human rights and the alleviation of suffering, as well as elevating the country's importance by fostering co-operation and engaging. Mulroney believed Canadian foreign policy should not take pride in standing alone and thereby achieve a false independence. The more appropriate approach to external affairs was to seek opportunities for collaboration with the United States and other powerful countries through multilateral organizations like the United Nations and, more narrowly, through ad hoc coalitions.

In addition to policy, Canada's Somalia engagement is notable because at times the decision making was unknowingly based on incomplete information. The government accepted the wrong task when it committed to the first UN mission to Somalia in August 1992. A Canadian High Commission in Nairobi team learned the assignment would involve stabilization, not the desired famine relief role. The pace of events, lack of personnel, and inexperience in the Horn made it hard for the government to stay informed. Talks with UN officials could not make up for this shortcoming. The Somalia case demonstrates the need for superior intelligence gathering and analysis tools before the country commits itself to missions in unfamiliar and distant regions and gets caught up in an undesirable or unsuitable task, and for expansion of Canada's foreign service so that this side of foreign policy is better supported. Canada may have difficulty leading or supporting stabilization missions to other failed states without independent access to timely and specific information.

The large August and December commitments emphasized the importance of prime ministerial leadership. In May, Mulroney's senior officials advised against a role in Somalia since it was too risky. Nonetheless, Mulroney decided in August, even though the situation was not improved, that the government should support the UN's first Somalia operation because of the calls from the domestic media to do more and the criticism of the international community's neglect of the Somali famine and civil war. Mulroney did not impair the decision-making process, but when we step back from the Somalia case it becomes clear that politicians' influence can be detrimental.

This seems to have been the case with the US war against Iraq in 2003. Political pressure on decision-making and intelligence processes, especially over whether weapons of mass destruction were present in Iraq, may explain why US and UK assessments (and Canada's, though it missed the war) so closely reflected the erroneous Washington political line.

In December 1992, Mulroney decided that Canada should agree to Bush's troop request because it would enable Canada to be more closely associated with Washington's decision making, especially when it affected Canadian interests. Mulroney understood that if Canada wanted to play it had to stick with the United States, and he was not uncomfortable with the use of force in humanitarian interventions, particularly after the coalition victory in the Persian Gulf War (1990-91). He was one of the first to recognize that the end of the Cold War (ca. 1989) and the Gulf success fundamentally changed the nature of international relations and the process by which Canada's interests would be pursued. Mulroney strongly supported multilateralism, another reason why the UN-sanctioned, US-led coalition had appeal. This was why he asked his advisers to consider taking a significant role in the second UN mission to Somalia in spring 1993 and why it was difficult to convince him to withdraw.

This book has considered both the political and military aspects of government decision making regarding peace operations in order to gain a fuller understanding of why and how Canada committed to the first UN mission and the Unified Task Force, and not to the second UN effort. Other studies have concentrated on "why" Canada engaged in peacekeeping and have described its strong record of participation, but this study discusses a situation in which Canada was the only nation to refuse a blue helmet role (in April-May 1992). The prime minister made this choice because the bureaucracy and military believed the risk was too great, and the crisis and the mission were not high priorities in Canada. Military leaders and the National Defence Headquarters Joint Staff provided advice and analysis that furthered the prime minister's decision making. The Canadian Forces' role within government in determining which operations and personnel are chosen (or not chosen) adds to our understanding of the country's UN and non-UN coalition commitments.

On the Somalia file, the Department of National Defence and Canadian Forces side and the Prime Minister's Office/Privy Council Office/External Affairs side of the government co-operated rather than competed. Although there were disagreements on points of policy – such as whether the Unified Task Force should disarm the Somali factions – these debates had a single purpose: to determine the best way to pursue Canada's interests. For example, when External Affairs learned in July that the United Nations needed battalions for Somalia, National Defence determined that the Canadian Forces had troops available and identified their roles and the periods for which they could be sustained. Commitments were never inflicted on the Canadian Forces. National

Defence did not object to the government's desire to engage, and Mulroney did not overextend the Canadian Forces. It was up to the military to determine what could be done and up to the rest of the government (with the prime minister having the final say) to decide whether Canada should take part.

The activities of the Unified Task Force and Canadian Forces contingent have broader significance because their accomplishments were precedent setting. The co-operation established with local parties and NGOs in Somalia is the best example. The Forces tried to stabilize the Beledweyne humanitarian relief sector while also encouraging locals to initiate and take responsibility for long-term peace building and national reconstruction. Colonel Serge Labbé, commander of the Canadian Joint Force Somalia, believed the Forces' proper role was to support the Somalis, who had to adopt and sustain the initiatives. They put Somalis front and centre, sat with faction leaders and other prominent Somalis, gave their concerns honest hearings, and helped authority figures with genuine popular support advance the community's interest. Like much of the coalition, the Canadians established effective co-ordination mechanisms with the NGOs working in their area. The soldiers did not try to dominate aid efforts; rather, they sought to meet agency requirements so that the humanitarians could feed, train, and care for the local population.

Other failed state interventions with Canadian Forces participation have adopted this principle, such as the NATO-commanded coalition in Afghanistan. It too required the "leading from behind" collaborative method used in Somalia. The Canadian troops that deployed to Kabul in 2003 and Kandahar in 2005 acted in support of the local Afghan authorities with the understanding that these leaders would be responsible for continuing government services after coalition forces left. If the Afghans did not feel in charge and take ownership over the rebuilding process, they could have become dependent and unwilling to apply themselves to learn the skills required to move their country forward. For policy makers and the military, the principle of acting in support was easier to implement in Afghanistan than in Somalia. For the former, a respected and responsible figure (President Hamid Karzai) stepped forward to serve as the Afghan face of the process. And there was no pressure to push harder than the Afghans wanted, the fatal error committed in Somalia, since the international community had accepted its involvement would last for many years.

The Canadian Joint Force Somalia approach of pursuing enhanced co-operation with the Somalis, humanitarian relief organizations, and the Canadian Forces Environments (new then but now standard to Canadian expeditions) was a precursor for what has been done in Afghanistan. Initially, with no Department of External Affairs and Canadian International Development Agency personnel in Somalia, Labbé sought coalition assistance to set up an international "3-D" (defence, development, diplomacy) effort. He contacted Robert Oakley, special envoy of the president to Somalia.

At Labbé's request, Oakley provided political advisers and Kim Maynard, a member of the US government Office of Foreign Disaster Assistance's Disaster Assistance Response Team, as a full-time development representative.[3]

Subsequently, Labbé and Canadian High Commissioner Lucie Edwards forged a close working relationship. Edwards sent Matt Bryden, an expert in Somali culture, to advise Labbé for ten days each month,[4] and pledged her full support from a political and development perspective. Labbé assigned a liaison officer, Lieutenant-Commander H.W. McEwan, full time to the High Commission in Nairobi, thereby establishing Canadian 3-D. The Canadian Joint Force Somalia also did direct developmental work. For example, as was noted in the previous chapter, money was accessed from the High Commission Canada Fund and the World Food Programme to build schools, and the UN Children's Fund was brought in for the testing and selection of the teachers.[5] Edwards was proud, she wrote on 2 June 1993, shortly before the Canadian Forces withdrawal, of the "collegial relations between the Canadian military contingent in Somalia and this mission [the High Commission]," which was "truly a model of interdepartmental cooperation."[6] It is not surprising that in Kandahar, which was war torn, loosely governed, and underdeveloped, the Canadian 3-D approach was similar.

The incidents during the Somalia operation have had deep ramifications for Canada's military. Public relations, for example, have changed. Senior military leaders recognized at the time that the public and media expected greater accountability and transparency. As a result, the Canadian Forces has become more open and proactive in terms of media relations and the release of information to the public. The lessons learned had major implications for the preparation of rules of engagement and aide-mémoire/soldier cards. The Forces did not fully understand the rules/soldier cards and the range of potential threats, such as looters, in failed-state environments. The rapid transition to peace enforcement created confusion about the use of arms. This was the key, perhaps preventable, mistake that the Canadian military made on Operation Deliverance. Since Somalia, the chief of the defence staff has been responsible for approving the cards, and the military is now intensely aware of the need to be absolutely sure that the rules are calibrated correctly and are appropriate to the situation on the ground.

The incidents during the Somalia mission shook Canadian Forces confidence as well as the confidence of the Canadian public in the Forces. Many successful operations and sacrifices will be required to win back public confidence, though this process appears to have started already. Like all Canadians, members of the Forces found it hard to believe that some of their own could be responsible for the incident committed on 16 March 1993. But this book has argued that the Somalia mission was, for the most part, handled professionally and competently. That professionalism remains inherent to the Canadian Forces.

Notes

Introduction

1 According to Tom Keating, multilateralism refers to "multilateral diplomacy and to policies supporting the establishment and maintenance of institutions and associations that facilitate and support the practice of multilateral diplomacy." See Tom Keating, *Canada and World Order: The Multilateralist Tradition in Canadian Foreign Policy*, 2nd ed. (Toronto: Oxford University Press, 2002), 4.

2 Denis Stairs, "Choosing Multilateralism: Canada's Experience after World War II," presentation to the North-South Co-operative Security Dialogue, Beijing, June 1982, *CANCAPS Paper #4* (Toronto: Canadian Consortium on Asia-Pacific Security, 1994), 2, 5.

3 Lester B. Pearson, *Mike: The Memoirs of the Rt. Hon. Lester B. Pearson*, vol. 2, *1948-57*, ed. John A. Munro and Alex I. Inglis (Toronto: Signet, 1975), 37.

4 Ibid., 2:33.

5 Ibid., 2:32.

6 Andrew Cohen, "Pearsonianism," in *Pearson: The Unlikely Gladiator*, ed. Norman Hillmer (Montreal and Kingston: McGill-Queen's University Press, 1999), 158.

7 Norman Hillmer, "Peacekeeping: Canadian Invention, Canadian Myth," in *Welfare States in Trouble: Historical Perspectives on Canada and Sweden*, ed. Sune Akerman and J.L. Granatstein (Uppsala: Swedish Science Press, 1995), 161, 165.

8 Interview with Deputy Minister of National Defence Jim Judd, NDHQ, Ottawa, 31 August 2000.

9 Interview with Canadian permanent representative to the United Nations Ambassador Paul Heinbecker, 16 August 2002. Heinbecker was chief foreign policy adviser to Prime Minister Mulroney and assistant secretary to Cabinet for foreign and defence policy until August 1992.

10 Brian Stevenson, *Canada, Latin America, and the New Internationalism: A Foreign Policy Analysis, 1968-1990* (Montreal and Kingston: McGill-Queen's University Press, 2000), 225-26.

11 Joe Clark, "Canada's New Internationalism," in *Canada and the New Internationalism*, ed. John Holmes and John Kirton (Toronto: Canadian Institute of International Affairs, 1988), 10.

12 Geoffrey Pearson, "Canadian Attitudes to Peacekeeping," in *Peacekeeping: Appraisals and Proposals*, ed. Henry Wiseman (New York: Pergamon, 1983), 122.

13 Nicholas Gammer, *From Peacekeeping to Peacemaking: Canada's Response to the Yugoslav Crisis* (Montreal and Kingston: McGill-Queen's University Press, 2001), 5, 114.

14 Keating, *Canada and World Order*, 168.

15 Gammer, *From Peacekeeping to Peacemaking*, 55, 67; and Norman Hillmer and Dean Oliver, "The NATO-United Nations Link: Canada and the Balkans, 1991-95," in *A History of NATO: The First Fifty Years*, ed. Gustav Schmidt (London: Palgrave, 2001), 1:71, 346n2.

16 David Cox, "Peacekeeping: The Canadian Experience," *Peacekeeping: International Challenge and Canadian Response*, with Alastair Taylor and J.L. Granatstein (Toronto: Canadian

Institute of International Affairs, 1968), 53-55; and J.L. Granatstein, "Canada: Peacekeeper – A Survey of Canada's Participation in Peacekeeping Operations," *Peacekeeping: International Challenge and Canadian Response*, with Alastair Taylor and David Cox (Toronto: Canadian Institute of International Affairs, 1968), 182-83.

17 Sean M. Maloney, *Canada and UN Peacekeeping: Cold War by Other Means, 1945-1970* (St. Catharines: Vanwell, 2002), xii.

18 J.L. Granatstein, "Peacekeeping: Did Canada Make a Difference? And What Difference Did Peacekeeping Make to Canada?" in *Making a Difference? Canada's Foreign Policy in a Changing World Order*, ed. John English and Norman Hillmer (Toronto: Lester, 1992): 231-32.

19 Norman Hillmer, "Canadian Peacekeeping: New and Old," *Peacekeeping 1815 to Today*, proceedings of the 21st Colloquium of the International Commission of Military History (Ottawa: Canadian Commission of Military History, 1995), 543, 544, 546.

20 Norman Hillmer and J.L. Granatstein, *Empire to Umpire: Canada and the World to the 1990s* (Toronto: Copp Clark Longman, 1994), 322.

21 Hillmer, "Peacekeeping: Canadian Invention, Canadian Myth," 159-60, 168.

22 Granatstein, "Peacekeeping: Did Canada Make a Difference?" 234.

Chapter 1: Food for Thought

1 Yves Fortier, "Canada and the United Nations: A Half-Century Partnership," O.D. Skelton Memorial Lecture (Montreal, 6 March 1996): 3, 7. Cited from www.dfait-maeci. gc.ca/skelton/lectures-en.asp.

2 The five permanent members were China, France, Russia, United Kingdom, and the United States. See Anthony Parsons, "The UN and the National Interests of States," in *United Nations, Divided World: The UN's Roles in International Relations*, ed. Adam Roberts and Benedict Kingsbury, 2nd ed. (Oxford: Clarendon, 1996), 117-19.

3 Ernst B. Haas, "Collective Conflict Management: Evidence for a New World Order?" in *Collective Security in a Changing World*, ed. Thomas G. Weiss (Boulder, CO: Lynne Rienner, 1993), 65.

4 Interview with Assistant Deputy Minister (Policy and Communications) Dr. Kenneth Calder, at NDHQ in Ottawa, 10 March 2000.

5 Cited in Louise Crosby, "Stronger Ties to the US Hallmark of PM's New World Order," *Ottawa Citizen*, 21 November 1992: B5.

6 Brian Mulroney, Address on the Occasion of the Centennial Anniversary Convocation of Stanford University, Stanford, California (29 September 1991): 6.

7 Ibid., 6.

8 Barbara McDougall, "Canada and the New Internationalism," *Canadian Foreign Policy* 1, 1 (Winter 1992-93): 2, 4.

9 Dag Hammarskjöld, "The UNEF [UN Emergency Force I] Experience Report, October-November 1958," *The Public Papers of the Secretaries-General of the United Nations*, vol. 4, *Dag Hammarskjöld, 1958-1960*, ed. and comp. Andrew W. Cordier and Wilder Foote (New York: Columbia University Press, 1974), 284, 288, 291.

10 Alan James, *Peacekeeping in International Politics* (New York: St. Martin's, 1990), 5.

11 Ibid., 4-5; and Alan James, "The History of Peacekeeping: An Analytical Perspective," *Canadian Defence Quarterly* (September 1993): 13, 16.

12 Barbara McDougall, "Meeting the Challenge of the New World Order," *International Journal*, 47, 3 (Summer 1992): 477.

13 Louis A. Delvoie, "Canada and Peacekeeping: A New Era?" *Canadian Defence Quarterly* 20, 2 (October 1990): 9, 11; and Department of National Defence, *Canadian Defence Policy 1992* (Ottawa: April 1992), 4.

14 Steven R. Ratner, *The New UN Peacekeeping: Building Peace in Lands of Conflict after the Cold War* (New York: St. Martin's, 1996), 123.

15 Brian D. Smith and William Durch, "UN Observer Group in Central America," in *The Evolution of UN Peacekeeping: Case Studies and Comparative Analysis*, ed. William Durch (New York: St. Martin's, 1993), 436, 453.

16 Fen Osler Hampson, "The Pursuit of Human Rights: The United Nations in El Salvador," *UN Peacekeeping, American Policy and the Uncivil Wars of the 1990s*, ed. William J. Durch (New York: St. Martin's, 1996), 69, 80.
17 Jocelyn Coulon, *Soldiers of Diplomacy: The United Nations, Peacekeeping, and the New World Order*, trans. Phyllis Aronoff and Howard Scott (Toronto: University of Toronto Press, 1994), 42; and James A. Schear, "Riding the Tiger: The United Nations and Cambodia's Struggle for Peace," in *UN Peacekeeping, American Policy and the Uncivil Wars of the 1990s*, ed. William J. Durch (New York: St. Martin's, 1996), 146.
18 Barbara McDougall, "Peacekeeping, Peacemaking and Peacebuilding," address to the House of Commons Standing Committee on External Affairs and International Trade, External Affairs and International Trade Canada, *Statement 93/11* (17 February 1993): 5; and Barbara McDougall, "Peacekeeping and the Limits of Sovereignty," address to a seminar of the Centre québécois de relations internationales," External Affairs and International Trade Canada, *Statement 92/58* (2 December 1992): 4.
19 Norman Hillmer and Grant Dawson, "Canada and Peacekeeping in the 1990s: A Search for Strategy," unpublished ms (2002), 10; Grant Dawson, "Still Committed: Canada's Response to the Changes in UN and non-UN Peacekeeping in the 1990s," *Mémoire de Guerre et Construction de la Paix. Mentalités et Choix Politiques, Belgique-Europe-Canada*, ed. Serge Daumain and Eric Remacle (New York: Peter Lang, 2006), 207.
20 William J. Durch and James A. Schear, "Faultlines: UN Operations in the Former Yugoslavia," *UN Peacekeeping, American Policy and the Uncivil Wars of the 1990s*, ed. William J. Durch (New York: St. Martin's, 1996), 253.
21 Boutros Boutros-Ghali, "Further Report of the Secretary-General Pursuant to Security Council Resolution 721 (1991)," United Nations document S/23592 (15 February 1992): para. 28. Cited in Kofi Annan, "Report of the Secretary-General Pursuant to General Assembly Resolution 53/35: The Fall of Srebrenica," United Nations document A/54/549 (15 November 1999): para. 13.
22 Interview with Canadian International Development Agency official Chris Liebich, at CIDA in Hull, 22 September 2000.
23 Jarat Chopra, Åge Eknes, and Toralv Nordbø, *Fighting for Hope in Somalia* (Oslo: Norwegian Institute of International Affairs, 1995), 20.
24 David D. Laitin, "Somalia: Civil War and International Intervention," in *Civil Wars, Insecurity and Intervention*, ed. Barbara F. Walter and Jack Snyder (New York: Columbia University Press, 1999), 147; and Eric Hooglund, "Government and Politics," in *Somalia: A Country Study*, ed. Helen Chapin Metz, 4th ed. (Washington, DC: Federal Research Division, 1993), 153, 163.
25 Thomas Ofcansky, "National Security," in *Somalia: A Country Study*, ed. Helen Chapin Metz, 4th ed. (Washington, DC: Federal Research Division, 1993), 182.
26 Hooglund, "Government and Politics," 164, 166; and David Carment, Patrick James, and Zeynep Taydas, *Who Intervenes? Ethnic Conflict and Interstate Crisis* (Columbus: Ohio State University Press, 2006) 95-96.
27 Chopra, Eknes, and Nordbø, *Fighting for Hope in Somalia*, 25.
28 Jonathan Manthorpe, "Beyond Hope," *Montreal Gazette*, 21 March 1991: A11.
29 Samuel M. Makinda, *Seeking Peace from Chaos: Humanitarian Intervention in Somalia* (Boulder, CO: Lynne Rienner, 1993), 12-13.
30 Mary-Jane Fox, "Political Culture in Somalia: Tracing Paths to Peace and Conflict" (PhD diss., Uppsala University, Uppsala, Sweden), 101, 137, 150-51.
31 Laitin, "Somalia: Civil War and International Intervention," 157.
32 Ibid., 153, 157-58.
33 Makinda, *Seeking Peace from Chaos*, 18.
34 Thomas G. Weiss, *Military-Civilian Interactions: Intervening in Humanitarian Crisis* (Boulder, CO: Rowman and Littlefield, 1999), 71-2.
35 Chopra, Eknes, and Nordbø, *Fighting for Hope in Somalia*, 22-24.
36 Laitin, "Somalia: Civil War and International Intervention," 158-59; and John Drysdale, *Whatever Happened to Somalia?* (London: HAAN Associates, 1994), 25, 36.

37 Boutros Boutros-Ghali, "Introduction," *United Nations and Somalia, 1992-1996* (New York: United Nations, 1996), 12; and Jane Perlez, "Slaughter Continues and the World Turns Its Back," *Vancouver Sun*, 4 January 1992, B6, New York Times News Service.
38 Drysdale, *Whatever Happened to Somalia?* 30-31, 43, 57; and Boutros-Ghali, "Introduction," 14.
39 Terrance Lyons and Ahmed I. Samatar, *Somalia: State Collapse, Multilateral Intervention, and Strategies for Political Reconstruction* (Washington, DC: Brookings, 1995), 22; and Said S. Samatar, *Somalia: A Nation in Turmoil* (1991; London: Minority Rights Group International, 1995): 10. See also the attached update, "Somalia and Somaliland," unnumbered pages, 4.
40 Catherine Besteman, *Unravelling Somalia: Race, Violence, and the Legacy of Slavery* (Philadelphia: University of Pennsylvania Press, 1999), 22, 229-30.
41 United Nations, "United Nations Operation in Somalia I and II (UNOSOM I and II)," *The Blue Helmets: A Review of United Nations Peacekeeping*, 3rd ed. (New York: United Nations, 1996), 288.
42 Mohamed Sahnoun, *Somalia: The Missed Opportunities* (Washington, DC: United States Institute of Peace Press, 1994), 10. See also Lyons and Samatar, *Somalia: State Collapse*, 29.
43 Peter Wallensteen, *Understanding Conflict Resolution: War, Peace and the Global System* (London: Sage, 2002), 244, 246.
44 Brian Mulroney, "Global Report: World Political Review," address to the Commonwealth Heads of Government Meeting, Harare, Zimbabwe (16 October 1991): 2.
45 Wilfrid-Guy Licari, "Foreign Policy Update – Africa and Middle East," memorandum GGD-0029 from External Affairs Africa and Middle East Bureau to Policy Planning Staff (12 February 1992): 2.
46 External Affairs, "Visit of Somali Prime Minister to Canada," telex GAA-0351 to the Permanent Mission to the UN in New York (12 April 1991): 1; and External Affairs, "Call by Somaliland Foreign Minister on Embassy Representative," telex GAA-0895 to Embassy in The Hague (21 August 1991): 1. Cited from files of the Department of Foreign Affairs and International Trade (DFAIT), 20-1-2-Somali, vol. 4.
47 Louise Fréchette, "Statement to the Donor's Meeting for the Special Emergency Programme for the Horn of Africa," New York (28 January 1992): 3.
48 External Affairs, "Call by Somaliland Foreign Minister on Embassy Representative," telex GAA-0895 to Embassy in The Hague (21 August 1991): 1. Cited from files of DFAIT, 20-1-2-Somali, vol. 4.
49 Fréchette, "Statement to the Donor's Meeting," 2, 4.
50 Tim Martin, "Costs of Somalia Crisis," memorandum GAA-0129 (5 February 1993): 1. Cited from files of DFAIT, 20-1-2-Somali, vol. 6.
51 Permanent Mission to the UN in New York, "Somalia," telex WKGR-1806 to External Affairs (7 January 1992): 1. Cited from files of DFAIT, 38-11-1-Somali, vol. 2.
52 Nancy Kassebaum and Paul Simon, "Save Somalia from Itself," *New York Times*, 2 January 1992: A21.
53 Permanent Mission in New York, "Somalia" (7 January 1992): 1.
54 The Iran-Iraq war lasted from 1980 to 1988. The UN Iran-Iraq Military Observer Group deployed in August 1988. See Paul Lewis, "Somalia First Test for Ghali," *Winnipeg Free Press*, 12 January 1992: A11, New York Times News Service.
55 Editorial, "Help Needed for Forsaken Somalia," *New York Times*, 9 February 1992: A16.
56 Interview with Canadian permanent representative to the United Nations Ambassador Paul Heinbecker, 16 August 2000.
57 Mulroney, "Global Report," 3.
58 External Affairs, "McDougall to Meet UN Secretary-General, Dr. Boutros Boutros-Ghali in New York," *News Release* 9 (10 January 1992): 1; and CBC Newsworld, special broadcast, "Mission to Somalia," transcript of press conference by Barbara McDougall and Marcel Masse (4 December 1992): 1. Cited from files of DFAIT, 21-14-6-UNOSOM, vol. 7.
59 Permanent Mission to the UN in New York, "Meeting with James Jonah," telex WKGR-4338 to External Affairs (20 January 1992): 4. Cited from files of DFAIT, 38-11-UN, vol. 65.
60 Permanent Mission to the UN in New York, "Meeting with James Jonah" (20 January 1992): 4; and Louise Fréchette, "Letter to UN Secretary-General Boutros Boutros-Ghali" (13 March 1992): 1. Cited from files of DFAIT, 38-11-1-Somali, vol. 2.

61 Chapter VII is concerned with aggression and threats to peace and contains the Charter's enforcement provisions. See United Nations, S/RES/733 (23 January 1992): operative paras. 4-5. Cited from United Nations, *United Nations and Somalia, 1992-1996* (New York: United Nations, 1996). (Hereafter *UN and Somalia.*)

62 Licari, "Foreign Policy Update – Africa and Middle East," 1.

63 David Cortright and George A. Lopez, *The Sanctions Decade: Assessing UN Strategies in the 1990s* (Boulder, CO: Lynne Rienner, 2000), 184-86.

64 Jane Perlez, "UN Sees Danger of Somali Famine," *New York Times*, 27 February 1992: A3.

65 Permanent Mission in New York, "Meeting with James Jonah" (20 January 1992): 2.

66 Permanent Mission in New York, "Somalia" (7 January 1992): 2.

67 Cited in "Security in Somalia," *Secretariat News* (July-August 1993): 12.

68 Jonathan Stevenson, *Losing Mogadishu: Testing US Policy in Somalia* (Annapolis: Naval Institute Press, 1995), 38.

69 Oto Denes, *Draft Report of the SEPHA Preparatory Mission for the 1992 Assistance Programme*, SEPHA/Fax/91-381 (30 December 1991): 5. Cited from files of DFAIT, 38-11-UN, vol. 65.

70 Cited in "Somalia Too Deadly, Immediate Evacuation Urged by Staff Union," *Secretariat News* (January 1992): 5.

71 Jonah was UN under-secretary-general (USG) for Africa. In February 1992, he became USG of the Department of Political Affairs. See Permanent Mission in New York, "Meeting with James Jonah" (20 January 1992): 3.

72 Aidan Hartley, "Doomed to Chaos," *Montreal Gazette*, 19 February 1992: A10.

73 "Call for Security Force in Somalia," *The Times* (London), 7 January 1992: A8; and Jane Perlez, "As Fighting Rages On, African Neighbour Seeks a Truce" *New York Times*, 6 January 1992: A2.

74 Allen G. Sens, *Somalia and the Changing Nature of Peacekeeping: The Implications for Canada*, study prepared for the Commission of Inquiry into the Deployment of Canadian Forces to Somalia (Ottawa: Public Works and Government Services Canada, 1997), 124.

75 Paul F. Diehl, *International Peacekeeping* (Baltimore: Johns Hopkins University Press, 1994), 168.

76 "Somalia Peace Elusive," *Secretariat News* (February 1992): 11.

77 Special Emergency Programme for the Horn of Africa, *Consolidated Inter-Agency Appeal* (New York: United Nations, 1 February 1992), 6.

78 Cited in "Somalia Too Deadly," *Secretariat News*, 5.

79 Hampson, "The Pursuit of Human Rights," 75.

80 Mohamed Sahnoun, "Flashlights over Mogadishu," *New Internationalist* no. 262 (December 1994): 9.

81 Rakiya Omaar and Alex de Waal, "Who Prolongs Somalia's Agony?" *New York Times*, 26 February 1992: A21.

82 Paul Lewis, "Warring Somali Factions Reach a Truce," *New York Times*, 15 February 1992: A5.

83 Boutros Boutros-Ghali, "Report to the Security Council on the Situation in Somalia," S/23693 (11 March 1992): para. 74. Cited from *UN and Somalia.*

84 United Nations, S/RES/746 (17 March 1992): operative para. 7. Cited from *UN and Somalia.*

85 Permanent Mission to the UN in New York, "Somalia: Canadian Permanent Representative Meeting with Under-Secretary-General James Jonah," telex WKGR-3337 to External Affairs (13 March 1992): 2. Cited from files of DFAIT, 38-11-1-Somali, vol. 2.

86 Fréchette, "Letter to UN Secretary-General Boutros-Ghali" (13 March 1992): 1-2.

87 Norman Hillmer, "Canadian Peacekeeping: New and Old," *Peacekeeping 1815 to Today*, proceedings of the 21st annual Colloquium of the International Commission of Military History (Ottawa: Canadian Commission of Military History, 1995), 545.

88 Paul Diehl, "With the Best of Intentions: Lessons from UNOSOM I and II," *Studies in Conflict and Terrorism* 19, 2 (April-June 1996): 154.

89 Permanent Mission in New York, "Somalia: Canadian Permanent Representative Meeting with Under-Secretary-General James Jonah," 3-4.

90 David Hannay, "Statement on Somalia on behalf of the United Kingdom to the Security Council," provisional verbatim record of Security Council meeting, United Nations document S/PV.3060 (17 March 1992): 57.
91 Alexander F. Watson, "Statement on Somalia on behalf of the United States to the Security Council," provisional verbatim record of Security Council meeting, United Nations document S/PV.3060 (17 March 1992): 48, 49-50.
92 Peter A. Van Brakel, "Somalia: Security Council Informals," secure fax from Permanent Mission in New York to External Affairs (17 March 1992): 2. Cited from files of DFAIT, 38-11-1-Somali, vol. 2.
93 Peter Hohenfellner, "Statement on Somalia on behalf of Austria to the Security Council," provisional verbatim record of Security Council meeting, S/PV.3060 (17 March 1992): 42.
94 Boutros-Ghali, "Report," S/23693 (11 March 1992): para. 73.
95 United Nations, "Transcript of Press Conference by Secretary-General Boutros Boutros-Ghali, held at Headquarters Today," press release, SG/SM/4718 (19 March 1992): 1.

Chapter 2: The Canadian Forces and the Recommendation to Stay out of Somalia

1   Herman J. Cohen, *Intervening in Africa: Superpower Peacemaking in a Troubled Continent* (New York: St. Martin's, 2000), 207.
2   United Nations, "Assessment of Member States' Contributions for the Financing of the United Nations Operation in Somalia (UNOSOM) from 1 May 1992 to 30 April 1993," ST/ADM/SER.B/393 (22 December 1992): 5.
3   Peter J. Schraeder, "The Horn of Africa: United States Foreign Policy in an Altered Cold War Environment," *Middle East Journal* 46, 4 (Autumn 1992): 586.
4   The $1.7 billion figure is in US dollars. See Mats Berdal and Michael Leifer, "Cambodia," in *The New Interventionism, 1991-1994: The United Nations Experience in Cambodia, Former Yugoslavia, and Somalia*, ed. James Mayall (Cambridge: Cambridge University Press, 1996), 25.
5   Herman Cohen, "Intervention in Somalia," in *The Diplomatic Record, 1992-93*, ed. Allan E. Goodman (Boulder, CO: Westview Press, 1995), 54.
6   Paul Tellier, "Somalia: Observer Mission and Peacekeeping Force – Will Canada Be Asked?" memorandum for the Prime Minister (7 May 1992): 1.
7   United Nations, S/RES/733 (23 January 1992): operative para. 5. Cited from United Nations, *The United Nations and Somalia, 1992-1996* (New York: United Nations, 1996). (Hereafter *UN and Somalia.*)
8   Fatun Mohammed Hassan, "Approaches to the Problems of Somalia," annex to "Letter from the Chargé d'affaires A.I. of the Permanent Mission of Somalia to the United Nations to the President of the Security Council," United Nations document S/23507 (3 February 1992): 4.
9   Ike Nwachukwu, "Statement on Somalia on behalf of the Organization of African Unity to the Security Council," provisional verbatim record of Security Council meeting, S/PV.3060 (17 March 1992): 12.
10 United Nations, S/RES/746 (17 March 1992): operative paras. 6-7; and Boutros Boutros-Ghali, "Report to the Security Council on the Situation in Somalia," S/23693 (11 March 1992): para. 73. Both documents cited from *UN and Somalia*.
11 The Royal Canadian Air Force, Royal Canadian Navy, and Canadian Army were formally unified into the single-service CF in February 1968.
12 Major S.L. James, "Joint/Combined Doctrine Review Presentation" (22 January 1991), Annex F to *Joint Doctrine Board Minutes of 22 January 1991 Meeting*, 1150-110/J244 (DGFD) (6 February 1991): 1.
13 Gary Garnett, "The Evolution of the Canadian Approach to Joint and Combined Operations at the Strategic and Operation Level," *Canadian Military Journal* 3, 2 (Winter 2002): 3.
14 The North American Aerospace Defence Command, a bilateral military organization involving Canada and the United States, was called the North American Air Defence Agreement until 1981. Cited from interview with Rear-Admiral (ret'd) Bruce Johnston, in Ottawa, 18 January 2001.
15 Todd Fitzgerald and Michael A. Hennessy, "An Expedient Reorganization: The NDHQ J-Staff System in the Gulf War," *Canadian Military Journal* 4, 1 (Spring 2003): 24.

16 Interview with Colonel (ret'd) Mike O'Brien, in Mountain, Ontario, 2 December 2000.
17 Ian Douglas, "Peacekeeping Operations (PKO) Review – Interim Report," Service Paper by the Special Peacekeeping Assistant to DCDS (14 February 1991): 7. Attached to J.M.D. Henrie, "DM/CDS Briefing – 20 February 1991 – Peacekeeping Operations," 1450-1 (NDHQ Sec Co-ordination) (14 February 1991): 1-2. The author thanks Al Balfour for providing the information.
18 A civil-military staff system, the matrix came into being when the previously separate military and departmental headquarters were merged in October 1972, creating NDHQ.
19 Mike O'Brien, "'NDHQ Crisis Management System' – Director-General Military Plans and Operations Presentation to Canadian Forces Command and Staff College," unpublished ms (27 March 1991), 15. The author thanks Al Balfour for providing the information.
20 United Nations, "Secretary-General Addresses First International Youth Leadership Conference, in Montreal, on 'Nationalism and Globalization,'" press release, SG/SM/4756 (22 May 1992): 3.
21 Sean M. Maloney, "Purple Haze: Joint Planning in the Canadian Forces from Mobile Command to J-Staff, 1975-1991 (Part 1)," *Army Doctrine and Training Bulletin* 5, 4 (Winter 2002-3): 58.
22 Testimony of Commodore David Cogdon to the Somalia Inquiry, 25 October 1995. Cited from *Information Legacy: A Compendium of Source Material from the Commission of Inquiry into the Deployment of Canadian Forces to Somalia* (Ottawa: Public Works and Government Services Canada, 1997), 9:1657. (Hereafter *Information Legacy*.)
23 Interview with Rear-Admiral (ret'd) Bruce Johnston, in Ottawa, 2 June 2000.
24 Douglas Bland, *Chiefs of Defence: Government and the Unified Command of the Canadian Armed Forces* (Toronto: Canadian Institute of Strategic Studies, 1995), 191.
25 Interview with Lieutenant-General (ret'd) David Huddleston, 18 December 2001.
26 Testimony of Colonel (ret'd) Mike O'Brien to the Somalia Inquiry, 26 October 1995. Cited from *Information Legacy*, 10:1872. The principal Joint Staff implementers were DCDS Lieutenant-General David Huddleston, COS J3 Commodore Bruce Johnston, and J3 Operations Colonel Mike O'Brien.
27 Mike O'Brien, "Briefing Note for the DM/CDS: The Role of the Joint Staff," draft memorandum 3350/165-F18 (ACOS J3) (15 May 1991): 2. The author thanks Al Balfour for providing the information.
28 David Huddleston, "Briefing Note for the DM/CDS: The Role of the Joint Staff," memorandum 3350/165-F18 (DCDS) (21 May 1991): 1. The author thanks Al Balfour for providing the information.
29 Bruce Johnston, "Staffing the Joint Staff," informal memorandum (25 February 1991): 1. The author thanks Al Balfour for providing the information.
30 Prior to mid-summer 1992, the JSAT had been called the Crisis Action Team.
31 Johnston, interview, 2 June 2000.
32 Department of National Defence, *NDHQ Joint Staff Standard Operating Procedures*, 3121-900 (COS J3/DGMPO) (Ottawa: DND, August 1993), 6. Access to Information request, Department of National Defence.
33 Testimony of Commodore David Cogdon to the Somalia Inquiry, 25 October 1995. Cited from *Information Legacy*, 9:1664.
34 NDHQ was trying to reduce its number of generals/admirals. From mid-1992 to February 1993, the DCDS was down-ranked to a two-star position and renamed DCDS (Intelligence, Security, Operations). The force development part of the old DCDS was hived off and a new post, Chief of Force Development, established under the VCDS. The DCDS (ISO) reported to the VCDS and was not a group principal. Cited from Interview with Admiral (ret'd) John Anderson, former Chief of the Defence Staff, 11 September 2004.
35 Johnston, interview, 2 June 2000.
36 Alain Forand, "Presentation to the Canadian Forces Command and Staff School," unpublished ms (May 1991), 11. The author thanks Al Balfour for providing the information.
37 Ibid., 7-8, 10.
38 Ibid., 15-6.
39 Huddleston, "Briefing Note for the DM/CDS," 2.
40 DND, *NDHQ Joint Staff Standard Operating Procedures*, 1-2.

41 Ibid., 5, 6.
42 Mike O'Brien, "The Canadian Joint Staff System after Op Friction," unpublished ms (6 January 1991): 1. The author thanks Al Balfour for providing the information.
43 Johnston, interview, 2 June 2000.
44 Johnston, interview, 20 February 2001.
45 Interview with Deputy Chief of the Defence Staff Lieutenant-General Raymond Henault, at NDHQ in Ottawa, 15 February 2001.
46 Charles Oliviero, "Operation Deliverance: International Success or Domestic Failure," *Canadian Military Journal* 2, 2 (Summer 2001): 58n26.
47 Jean Morin and Richard H. Gimblett, *The Canadian Forces in the Persian Gulf: Operation Friction 1990-1991* (Toronto: Dundurn Press, 1997) 37.
48 Interview with Colonel (ret'd) Mike Houghton, in Ottawa, 27 April 2000.
49 *The Journal* with Brian Stewart, CBC transcript, 5 March 1992, 1, 3, 5.
50 Testimony of Colonel (ret'd) Mike Houghton to the Somalia Inquiry, 12 February 1996. Cited from *Information Legacy*, 44:8661.
51 United Nations, *Report of the United Nations Technical Team to Somalia, 21 March to 3 April 1992* (5 April 1992): para. 8b. Cited from *Information Legacy*, document DND122543.
52 Houghton testimony. Cited from *Information Legacy*, 44:8655.
53 Interview with Colonel (ret'd) John Bremner, in Ottawa, 31 July 2000.
54 Houghton, interview, 27 April 2000.
55 Boutros-Ghali, "Report on the Situation in Somalia," S/23693 (11 March 1992): paras. 73-4; and United Nations, S/RES/746 (17 March 1992): operative paras. 6-7. Both documents cited from *UN and Somalia*.
56 External Affairs, letter IDD-0050 from Michael Brock to Larry Murray (18 March 1992): 1. Cited from *Information Legacy*, document NS085469.
57 Testimony of Commodore David Cogdon to the Somalia Inquiry, 25 October 1995. Cited from *Information Legacy*, 9:1681.
58 Mike Houghton, e-mail message to author, 4 May 2001.
59 Boutros Boutros-Ghali, "Report to the Security Council on the Situation in Somalia," S/23829 (21 April 1992): paras. 24-9. Cited from *UN and Somalia*.
60 John de Chastelain and Robert Fowler, "Projected UN Operation in Somalia (UNOSOM)," briefing note to Minister of National Defence Marcel Masse (1 May 1992): paras. 1, 4. Cited from *Information Legacy*, document #DND000874.
61 Houghton testimony, 12 February 1996. Cited from *Information Legacy*, 44:8682.
62 Ibid., 8682, 8684.
63 Ibid., 8657.
64 Ibid., 8682.
65 O'Brien, interview, 13 May 2000.
66 Houghton, e-mail message to author, 4 May 2001.
67 Houghton testimony. Cited from *Information Legacy*, 44:8680; and Houghton, interview, 27 April 2000.
68 Confidential interview with UN officer involved in UNOSOM I and II, 8 June 2001.
69 Houghton testimony. Cited from *Information Legacy*, 44:8680.
70 Boutros-Ghali, "Report on the Situation in Somalia," S/23829 (21 April 1992): para. 26.
71 Ali Mahdi Mohamed, letter dated 29 February 1992, and Abdi Osman Farah, letter dated 1 March 1992, annex IV:A-B to Boutros-Ghali, "Report on the Situation in Somalia," S/23693 (11 March 1992). Cited from *UN and Somalia*, 133.
72 Ioan Lewis and James Mayall, "Somalia," in *The New Interventionism, 1991-1994: The United Nations Experience in Cambodia, Former Yugoslavia, and Somalia*, ed. James Mayall (Cambridge: Cambridge University Press, 1996), 123.
73 Boutros-Ghali, "Report on the Situation in Somalia," S/23829 (21 April 1992): para. 28.
74 United Nations, S/RES/751 (24 April 1992): operative para. 3. Cited from *UN and Somalia*.
75 Boutros-Ghali was secretary-general, Jonah was one of two under-secretaries-general in charge of the Department of Political Affairs, and Annan was assistant-secretary-general of the Department of Peacekeeping Operations. See Marrack Goulding, *Peacemonger* (London: John Murray, 2002), 276.

76 Permanent Mission in New York, "UN Technical Assistance to Somalia," telex WKGR-3467 to External Affairs (7 April 1992): 3. Cited from files of the Department of Foreign Affairs and International Trade (DFAIT), 38-11-1-Somali, vol. 2.

77 Boutros Boutros-Ghali, "Report to the Security Council on the Situation in Somalia," S/24343 (22 July 1992): paras. 13-14.

78 Testimony of Deputy Minister Robert Fowler to the Somalia Inquiry, 21 February 1996. Cited from *Information Legacy* 50:10175.

79 Testimony of Colonel John Bremner to the Somalia Inquiry, 24 October 1995. Cited from *Information Legacy*, 8:1481.

80 De Chastelain and Fowler, "Projected UN Operation in Somalia (UNOSOM)" (1 May 1992): paras. 7-9. Cited from *Information Legacy*, document #DND000874.

81 All criteria cited from Department of National Defence, *Challenge and Commitment: A Defence Policy for Canada* (Ottawa: Supply and Services Canada, 1987) 24.

82 Bremner testimony. Cited from *Information Legacy* 8:1489.

83 Interview with Rick Burton at NDHQ, in Ottawa, 23 November 1999. Burton was the executive assistant (1989-91) and special adviser (1991-93) to Deputy Minister Robert Fowler.

84 Interview with Lieutenant-Colonel (ret'd) Anthony Anderson, in Ottawa, 22 October 1999. Anderson was on secondment to EAITC from 1990 to 1993, where he headed its one- to two-person Peacekeeping Section.

85 Permanent Mission to the UN in New York, "Somalia: UNOSOM Peacekeeping," telex WKGR-5881 to External Affairs (6 May 1992): 2. Cited from files of DFAIT, 21-14-6-UNOSOM, vol. 2.

86 Bremner, interview, 19 April 2000.

87 Interview with Canadian permanent representative to the United Nations Ambassador Paul Heinbecker, 16 August 2002.

88 Michael Brock, "Somalia," memorandum to Assistant Deputy Minister (Political and International Security) Jeremy Kinsman (4 May 1992): 1. Cited from files of DFAIT, 21-14-6-UNOSOM, vol. 2.

89 Glen Shortliffe, e-mail message to author, 27 October 2005.

90 Interview with former Chief of Staff of the Prime Minister's Office Hugh Segal, in Montreal, 28 June 2000.

91 Anderson, interview, 22 October 1999.

92 Interview with Assistant Deputy Minister (Policy) Dr. Kenneth Calder, at NDHQ in Ottawa, 10 March 2000.

93 *Dishonoured Legacy: The Lessons of the Somalia Affair*, report of the Commission of Inquiry into the Deployment of Canadian Forces to Somalia, vol. 1 (Ottawa: Public Works and Government Services Canada, 1997), 239.

Chapter 3: "Do Something Significant"

1 Boutros Boutros-Ghali, "Report of the Secretary-General on the Situation in Bosnia-Herzegovina," S/24333 (21 July 1992): para. 13; and United Nations, S/RES/767 (27 July 1992): preambular para. 4. Cited from United Nations, *United Nations and Somalia, 1992-1996* (New York: United Nations, 1996). (Hereafter *UN and Somalia*.)

2 Manon Tessier and Michel Fortmann, "The Conservative Approach to International Peacekeeping," in *Diplomatic Departures: The Conservative Era in Canadian Foreign Policy, 1984-93*, ed. Kim Richard Nossal and Nelson Michaud (Vancouver: UBC Press, 2001), 114, 125.

3 Interview with former Chief of Staff of the Prime Minister's Office Hugh Segal, in Montreal, 28 June 2000.

4 Jim Gervais, "Land Force in Transition: Challenges and Opportunities, Part 2," *Canadian Defence Quarterly* 22, 2 (October 1992): 6-7; and Government of Canada, "Canada to Withdraw Troops from Cyprus," *News Release* 231 (11 December 1992): 1.

5 Mark Schacter with Phillip Haid, "Cabinet Decision-Making in Canada: Lessons and Practice," Institute on Governance research paper (Ottawa: April 1999): 9. Cited from www.igvn.ca.

6 Interview with Derek Burney, former Chief of Staff to Prime Minister Brian Mulroney and former Canadian Ambassador to the United States, in Ottawa, 8 December 2005.

7   Segal, interview, 28 June 2000.
8   In the Canadian federal government, the centre consists of the following: the Prime Minister and his/her Office, the Cabinet, and the central agencies (Privy Council Office, Department of Finance, Treasury Board Secretariat, Public Service Commission, and Intergovernmental Affairs Secretariat). See Donald J. Savoie, *Governing from the Centre: The Concentration of Power in Canadian Politics* (Toronto: University of Toronto Press, 2001), 3, 7; and Evan Potter, "A Question of Relevance: Canada's Foreign Policy and Foreign Service in the 1990s," in *Canada among Nations, 1993-94: Global Jeopardy*, ed. Christopher J. Maule and Fen Osler Hampson (Ottawa: Carleton University Press, 1993), 37-38.
9   Peter C. Newman, *The Secret Mulroney Tapes: Unguarded Confessions of a Prime Minister* (Toronto: Random House Canada, 2005), app. C, 453-54.
10 The same transformation in attitudes occurred during the Progressive Conservative government of Joe Clark (1979-80). See Jeffrey Simpson, *Discipline of Power: The Conservative Interlude and the Liberal Restoration*, 2nd ed. (Toronto: University of Toronto Press, 1996), 143.
11 An example is Newman's *The Secret Mulroney Tapes*. See Jane Taber, "Mulroney Feels Book Author 'Betrayed' Him," *Globe and Mail*, 13 September 2005: A4; and Jeffrey Simpson, "Mr. Mulroney, Hoist by His Own Petard," *Globe and Mail*, 13 September 2005: A21.
12 Interview with former Clerk of the Privy Council Glen Shortliffe, in Ottawa, 21 July 2000.
13 Morden was under-secretary of state for External Affairs (the deputy minister), Kinsman/Lavertu were assistant deputy ministers (ADMs) (Political and International Security), and Moher was director general of the International Security Bureau. De Chastelain was chief of the defence staff, Fowler was deputy minister, Calder was ADM (Policy and Communications), and Murray was associate ADM (Policy and Communications). Tellier/Shortliffe were clerks of the Privy Council and Heinbecker/Judd were assistant secretaries to Cabinet for foreign and defence policy.
14 Institute on Governance, "Government Decision-Making in Canada – Players, Processes, Institutions: Central Agencies in Decision-Making," report of study tour by the Secretariat of the Cabinet of Ministers of Ukraine (Ottawa: January 2001): 13. Cited from www.igvn.ca.
15 Boutros-Ghali, "Report on the Situation in Bosnia-Herzegovina," S/24333 (21 July 1992): para. 13. Cited from *UN and Somalia*.
16 Interview with Deputy Secretary-General of the United Nations Louise Fréchette, in New York City, 16 June 2000.
17 Interview with former Assistant Deputy Minister (Political and International Security) Jeremy Kinsman, 21 August 2000.
18 Anthony Anderson, "Canadian Response to an Informal Request by the United Nations to Contribute Five Observers," memorandum IDR-1737 to the Secretary of State for External Affairs (30 April 1992): 3. Access to Information request, Department of Foreign Affairs and International Trade.
19 Paul Tellier, "Somalia: Observer Mission and Peacekeeping Force – Will Canada Be Asked?" memorandum for the prime minister (7 May 1992): 1-2. Access to Information request, Privy Council Office.
20 Emphasis in original. Barbara McDougall, "RE: your memorandum IDR-1737 of 30 April," handwritten note to Michael Burke (6 May 1992): 1. Access to Information request, Department of Foreign Affairs and International Trade.
21 Brian Mulroney, "World Peace Demands a Stronger United Nations Role," *Canadian Speeches: Issues of the Day* 6, 4 (June-July 1992): 32.
22 Interview with former Under-Secretary of State for External Affairs Reid Morden, in Ottawa, 7 September 2000.
23 Confidential interview, 25 January 2002.
24 Confidential interview, 26 June 2000.
25 Kinsman, interview, 21 August 2000.
26 Greg McLaughlin, *The War Correspondent* (London: Pluto Press, 2000), 194, 196; Piers Robinson, "The Policy-Media Interaction Model: Measuring Media Power during Humanitarian Crisis," *Journal of Peace Research*, 37, 5 (September 2000): 614; and Brian Patrick Hoey, "Humanitarian Intervention in Somalia, 1992-1994: Elite Newspaper

Coverage, Public Opinion, and United States Foreign Policy" (PhD diss., University of Maryland, College Park, 1995), 133-34, 151.

27 Newman, *The Secret Mulroney Tapes*, 38, 251-52, 263, 258.

28 Interview with Mark J. Moher, former Director General of the International Security Bureau, at DFAIT in Ottawa, 21 December 2000.

29 Kenneth D. Bush, "Somalia: When Two Anarchies Meet," in *Canada and Missions for Peace: Lessons from Nicaragua, Cambodia, and Somalia*, ed. Gregory Wirick and Robert Miller (Ottawa: International Development Research Centre, 1998), 91.

30 Interview with former Eastern/Southern Africa Division Deputy Director Edward Willer, in Ottawa, 6 December 1999.

31 Philip Johnston, *Somalia Dairy: The President of CARE Tells One Country's Story of Hope* (Atlanta: Longstreet Press, 1994), 54.

32 Michael Ignatieff, "The Stories We Tell: Television and Humanitarian Aid," in *Hard Choices: Moral Dilemmas in Humanitarian Intervention*, ed. Jonathan Moore (New York: Rowman and Littlefield, 1998), 290, 293.

33 Rony Brauman, "When Suffering Makes a Good Story," in *Somalia, Rwanda, and Beyond: The Role of the International Media in Wars and Humanitarian Crises*, ed. Edward R. Girardet (Dublin: Crosslines Communications, 1995), 141, 143.

34 Cited in CBC, *News in Review* with Knowlton Nash, "Somalia: War and Starvation" (October 1992). Findlay's report, "The Face of Famine," originally appeared as part of a feature report entitled "Somalia: The Desperate Struggle" in CBC, *The National* with Peter Mansbridge (26 May 1992). See also: http://archives.cbc.ca/IDCC-1-71-723-4333/conflict_war/somalia/x.

35 Reuters, "Famine, War Create Living Hell," *Ottawa Citizen*, 6 August 1992: A12; and Michael Young, "Some Children May Never Recover," *Calgary Herald*, 10 December 1992: A5.

36 Lewis MacKenzie, "Peacekeeping: Into the Grey Zone," in *Canadian Forces and the Modern World*, ed. David E. Code and Ian Cameron (Ottawa: Conference of Defence Associations Institute, 1993), 35.

37 Ignatieff, "The Stories We Tell," 301.

38 John Stackhouse of the *Globe and Mail* and Paul Watson of the *Toronto Star* were two Canadian exceptions to this general rule. Cited from Barton, interview, 31 May 2000.

39 Interview with former principal spokesperson for CARE USA in Somalia Rick Grant, 30 March 2002. Grant worked for CARE USA in Somalia from August 1992 to January 1993.

40 Joseph Hall, "Canada Can Still Help, Aid Teams Say," *Toronto Star*, 30 August 1992: A1.

41 Glen Shortliffe, "Canadian Involvement in Somalia," memorandum for the prime minister (18 August 1992): 1-2. Access to Information request, Privy Council Office.

42 Interview with World Food Programme senior press officer in Nairobi Brenda Barton, 31 May 2000. A Canadian, Barton was the Regional Information Officer in Nairobi as of August 1992. She supervised all press activities in sub-Saharan Africa for the World Food Programme.

43 Jane Perlez, "Deaths in Somalia Outpace Delivery of Food," *New York Times*, 19 July 1992: A1, A8. Reprinted the next day on the front page of the *Globe and Mail*.

44 Editorial, "The Hell Called Somalia," *New York Times*, 23 July 1992: A22.

45 Reid Miller, "Smell of Death Haunts Desolate Somalian City," *Ottawa Citizen*, 7 August 1992: A6.

46 Perlez, "Deaths in Somalia Outpace Delivery of Food," A1.

47 Interview with former Canadian Ambassador to Ethiopia Francis Filleul, Ottawa, 16 September 2000.

48 Tim Martin, "Situation in Somalia," memorandum GAA-1433 for the Secretary of State for External Affairs (21 August 1992), 4; and Tim Martin, "Costs of Somalia Crisis," memorandum GAA-0129 (5 February 1993), 1. Both cited from DFAIT, 20-1-2-Somali, vol. 6.

49 Interview with Deputy Minister of National Defence Jim Judd, NDHQ, Ottawa, 31 August 2000.

50 Editorial, "Don't Forget Somalia," *Montreal Gazette*, 22 July 1992: B2.

51 Editorial, "If Sarajevo, Why Not Somalia?" *Globe and Mail*, 22 July 1992: A12.

52 Barbara McDougall, "A Few Parting Shots," interview by Anthony Wilson-Smith and E. Kaye Fulton, *Maclean's* (5 July 1993): 10.

53 Hassan A. Mohamed, "The Socio-Cultural Adaptation of Somali Refugees in Toronto: An Explanation of Their Integration Experiences" (DEd diss., University of Massachusetts, Amherst, 2001), 49, 126-7; and Martin, "Costs of Somalia Crisis," 5 February 1993: 2.

54 Gerald E. Shannon, "Canadian Statement to the Co-ordination Meeting on Assistance for Somalia, Geneva," 12 October 1992: 1. Cited from files of DFAIT, 38-11-1-Somali-2, vol. 1.

55 Editorial, "A Safe Haven," *Toronto Star*, 31 July 1992: A22.

56 Cited in Editorial, "Helping Somalis," *Toronto Star*, 8 August 1992: C2.

57 "Helping Somalis," *Toronto Star*, 8 August 1992: C2; and Mohamed Farah, "Valcourt's Sarcasm Denies Reality," letter to editor, *Toronto Star*, 19 August 1992: A18.

58 "Somali Son's Plea," photograph, *Ottawa Citizen*, 8 August 1992: A3. Emphasis and ellipses in original.

59 Editorial, "Africa's Forgotten War," *Toronto Star*, 1 August 1992: B2.

60 Martin, "Situation in Somalia," 21 August 1992: 4.

61 "United Nations Head Charges Yugoslavia Bias," *Facts on File*, 52, 2700 (20 August 1992): 623.

62 Phillip Corwin, *Dubious Mandate: A Memoire of the United Nations in Bosnia, Summer 1995* (Durham: Duke University Press, 1999), xv.

63 Morden, interview, 7 September 2000.

64 Marc Perron, "Somalia Update," memorandum (29 July 1992): 1. Cited from files of DFAIT, 21-14-6-UNOSOM, vol. 2.

65 United Nations, S/RES/767 (27 July): operative para. 12. Cited from *UN and Somalia*.

66 Boutros Boutros-Ghali, "Report to the Security Council on the Situation in Somalia," S/24343 (22 July 1992): paras. 57-61. Cited from *UN and Somalia*. Boutros-Ghali later recommended the creation of a fifth zone to be based in the town of Mandera, Kenya (see Chapter 6).

67 Segal, interview, 28 June 2000.

68 Captain (Navy) Ken McMillan, "Humanitarian Assistance Somalia – Record of Decisions," memorandum 3351-l (28 July 1992): para. 1. Cited from *Information Legacy: A Compendium of Source Material from the Commission of Inquiry into the Deployment of Canadian Forces to Somalia* (Ottawa: Public Works and Government Services Canada, 1997), document DND002116.

69 Segal, interview, 28 June 2000.

70 Barbara McDougall and Marcel Masse, "Memorandum to the Prime Minister" (July 1992): 2. Cited from files of DFAIT, 38-11-1-Somali, vol. 4. This memorandum is undated but refers to the secretary-general's 22 July report. It also mentions in the future tense a démarche with France that Masse conducted on 30 July. This suggests that the document was prepared in late July. See also Marcel Masse, "Talking Points: Possible Humanitarian Assistance to Somalia" (30 July 1992): 1. Cited from files of DFAIT, 21-14-6-UNOSOM, vol. 2.

71 Kinsman, interview, 21 August 2000.

72 Brian Mulroney, "Letter to Secretary-General Boutros Boutros-Ghali" (13 August 1992): 1. Cited from files of DFAIT, 38-11-1-Somali, vol. 2.

73 Shortliffe, "Canadian Involvement in Somalia," 2.

74 High Commission in Nairobi, "Airlift to Somalia," telex WADA-0766 to External Affairs (6 August 1992): 3. Cited from files of DFAIT, 38-11-1-Somali, vol. 2.

75 Prime Minister's Office, "Canada to Provide Additional Help to Somalia," *News Release* (21 August 1992): 1.

76 Shortliffe, "Canadian Involvement in Somalia," 2.

77 Shortliffe, interview, 21 July 2000.

78 Douglas Fraser, "Somalia/UNOSOM: Request for Troops," COSICS message C-PRMNY-WKGR-0599 to External Affairs (25 August 1992): 1. Cited from files of DFAIT, 21-14-6-UNOSOM, vol. 3.

79 Douglas Fraser, "Somalia/UNOSOM: Official Request," COSICS message C-PRMNY-WKGR-0617 to External Affairs (31 August 1992): 1. Cited from files of DFAIT: 21-14-6-UNOSOM, vol. 3.

80 Permanent Mission in New York, "Somalia: Resolution 767 Adopted," secure fax WKGR-3865 to External Affairs Eastern and Southern Africa Division (27 July 1992): 2. Cited from files of DFAIT, 21-14-6-UNOSOM, vol. 2.

81 Ross G. Hynes, "Somalia," COSICS message [no number] to External Affairs at 18:28 (27 July 1992): 1. Cited from files of DFAIT, 38-11-1-Somali, vol. 2. Also Martin, "Situation in Somalia," (21 August 1992): 4.

82 Ross G. Hynes, "Somalia," COSICS message [no number] to External Affairs at 17:34 (27 July 1992): 2. Cited from files of DFAIT, 38-11-1-Somali, vol. 2.

83 Brian Mulroney, "Letter to United States President George Bush" (14 August 1992) 2; and "Letter to United Kingdom Prime Minister John Major" (14 August 1992) 2. Cited from files of DFAIT, 38-11-1-Somali, vol. 2.

84 William J. Durch, "Introduction to Anarchy: Humanitarian Intervention and 'State-Building' in Somalia," in *United Nations Peacekeeping, American Policy and the Uncivil Wars of the 1990s*, ed. William Durch (New York: St. Martin's, 1996), 317.

85 *MacNeil-Lehrer NewsHour* with Robert MacNeil and James Lehrer, "Perot's Partisans; Lowering Your Guard; Misery's Cradle," transcript # 4383, Public Broadcasting Service (22 July 1992).

86 John L Hirsch and Robert B. Oakley, *Somalia and Operation Restore Hope: Reflections on Peacemaking and Peacekeeping* (Washington: United States Institute of Peace Press, 1995), 38-39.

87 Ioan Lewis and James Mayall, "Somalia," in *The New Interventionism, 1991-1994: The United Nations Experience in Cambodia, Former Yugoslavia, and Somalia*, ed. James Mayall (Cambridge: Cambridge University Press, 1996), 110.

88 Interview with Canadian permanent representative to the United Nations Ambassador Paul Heinbecker, 16 August 2002.

89 Boutros Boutros-Ghali, "Report to the Security Council on the Situation in Somalia," S/24480 (24 August 1992): para. 37; and "Addendum," S/24480/Add.1 (28 August 1992): para. 1. Cited from *UN and Somalia*.

Chapter 4: The Humanitarian Airlift Takes Flight

1 Interview with Assistant Deputy Minister (Policy and Communications) Dr. Kenneth Calder, at NDHQ in Ottawa, 10 March 2000.

2 The figure quoted by Fowler may be high. In mid-1992, the most common estimate was 1,000-2,000 deaths daily. See testimony of Ambassador Robert Fowler to the Somalia Inquiry, 21 February 1996. Cited from *Information Legacy: A Compendium of Source Material from the Commission of Inquiry into the Deployment of Canadian Forces to Somalia* (Ottawa: Public Works and Government Services Canada, 1997), 50:10166, 10176. (Hereafter *Information Legacy*.)

3 United Nations, S/RES/751 (24 April 1992): operative paras. 3-4; and Boutros Boutros-Ghali, "Addendum 2 to Report to the Security Council on the Situation in Somalia," S/23829/Add.2 (24 April 1992): para. 2. Both documents cited from United Nations, *United Nations and Somalia, 1992-1996* (New York: United Nations, 1996). (Hereafter *UN and Somalia*.)

4 Department of National Defence (DND), *Canadian Defence Policy 1992* (Ottawa: DND, 1992), 34.

5 Marrack Goulding, "Guide to the Use of Force by UNIFIL Military Personnel," coded cable MSC-842, to Force Commander Brigadier-General Imtiaz Shaheen (2 September 1992): 1. Cited from *Information Legacy*, document DND009842.

6 F.T. Liu, *United Nations Peacekeeping and the Non-Use of Force*, International Peace Academy Occasional Paper (Boulder, CO: Lynne Rienner, 1992), 29.

7 United Nations, S/RES/775 (28 August 1992): operative para. 5. Cited from *UN and Somalia*.

8 John Drysdale, *Whatever Happened to Somalia?* (London: HAAN Associates, 1994), 45-6.

9 Colonel Jim Cox, fax to J3 Peacekeeping Colonel Mike Houghton (December 1992): 4. The author thanks Brigadier-General (ret'd) Cox for providing the information.

10 Marrack Goulding, cover letter for "Guide to the Use of Force by UNIFIL" (2 September 1992): 1. Cited from *Information Legacy*, document DND009842.

11 Maurice Baril, "United Nations Operation in Somalia," United Nations fax MSF-9617-08 to Canada's Permanent Mission to the United Nations in New York (25 August 1992): 1. Cited from files of the Department of Foreign Affairs and International Trade (DFAIT), 21-14-6-UNOSOM, vol. 3.

12   Alan James, "Humanitarian Aid Operations and Peacekeeping," in *The Politics of International Humanitarian Aid Operations*, ed. Eric A. Belgrad and Nitza Nachmias (Westport, CT: Praeger, 1997), 55-56.

13   Under Security Council resolution 425 (19 March 1978), UNIFIL was to verify the withdrawal of Israel's armed forces from southern Lebanon and help restore peace. Israel did not co-operate.

14   United Nations, "United Nations Interim Force in Lebanon (UNIFIL)," *The Blue Helmets: A Review of United Nations Peacekeeping*, 3rd ed. (New York: United Nations, 1996), 112.

15   Boutros Boutros-Ghali, "Report of the Secretary-General on the Situation in Somalia," S/23829 (21 April 1992): para. 58. Cited from *UN and Somalia*.

16   Boutros Boutros-Ghali, "Introduction," *United Nations and Somalia*, 24.

17   Cited in *Meeting New Challenges: Canada's Response to a New Generation of Peacekeeping*, Report of Standing Senate Committee on Foreign Affairs, Subcommittee on Security and National Defence, 3rd session, 34th Parliament (Ottawa: Canada Communications Group, 1993), 37.

18   Stanley Hoffmann, "The Hell of Good Intentions," *Foreign Policy* 29 (Winter 1977): 8.

19   United Nations, "Secretary-General 'Shocked and Concerned' over Situation in Somalia," press release SG/SM/4682 (27 December 1991): 2.

20   James, "Humanitarian Aid Operations and Peacekeeping," 59.

21   United Nations, "More World Food Programme Aid Arrives in Somalia," press release WFP/801 (12 June 1992): 1.

22   The DPKO military desk officer for UNOSOM was Major Nauludole Mataitini (Fijian Army). See Elisabeth Lindenmayer, "Somalia: A New Role for United Nations Peacekeepers," New York, September 1992. Cited in *Information Legacy*, document DND006580.

23   Interview with United Nations Deputy Secretary-General Louise Fréchette, at UN headquarters in New York, 16 June 2000.

24   Lieutenant-General Maurice Baril, "Le Canada, les Casques bleus et le maintien de la paix," interview by Francois Taschereau, *bout de papier* 12, 4 (Winter 1995): 17. Translated for the author by Alex Lazarow.

25   Boutros Boutros-Ghali, "Setting a New Agenda for the United Nations," interview by Carolyn Reynolds et al., *Journal of International Affairs* 46, 2 (Winter 1993): 292; and Boutros Boutros-Ghali, "Empowering the United Nations," *Foreign Affairs* 72, 5 (Winter 1992): 91.

26   William Durch, "Epilogue: Peacekeeping in Uncharted Territory," in *The Evolution of United Nations Peacekeeping: Case Studies and Comparative Analysis*, ed. William Durch (New York: St. Martin's, 1993), 472.

27   UNIFIL statistic as of June 2005. The United Nations Protection Force was third at 211, the United Nations Peacekeeping Force in Cyprus was fourth at 174, the United Nations Mission in Sierra Leone was fifth at 164, and UNOSOM II was sixth at 151. See United Nations, "Peacekeeping Fatalities by Mission and Incident Type" (30 June 2005). Cited from http://www.un.org/Depts/dpko/fatalities/fatal2.htm.

28   Alan James, "Problems of Internal Peacekeeping," *Diplomacy and Statecraft* 5, 1 (March 1994): 33.

29   Paul F. Diehl, *International Peacekeeping*, 2nd ed. (Baltimore: Johns Hopkins University Press, 1994), 200.

30   Fifty observers were deployed by 23 July. Patrolling took place along the "Green Line" dividing north (Ali Mahdi) and south (Aidid) Mogadishu. In the south, patrolling started on 15 August, in the seaport area on the 16th, and in the north on the 19th. Monitoring stopped on 30 September because of the increasing number of violations and rising hostility. Cited from Imtiaz Shaheen et al., "Political and Military Events in Somalia: From Cease-fire Agreement to Resolution Multi-national Force Deployment, 3 March-3 December 1992," unpublished ms (15 December 1992), 18. The author thanks to Brigadier-General (ret'd) Jim Cox for providing the information.

31   Mohamed Sahnoun, "Prevention in Conflict Resolution: The Case of Somalia," *Irish Studies in International Affairs* 5 (1994): 9.

32 Cited in Jonathan Stevenson, "Hope Restored in Somalia?" *Foreign Policy* 91 (Summer 1993): 146; and Mohamed Sahnoun, *Somalia: The Missed Opportunities* (Washington: United States Institute of Peace, 1994), 25.
33 Rakiya Omaar, "Somalia: At War with Itself," *Current History* (May 1992): 234.
34 Interview with the former first Special Representative of the Secretary-General to Somalia Ambassador Mohamed Sahnoun, in Ottawa, 7 August 2001.
35 Stevenson, "Hope Restored in Somalia?" 154.
36 John Hirsch and Robert Oakley argue Sahnoun generated grassroots support for the United Nations. See *Somalia and Operation Restore Hope: Reflections on Peacemaking and Peacekeeping* (Washington, DC: United States Institute of Peace, 1995), 22.
37 David B. Carment, "Rethinking Peacekeeping: The Bosnia and Somalia Experience," in *Canada Among Nations 1996: Big Enough to Be Heard*, ed. Fen Osler Hampson and Maureen Appel Molot (Ottawa: Carleton University Press, 1996), 225, 231.
38 Confidential Interview with senior UNOSOM official, 10 March 2001.
39 Boutros Boutros-Ghali, "Report to the Security Council on the Situation in Somalia," S/24343 (22 July 1992): paras. 59, 56. Cited from *UN and Somalia.*
40 Ibid., para. 56.
41 Ibid., para. 61.
42 Interview with Deputy Minister of National Defence Jim Judd, at NDHQ in Ottawa, 31 August 2000.
43 J.M.D. Henrie, "Record of Daily Executive Meeting Regarding Somalia" (28 July 1992): paras. 3-4. Cited from *Information Legacy*, document DND299450.
44 Testimony of Ambassador Robert Fowler to the Somalia Inquiry, *Information Legacy*, 50:10157, 10200.
45 Henrie, "Record of Daily Executive Meeting": para. 2.
46 Robert H. Clark, "Aide-Mémoire on Somalia," memorandum 3451-1 (DI Pol 5) (29 July 1992): para. 8c. Cited from *Information Legacy*, document DND001198.
47 Ken McMillan, "Humanitarian Assistance Somalia – Record of Decisions" (28 July 1992): para. 2b. Cited from *Information Legacy*, document DND002116.
48 The three others were: the 5e Regiment d'artillerie légère du Canada (5th Regiment Royal Canadian Artillery), the 12e Régiment Blindé du Canada (12th Armoured Regiment of Canada), and the Royal Canadian Dragoons.
49 Rick H. Froh, "Option Analysis for a Security Battalion in Support of United Nations Humanitarian Assistance Operations in Somalia as Requested by CDS" (31 July 1992): paras. 5-6, 8, 11-12. Cited from *Information Legacy*, document DND002070. See also G.M. Whiting, "Option Analysis Somalia – Probable Tasks and Forces Available," memorandum 3351-l, J3 Plans (L)4 (29 July 1992): para. 7a. Cited from *Information Legacy.*
50 Froh, "Option Analysis for a Security Battalion": paras. 8a, 18.
51 Ibid., paras. 4, 5a-c, 8f.
52 Clark, "Aide-Mémoire on Somalia": paras. 8c, 11.
53 Cited in Rick H. Froh, "Option Analysis for a Security Battalion in Support of United Nations Humanitarian Assistance Operations in Somalia as Requested by CDS" (30 July 1992): para. 11, *De Faye Board of Inquiry on the Canadian Airborne Regiment Battle Group*, exhibit 110. Cited from *Information Legacy.*
54 Interview with Colonel (ret'd) John Bremner, at DFAIT in Ottawa, 19 April 2000.
55 John Bremner, "Interview with Colonel (ret'd) John Bremner," in Ottawa, 31 July 2000.
56 Clark, "Aide-Mémoire on Somalia": para. 8a-d.
57 W.D. Turnbull, "Briefing Note: Somalia," memorandum 3451-1 (DI Pol 4) (16 August 1992): para. 3. Cited from *Information Legacy*, document DND002543.
58 Verona Edelstein, "Somalia – Meeting with United Nations Special Representative for Somalia," telex GAA-1314 to High Commission in Nairobi (5 August 1992): para. 8. Cited from *Information Legacy*, document DND002582.
59 United Nations, S/RES/767 (27 July 1992): operative para. 2. Cited from *UN and Somalia.*
60 Interview with former Assistant Deputy Minister (Political and International Security) Jeremy Kinsman, 21 August 2000.

61 Interview with former Under-Secretary of State for External Affairs Reid Morden, in Ottawa, 7 September 2000.
62 Interview with Vice-Admiral (ret'd) Larry Murray, in Ottawa, 16 February 2000.
63 Julian Ozanne, "United Nations Will Send Troops to Guard Food Convoys in Somalia," *Financial Times* (London), 13 August 1992: A14.
64 United Nations, *Report of the Technical Mission to Somalia* (17 August 1992): 17. Cited from files of DFAIT, 21-14-6-UNOSOM, vol. 3.
65 Boutros Boutros-Ghali, "Report to the Security Council on the Situation in Somalia," S/24480 (24 August 1992): para. 15. Cited from *UN and Somalia*.
66 United Nations, S/RES/775 (28 August 1992): operative para. 4. Cited from *UN and Somalia*.
67 External Affairs, "Somalia: Meeting with United Nations Special Representative for Somalia," telex GAA-1314 to High Commission in Nairobi (5 August 1992): 4. Cited from files of DFAIT, 38-11-1-Somali, vol. 2.
68 High Commission in Nairobi, "Airlift to Somalia," telex WADA-0753 to External Affairs (3 August 1992): 1. Cited from files of DFAIT, 21-14-6-UNOSOM, vol. 2.
69 Embassy in Geneva, "Airlift to Somalia," telex YTGR-4230 to External Affairs and High Commission in Nairobi (7 August 1992): 1. Cited from files of DFAIT, 21-14-6-UNOSOM, vol. 2.
70 Interview with Brigadier-General (ret'd) Roy Mould, in Toronto, 28 December 2000.
71 Brian Mulroney, "Letter to United Nations Secretary-General Boutros Boutros-Ghali" (13 August 1992): 1. Cited from files of DFAIT, 38-11-1-Somali, vol. 2.
72 Office of the Prime Minister, "Canada to Provide Additional Help to Somalia," *News Release* (21 August 1992): 1.
73 Interview with Commodore Ken McMillan, in Ottawa, 17 November 2000.
74 B. Tremblay, "Fact Sheet – Canadian Forces Support, United Nations Humanitarian Assistance in Somalia" (14 August 1992): table 1, para 2-3. Cited from *Information Legacy*, document DND002551.
75 K.D. Hunt, "Assessment of Air Capabilities for Humanitarian Assistance for Somalia" (17 August 1992): para. 2. Cited from *Information Legacy*, document DND002546.
76 Stephen L. James, "Formation of Air Command: A Struggle for Survival" (MA diss., Royal Military College, Kingston, 1989), 14.
77 Stephen L. James, "The Air Force's Cold War Struggle with Its National Purpose," *Proceedings of the 3rd Annual Air Force Historical Conference*, ed. William March and Don Pearsons (Winnipeg: Department of National Defence, 1998), 91.
78 Interview with Brigadier-General (ret'd) Gordon Diamond, in Ottawa, 24 October 2001.
79 Jean Morin, "The Command and Control of the Air Transport Group during the Gulf War," *Proceedings of the 3rd Annual Air Force Historical Conference*, ed. William March and Don Pearsons (Winnipeg: Department of National Defence, 1998), 117.
80 Interview with former Commander of Air Command Lieutenant-General (ret'd) David Huddleston, 18 December 2000.
81 Mould, interview, 28 December 2000.
82 Interview with Lieutenant-General (ret'd) Lou Cuppens, 16 December 2000. Cuppens only referred to his discussion with Huddleston.
83 Mould, interview, 28 December 2000.
84 Charles R. Simonds, "External Military Involvement in the Provision of Humanitarian Relief in Ethiopia," in *Humanitarian Emergencies and Military Help in Africa*, ed. Thomas G. Weiss (New York: St. Martin's, 1990), 65, 68.
85 Jamie Robertson, "Canada – Please Help Us!" *Sentinel* 27, 6 (1991): 4.
86 D. Hinton, "Where There's a Need ATG Crews Will Travel," *Air Transport Group Newsletter* 4, 1 (Spring 1992): 11.
87 Huddleston, interview, 18 December 2000.
88 Department of National Defence, "Air Transport Group Aircraft Leave for Somalia," *News Release* (4 September 1992): 1.
89 John P. Jensen, "Airlift Control Element (ALCE) I," in *Canadian Joint Force Somalia: In the Line of Duty, 1992-93*, ed. Ron Pupetz (Ottawa: Department of National Defence, 1994), 36.

90 Interview with Brigadier-General (ret'd) Jeff Brace, 26 April 2002.
91 Jensen, "Airlift Control Element (ALCE) I," 37-38.
92 Jane MacDonald, "The First ALCE Commander," in *Canadian Joint Force Somalia: In the Line of Duty, 1992-93*, ed. Ron Pupetz (Ottawa: Department of National Defence, 1994), 34.
93 International Committee of the Red Cross, *The Fundamental Principles of the Red Cross and Red Crescent* (1 July 1996). Cited from www.icrc.org.
94 Jane MacDonald, "Operation Relief," in *Canadian Joint Force Somalia: In the Line of Duty, 1992-93*, ed. Ron Pupetz (Ottawa: Department of National Defence, 1994), 26.
95 Brace, interview, 26 April 2002.
96 Ibid.
97 Jensen, "Airlift Control Element (ALCE) I," 38.
98 Air Transport Command, "Operation Relief Situation Report # 8," telex to Air Command, National Defence Headquarters and External Affairs (19 September 1992): 3. Cited from files of DFAIT, 21-14-6-UNOSOM, vol. 4.
99 MacDonald, "Operation Relief," 27.
100 Ibid.; and interview with former High Commissioner to Nairobi (with accreditation to Somalia) Ambassador (ret'd) Larry Smith, at DFAIT in Ottawa, 11 July 2000.
101 Confidential interview with UNOSOM I official, at UN Headquarters in New York, 19 June 2000.
102 Associate Minister of National Defence Mary Collins, speech to Parliament, House of Commons, 3rd session, 34th Parliament, *Hansard* (7 December 1992): 14783.
103 Serge Labbé, "Somalia: Setting the Record Straight," unpublished ms (March 1994), ch. 1. The author thanks Colonel Serge Labbé for providing the information.
104 Brace, interview, 26 April 2002.
105 Murray, interview, 16 February 2000.
106 Simonds, "External Military Involvement in the Provision of Humanitarian Relief in Ethiopia," 72.
107 Interview with Brigadier-General (ret'd) David M. Jurkowski, in Ottawa, 25 February 2001.
108 Diamond, interview, 24 October 2001.

Chapter 5: Sticking with the (Wrong) Peacekeeping Mission

1 Li Daoyu, "Letter from the President of the Security Council to the Secretary-General," S/24452 (14 August 1992): 1. Cited from United Nations, *United Nations and Somalia, 1992-1996* (New York: United Nations, 1996). (Hereafter *UN and Somalia*.)
2 Boutros Boutros-Ghali, *Unvanquished: A US-UN Saga* (New York: Random House, 1999), 55.
3 Peter Hansen, "Report of the Technical Mission to Somalia" (21 August 1992): 19. Cited from files of the Department of Foreign Affairs and International Trade (DFAIT), 21-14-6-UNOSOM, vol. 3.
4 Boutros Boutros-Ghali, "Report to the Security Council on the Situation in Somalia," S/24480 (24 August 1992): para. 36. Cited from *UN and Somalia*.
5 Brian Mulroney, "Letter to United Nations Secretary-General Boutros Boutros-Ghali" (13 August 1992) 1-2. Cited from files of DFAIT, 38-11-1-Somali, vol. 2.
6 Spyros Economides and Paul Taylor, "Former Yugoslavia," in *The New Interventionism, 1991-1994: The United Nations Experience in Cambodia, Former Yugoslavia and Somalia*, ed. James Mayall (Cambridge: Cambridge University Press, 1996), 69.
7 Ibid., 72-73.
8 Barbara McDougall, "Address to the London Peace Conference on the Former Socialist Federal Republic of Yugoslavia," External Affairs and International Trade Canada *Statement 92/36* (26 August 1992): 2, 3.
9 United Nations, Organization of African Unity, League of Arab States, and Organization of the Islamic Conference, "Joint Communiqué on the Implementation of Security Council resolution 733 (1992)," United Nations press release IHA/431 (12 February 1992): 1. See also S/RES/746 (17 March 1992): preambular para. 10, and S/RES/751 (24 April 1992): preambular para. 9. All documents cited from *UN and Somalia*.
10 Interview with Chief of the Defence Staff General Maurice Baril, at NDHQ in Ottawa, 18 August 2000.

11   Interview with former second Special Representative of the Secretary-General to Somalia Ambassador Ismat Kittani, 28 July 2000.
12   Baril, interview, 18 August 2000.
13   High Commission in Nairobi, "Proposed International Conference on Somalia," telex WADA-0892 to External Affairs (10 September 1992): 2. Cited from files of DFAIT, 38-11-1-Somali-2, vol. 1.
14   Marc Perron, "Somalia," memorandum GGB-0182 to the Under-Secretary of State (22 September 1992): 2-3. Cited from files of DFAIT, 21-14-6-UNOSOM, vol. 4.
15   Boutros Boutros-Ghali, "Report to the Security Council on the Situation in Somalia," S/24343 (22 July 1992): paras. 42-3, 55. Cited from *UN and Somalia*.
16   John Noble, "Proposals for Assisting United Nations Co-ordination on Somalia and Humanitarian Issues," memorandum IMD-0263 to External Affairs Eastern/Southern Africa Division (21 October 1992): 1. Cited from files of DFAIT, 21-14-6-UNOSOM, vol. 4.
17   Ibid.
18   Nicholas Gammer, *From Peacekeeping to Peacemaking: Canada's Response to the Yugoslav Crisis* (Montreal and Kingston: McGill-Queen's University Press, 2001), 91.
19   David MacDonald, speech to Parliament, House of Commons, 3rd session, 34th Parliament, *Hansard* (7 December 1992): 14790.
20   H. John McDonald, "Letter to Prime Minister Brian Mulroney" (16 November 1992): 1. Deputy Executive Director of CARE Canada Nancy Gordon provided the author with this document from CARE Canada's archives.
21   Interview with Deputy Executive Director of CARE Canada Nancy Gordon, at CARE Canada headquarters in Ottawa, 28 April 2000.
22   Interview with former Assistant Deputy Minister (Political and International Security) Jeremy Kinsman, 21 August 2000.
23   Department of National Defence, "Canadian Airborne Regiment Going to Somalia," *News Release* 92/52 (2 September 1992): 1.
24   John de Chastelain, letter to author (3 April 2000): 3-4.
25   Vince Kennedy, "Staff Estimate Land Force Personnel Augmentation Requirements for Sustainment of Peacekeeping Operations," Land Force common document 3450-1 (G3 Plans) (16 October 1992): 9-10. The author thanks Al Balfour for providing the information.
26   Marcel Masse, "Testimony in Support of *The Study of Peacekeeping*," issue 9, eighth proceeding of the Standing Senate Committee on Foreign Affairs, Subcommittee on Security and National Defence, 3rd session, 34th Parliament (25 November 1992): 40.
27   Interview with former Minister of National Defence Marcel Masse," in Quebec City, 14 August 2000.
28   Department of National Defence, *Challenge and Commitment: A Defence Policy for Canada* (Ottawa: Supply and Services Canada, 1987), 25.
29   Department of National Defence, *Defence Policy 1991* (Ottawa: DND, September 1991), 12; and Department of National Defence, *Canadian Defence Policy 1992* (Ottawa: DND, April 1992), 24.
30   John de Chastelain, "Testimony in Support of *The Study of Peacekeeping*," issue 9, eighth proceeding of the Standing Senate Committee on Foreign Affairs, Subcommittee on Security and National Defence, 3rd session, 34th Parliament (25 November 1992): 39.
31   External Affairs, "Somalia: Views of SSDF Faction on Canadian Participation in UNOSOM," telex GAA-1467 to High Commission in Nairobi (25 September 1992): 2-3. Cited from files of DFAIT, 20-1-2-Somali, vol. 5.
32   High Commission in Nairobi, "Somalia: Horn of Africa Roundtable, 2 October – Political Developments," telex WAGR-0895 to External Affairs (30 September 1992): 4. Cited from files of DFAIT, 20-1-2-Somali, vol. 5.
33   High Commission in Nairobi, "Somalia: Meeting with the Somali Salvation Democratic Front (SSDF)," telex WAGR-0952 to External Affairs (14 October 1992): 5. Cited from files of DFAIT, 21-14-6-UNOSOM, vol. 4.
34   Gerald E. Shannon, "Statement to the Co-ordination Meeting on Assistance for Somalia (12-13 October), Palais des Nations, Geneva" (12 October 1992): 1. Cited from files of DFAIT, 38-11-1-Somali-2, vol. 1.

35 John Noble, "Somalia: Meetings with Jonah and Goulding," COSICS message C-EXOTT-IMD-0042 to Permanent Mission in New York (9 October 1992): 2. Cited from files of DFAIT, 38-11-1-Somali, vol. 2.
36 Noble, "Somalia: Meetings with Jonah and Goulding," 1.
37 Interview with former Clerk of the Privy Council Glen Shortliffe, in Ottawa, 21 July 2000.
38 Interview with former Chief of Staff of the Prime Minister's Office Hugh Segal, in Montreal, 28 June 2000.
39 Ibid.
40 Andrew Cooper, *Canadian Foreign Policy: Old Habits and New Directions* (Toronto: Prentice Hall, 1997), 185.
41 Noble, "Somalia: Meetings with Jonah and Goulding," 2.
42 Kent Vachon, "Somalia: Meeting with Sahnoun," COSICS message C-PRMNY-WKGR-0950 to External Affairs (16 October 1992): 2; and Nicole Rousseau, "Somalia," COSICS message C-PRMNY-WKGR-0913 to External Affairs (13 October 1992): 1. Both documents cited from files of DFAIT, 21-14-6-UNOSOM, vol. 4.
43 Vachon, "Somalia: Meeting with Sahnoun," 2.
44 Embassy in Geneva, "Somalia: United Nations Co-ordination Meeting on Humanitarian Assistance," telex YTGR-7112 to External Affairs (21 October 1992): 6-7. Cited from files of DFAIT, 38-11-1-Somali-2, vol. 2; and External Affairs, "Meeting with Former SRSG Sahnoun," telex GAA-1859 to High Commission in Nairobi (14 December 1992): 3. Cited from files of DFAIT, 20-1-2-Somali, vol. 5.
45 Embassy in Geneva, "Somalia: United Nations Co-ordination Meeting on Humanitarian Assistance," 11.
46 Interview with the former first Special Representative of the Secretary-General to Somalia Ambassador Mohamed Sahnoun, in Ottawa, 7 August 2001.
47 Baril, interview, 18 August 2000.
48 Samuel M. Makinda, *Seeking Peace from Chaos: Humanitarian Intervention in Somalia* (Boulder, CO: Lynne Rienner, 1993), 64.
49 Paul Watson, "Famine Diary," *Toronto Star*, 13 September 1992: F1; and John Prendergast, "Staving Off Hunger and Food Bandits in Somalia," *Wall Street Journal*, 17 September 1992: A16.
50 Baril, interview, 18 August 2000.
51 Interview with former High Commissioner to Nairobi (with accreditation to Somalia) Ambassador Lucie Edwards, 25 July 2000.
52 David Kern, "Incentives and Disincentives for Violence," in *Greed and Grievance: Economic Agendas in Civil Wars*, ed. Mats Berdal and David M. Malone (Boulder, CO: Lynne Rienner, 2000), 21; and Andrew S. Natsios, "Humanitarian Relief Intervention in Somalia: The Economics of Chaos," in *Learning from Somalia: The Lessons of Humanitarian Intervention*, ed. Walter Clarke and Jeffery Herbst (Boulder, CO: Westview Press, 1997), 85.
53 David Shearer, "Aiding or Abetting? Humanitarian Aid and Its Economic Role in Civil War," in *Greed and Grievance: Economic Agendas in Civil Wars*, ed. Mats Berdal and David M. Malone (Boulder, CO: Lynne Rienner, 2000), 195.
54 Christopher Clapham, "Being Peacekept," in *Peacekeeping in Africa*, ed. Oliver Murray and Roy May (Sydney: Ashgate, 1998), 305-6.
55 Jane Perlez, "United Nations Official in Somalia Quits in Dispute with Headquarters," *New York Times*, 28 October 1992: A6.
56 Susan D. Moeller, *Compassion Fatigue: How the Media Sell Disease, Famine, War and Death* (New York: Routledge, 1999), 135-36.
57 Walter Goodman, "Why It Took TV So Long to Focus on the Somalis," *New York Times*, 2 September 1992: C18; and Moeller, *Compassion Fatigue*, 138-39.
58 Embassy in Washington, "Somalia: [Assistant Secretary of State for African Affairs Herman] Cohen Appearance before the Congressional Committee," telex UNGR-2352 to External Affairs (18 September 1992): 4-5. Cited from files of DFAIT, 38-11-Somali, vol. 2.
59 Furio Colombo, "The Media and Operation Restore Hope in Somalia," in *Somalia, Rwanda, and Beyond: The Role of the International Media in Wars and Humanitarian Crises*, ed. Edward R. Girardet (Dublin: Crosslines Communications, 1995), 89.

60   Editorial, "Don't Forsake Somalia," *New York Times*, 4 November 1992: A30.
61   Interview with former UN Operation in Somalia I Deputy Force Commander Canadian Forces Brigadier-General Jim Cox, in Ottawa, 16 August 2000.
62   Matthew Bryden, e-mail to author, 18 September 2000.
63   Boutros Boutros-Ghali, "Letter to the President of the Security Council on the Situation in Somalia," S/24859 (27 November 1992). Cited in *UN and Somalia*, 209.

Chapter 6: Problems with the Expanded UN Operation
1   Imtiaz Shahêen et al., "Political and Military Events in Somalia, from Cease-fire Agreement to Resolution Multinational Force Deployment, 3 March-3 December 1992," unpublished ms (15 December 1992), 14. The author thanks Brigadier-General (ret'd) Jim Cox for providing the information.
2   Boutros Boutros-Ghali, "Report to the Security Council on the situation in Somalia," S/24480 (24 August): paras. 22, 25. Cited from United Nations, *United Nations and Somalia, 1992-1996* (New York: United Nations, 1996). (Hereafter *UN and Somalia*.)
3   Boutros-Ghali, "Report on the Situation in Somalia" (24 August): paras. 25, 31. Cited from *UN and Somalia*.
4   John Noble, "Somalia: Meetings with Jonah and Goulding," to Canadian Permanent Mission to the United Nations, COSICS message C-EXOTT-IMD-0042 (9 October 1992): para. 3. Cited from files of the Department of Foreign Affairs and International Trade (DFAIT), 38-11-1-Somali, vol. 2.
5   Confidential interview with UN officer involved in UNOSOM I and II, 27 February 2001.
6   High Commission in Nairobi, "Somalia/UNOSOM: Request for Troops," telex WAGR-0802 to External Affairs, Department of National Defence, and Privy Council Office (2 September 1992): 1-2. Cited from files of DFAIT, 21-14-6-UNOSOM, vol. 4.
7   Caroline Moorhead, *Dunant's Dream: War, Switzerland and the History of the Red Cross* (New York: Carroll and Graf, 1999), 686.
8   Cited in Moorhead, *Dunant's Dream*, 685.
9   Interview with former first Special Representative of the Secretary-General to Somalia Ambassador Mohamed Sahnoun, in Ottawa, 7 August 2001.
10   Boutros Boutros-Ghali, "Report to the Security Council on the Situation in Somalia," S/24343 (22 July 1992): para. 57a-d. Cited from *UN and Somalia*.
11   Interview with Canadian permanent representative to the United Nations Ambassador Paul Heinbecker, 16 August 2002.
12   Boutros Boutros-Ghali, "Introduction," *The United Nations and Somalia: 1992-1996* (New York: United Nations, 1996), 26; and United Nations, "Secretary-General Opens Photo Exhibit on 'Somalia's Cry,'" press release, SG/SM/4855 (17 November 1992): 1.
13   John Hirsch and Robert Oakley, *Somalia and Operation Restore Hope: Reflections on Peacemaking and Peacekeeping* (Washington, DC: United States Institute of Peace Press, 1995), 26.
14   Sahnoun, interview, 7 August 2001.
15   Boutros-Ghali, "Report on the Situation in Somalia," S/24480 (24 August): paras. 36-7; and Add. 1: para. 1. Both documents cited from *UN and Somalia*.
16   Sahnoun, interview, 7 August 2001.
17   United Nations, S/RES/775 (28 August 1992): operative paras. 2-3; and José Ayala Lasso, "Letter from the President of the Security Council to the Secretary-General," S/24532 (8 September 1992): para 1. Both documents cited from *UN and Somalia*.
18   Marrack Goulding, "The Evolution of United Nations Peacekeeping," *International Affairs* 69, 3 (1993): 458.
19   See Boutros Boutros-Ghali, "An Agenda for Peace: Preventive Diplomacy, Peacemaking and Peacekeeping," A/47/277 – S/24111 (17 June 1992): para. 20. Italics added. Cited from www.un.org.
20   Adam Roberts, "From San Francisco to Sarajevo: The United Nations and the Use of Force," *Survival* 37, 4 (Winter 1995-96): 15; and Kofi Annan, "Report of the Secretary-General Pursuant to General Assembly Resolution 53/35: The Fall of Srebrenica," United Nations document A/54/549 (15 November 1999): para. 505. Cited from www.un.org.

21 Innis Claude, "Peace and Security: Prospective Roles for the Two United Nations," *Global Governance* 2 (1996): 295.

22 Imtiaz Shaheen, letter to author, 3 March 2000, 1.

23 Sahnoun, interview, 7 August 2001.

24 Interview with Chief of the Defence Staff General Maurice Baril, at NDHQ in Ottawa, 18 August 2000.

25 Boutros Boutros-Ghali, *Unvanquished: A US-UN Saga* (New York: Random House, 1999), 56-7.

26 Cited in Philip Johnston, *Somalia Diary: The President of CARE Tells One Country's Story of Hope* (Atlanta: Longstreet Press, 1994), 39.

27 Samuel M. Makinda, *Seeking Peace from Chaos: Humanitarian Intervention in Somalia* (Boulder, CO: Lynne Rienner, 1993), 68-69.

28 Sahnoun, interview, 7 August 2001.

29 John Stackhouse, *Out of Poverty and into Something More Comfortable* (Toronto: Vintage Canada, 2001), 53. See also Andrew Bilski, "Wings of Hope," *Maclean's* (28 September 1992): 35.

30 United Nations, "United Nations Calls on Somali People to Co-operate with Special Representative to Save Lives, Defeat Famine and Strife, Pave Way for Reconciliation," press release, SG/SM/4848 (2 November 1992): 1. See also "Secretary-General Sends Message of Hope and Reassurance to Somali People, Saying United Nations Mandate is One of Peace and Co-operation," press release, SG/SM/4854 (13 November 1992).

31 High Commission in Nairobi, "Somalia: Somali National Alliance (SNA) Views," telex WAGR-0975 to External Affairs (21 October 1992): 2. Cited from files of DFAIT, 20-1-2-Somali, vol. 5.

32 Boutros Boutros-Ghali, "Letter from the Secretary-General to the President of the Security Council," S/24859 (27 November 1992). Cited in *UN and Somalia*, 207.

33 Jane Boulden, *The United Nations and Mandate Enforcement: Congo, Somalia, and Bosnia*, Martello Paper #20 (Kingston-Quebec City: Queen's University-Université Laval, 1999), 53.

34 Douglas Fraser, "Somalia/UNOSOM: Official Request," COSICS message C-PRMNY-WKGR-0617 to External Affairs (31 August 1992): 1. Cited from files of DFAIT: 21-14-6-UNOSOM, vol. 3.

35 Shashi Tharoor, "Should United Nations Peacekeeping Go 'Back to Basics'?" *Survival* 37, 4 (Winter 1995-96): 55.

36 John de Chastelain, letter to author, 20 September 2000, 1.

37 Interview with Lieutenant-General (ret'd) Paul Addy, in Ottawa, 7 February 2000.

38 John de Chastelain and Robert Fowler, "Somalia: United Nations Request for a Security Battalion" (2 September 1992): paras. 2-3. Cited from *Information Legacy: A Compendium of Source Material from the Commission of Inquiry into the Deployment of Canadian Forces to Somalia* (Ottawa: Public Works and Government Services Canada, 1997), document DND000885. (Hereafter *Information Legacy*.)

39 Interview with Vice-Admiral (ret'd) Larry Murray, Ottawa, 28 April 2000.

40 Testimony of Colonel John Bremner to the Somalia Inquiry, 24 October 1995. Cited from *Information Legacy*, 8:1572-73.

41 See Chapter 3 for more information on the first UN Technical Mission. Testimony of Colonel (ret'd) Mike Houghton to the Somalia Inquiry, 12 February 1996. Cited from *Information Legacy*, 44:8685.

42 Interview with Colonel (ret'd) Mike Houghton, in Ottawa, 27 April 2000.

43 Houghton, testimony. Cited from *Information Legacy*, 44:8686.

44 Ibid., 12:2261, and 44:8707.

45 Bernd Horn, *Bastard Sons: An Examination of Canada's Airborne Experience, 1942-1995* (St. Catharines: Vanwell, 2001), 192.

46 Addy, interview, 7 February 2000.

47 Murray, interview, 17 March 2000.

48 John de Chastelain, letter to author, 3 April 2000, 2.

49 Interview with Lieutenant-General (ret'd) David Huddleston, 18 December 2000.

50 Rick Froh, "Option Analysis for a Security Battalion in Support of United Nations Humanitarian Assistance Operations in Somalia as Requested by CDS" (31 July 1992): para. 19. Cited from *Information Legacy*, document DND002070. Froh raised the same objections in a different estimate prepared a day earlier for the CDS. See Rick Froh, "Option Analysis for a Security Battalion in Support of United Nations Humanitarian Assistance Operations in Somalia as Requested by CDS" (30 July 1992): para. 18, *De Faye Board of Inquiry on the Canadian Airborne Regiment Battle Group*, Exhibit #110. Both documents cited from *Information Legacy*.

51 Interview with Lieutenant-General (ret'd) Jim Gervais, in Ottawa, 12 July 2000.

52 Interview with Brigadier-General (ret'd) Ernest Beno, in Kingston, 24 May 2000.

53 Only three areas are mentioned because only three (Quebec, Central, and Western) had brigade groups. The Atlantic Area (established last, in fall 1992) had just one infantry unit, namely 2nd Battalion, Royal Canadian Regiment at CFB Gagetown. Testimony of Lieutenant-General (ret'd) James (Jim) Gervais to the Somalia Inquiry, 15 February 1996. Cited from *Information Legacy* 47:9397.

54 Testimony of General (ret'd) John de Chastelain to the Somalia Inquiry, 20 February 1996. Cited from *Information Legacy*, 49:9947.

55 W.I. Kennedy, "Briefing Notes: FMC to CDS, Operations Cordon and Dagger Planning" (4 September 1992): 3, para. 18. Cited from *Information Legacy*, document: DND131215. The date given on this document, "92/04/02," is not correct. Based on its contents, this is likely the briefing that took place on the 4th as mentioned in *Dishonoured Legacy: The Lessons of the Somalia Affair*, Report of the Commission of Inquiry into the Deployment of Canadian Forces to Somalia (Ottawa: Public Works and Government Services Canada, 1997), 3:719-20. (Hereafter cited as *Dishonoured Legacy*.)

56 Gervais, testimony to the Somalia Inquiry, 15 February 1996. Cited from *Information Legacy*, 47:9398.

57 Ibid.

58 *Dishonoured Legacy*, 2:494.

59 Confidential interview with senior government official, 26 June 2000.

60 De Chastelain, testimony to the Somalia Inquiry, 20 February 1996. Cited from *Information Legacy*, 49:9931.

61 De Chastelain, letter to author, 3 April 2000, 2.

62 Douglas Fraser, "UNOSOM Developments," COSICS message C-PRMNY-WKGR-0596 to External Affairs (25 August 1992): 1; and Fraser, "Somalia/UNOSOM: Official Request" (31 August 1992): 1. Both documents cited from files of DFAIT: 21-14-6-UNOSOM, vol. 3.

63 Michel Drapeau, "Record of Daily Executive Meeting Regarding Somalia" (3 September 1992): para. 3. Cited from *Information Legacy*, document DND299457.

64 Department of National Defence, "Canada Ready to Send Troops to Somalia," *News Release* 92/51 (28 August 1992): 1.

65 Robin W. Allen, "Combined and Joint Operations in Somalia," in *Multinational Naval Forces*, ed. Peter T. Haydon and Ann L. Griffiths (Halifax: Dalhousie University Centre for Foreign Policy Studies, 1996), 205.

66 Kennedy, "Briefing Notes" (4 September 1992): paras. 7c, 9, 16. Cited from *Information Legacy*, document DND131215.

67 Michel Drapeau, "Record of Daily Executive Meeting Regarding Somalia" (11 September 1992): para. 7. Cited from *Information Legacy*, document DND299550.

68 Gary Furrie, "Draft Warning Order – Operation Cordon," memorandum 3451-9-034/293 (2 September 1992): para. A-1. Cited from *Information Legacy*, document DND221319.

69 John Bremner, "Operation Cordon – United Nations Request to Deploy Canadian Security Battalion to Somalia," memorandum (26 October 1992): paras. 3-4. Cited from *Information Legacy*, document DND002210.

70 Drapeau, "Record of Daily Executive Meeting" (11 September 1992): para. 7. Cited from *Information Legacy*, document DND299550.

71 The mission still had 564 troops on 3 December, when it was suspended in favour of the US-led Unified Task Force. Boutros-Ghali approved "about 100 additional personnel" for the peacekeeping operation on 18 December. It had 634 and 715 all ranks as of 26 January

and 3 March 1993, respectively. Later that March it was subsumed into the United Nations Operation in Somalia II. See Boutros Boutros-Ghali, "Report of the Secretary-General in Pursuance of Paragraphs 18 and 19 of Resolution 794 (1992)," S/24992 (19 December 1992): para. 6; S/25168 (26 January 1993): para. 19; and S/25354 (3 March 1993): para. 5. Cited from *UN and Somalia*.

72 Sahnoun, interview, 7 August 2001.
73 Interview with former UN Operation in Somalia I Deputy Force Commander Brigadier-General Jim Cox, in Ottawa, 16 August 2000.
74 Addy, interview, 26 November 1999.
75 Michel Drapeau, "Record of Discussion on Reconnaissance Team Report – Somalia with the DM/CDS" (21 October 1992): para. 6. Cited from *Information Legacy*, document DND444016.
76 Shaheen, letter to author, 3 March 2000, 1.
77 *Dishonoured Legacy*, 3:749.
78 Mohamed Farah Aidid, letter to Prime Minister Brian Mulroney, 12 October 1992, 1. Cited from files of DFAIT: 21-14-6-UNOSOM, vol. 4.
79 Kent Vachon, "Somalia: Meeting with Sahnoun," COSICS message C-PRMNY-WKGR-0950 to External Affairs (16 October 1992): 1. Cited from files of DFAIT: 21-14-6-UNOSOM, vol. 4.
80 Bremner, "Operation Cordon – United Nations Request to Deploy Canadian Security Battalion to Somalia" (26 October 1992): paras. 4-5. Cited from *Information Legacy*, document DND002210.
81 Gary Furrie, "Deployment to Somalia – Delay," e-mail message to ADM (Mat) R. Sturgeon, Associate ADM (Mat) Major-General J. Adams, et al. (5 November 1992): paras. 1, 4. Cited from *Information Legacy*, control no. 823200.
82 Cited in Michel Drapeau, "Record of Daily Executive Meeting Regarding Somalia" (13 November 1992): para. 2. Cited from *Information Legacy*, document DND299507.
83 William Fuller, "Operation Cordon Deployment Movement Order," 3451-9-293 (J4 Move) (23 November 1992): para. 2. Cited from *Information Legacy*, document DND001650. All dates in this paragraph are from this document.

Chapter 7: Robust Militarism
1 Jonathan Stevenson, *Losing Mogadishu: Testing United States Policy in Somalia* (Annapolis, MD: Naval Institute Press, 1995), xii, 98-99.
2 Lawrence E. Casper, *Falcon Brigade: Combat and Command in Somalia and Haiti* (Boulder, CO: Lynne Rienner, 2001), 9-10.
3 Interview with former Special Envoy of the President to Somalia Ambassador (ret'd) Robert Oakley, 3 August 2000.
4 Interview with former Chief of Staff in the Prime Minister's Office Hugh Segal, in Montreal, 28 June 2000.
5 J.L. Granatstein and Norman Hillmer, *For Better or for Worse: Canada and the United States to the 1990s* (Toronto: Copp Clark Pitman, 1991), 316-17.
6 Interview with Deputy Minister of National Defence Jim Judd, in Ottawa at NDHQ, 31 August 2000.
7 Robert Fife, "Former PM Deflects Pressure to Lead Tories," *National Post*, 19 November 2002: A9.
8 Dieudonné Mouafo, Nadia Ponce Morales, and Jeff Heynen, eds., *Building Cross-Border Links: A Compendium of Canada-US Government Collaboration*, Action-Research Roundtable on Managing Canada-US Relations (Ottawa: Canada School of Public Service, 2004), 4.
9 Mike Trickey, "When Leaders Need Not Be Friends," *Ottawa Citizen*, 14 September 2002: A11.
10 Interview with Canadian permanent representative to the United Nations Ambassador Paul Heinbecker, 16 August 2002.
11 Brian Mulroney, "Address on the Occasion of the Centennial Anniversary Convocation of Stanford University," Stanford, California (29 September 1991): 6.
12 George Bush and Brent Scowcroft, *A World Transformed* (New York: Knopf, 1998), 448-49.

13 See Boutros Boutros-Ghali, "Letter dated 29 November to the President of the Security Council," S/24868 (30 November 1992). Cited from United Nations, *UN and Somalia, 1992-1996* (New York: United Nations, 1996), 211. (Hereafter cited as *United Nations and Somalia.*)

14 Heinbecker, interview, 16 August 2002.

15 Denis Stairs, "Canada in the 1990s: Speak Loudly and Carry a Bent Twig," *Policy Options* 22, 1 (January-February 2001): 45.

16 Brian Mulroney, "World Peace Demands Stronger United Nations Role," *Canadian Speeches: Issues of the Day* 6, 4 (June/July 1992): 31.

17 Barbara McDougall, speech to Parliament, House of Commons, 3rd session, 34th Parliament, *Hansard* (7 December 1992): 14772.

18 Glen Shortliffe, "Somalia: Situation Report," memorandum for the Prime Minister (11 December 1992): 3. Access to Information request, Privy Council Office.

19 Denis Stairs, "Lester B. Pearson and the Meaning of Politics," in *Pearson: The Unlikely Gladiator*, ed. Norman Hillmer (Montreal and Kingston: McGill-Queen's University Press, 1999), 34, 38-39.

20 Gordon S. Smith, "Establishing Canada's Priorities," in *Canada among Nations 2004: Setting Priorities Straight*, ed. David Carment, Fen Osler Hampson, and Norman Hillmer (Montreal and Kingston: McGill-Queen's University Press, 2005), 47.

21 An exception was the US-led Multinational Force and Observers stationed in the Sinai Peninsula (1971-present). Cited from interview with former Under-Secretary of State for External Affairs Reid Morden, in Ottawa, 7 September 2000.

22 Interview with former Clerk of the Privy Council Glen Shortliffe, in Ottawa, 21 July 2000.

23 Morden, interview, 7 September 2000.

24 Ibid.

25 Kent Vachon, "Somalia: Security Council Deliberations and Options for UNOSOM," COSICS message C-PRMNY-WKGR-1394 to External Affairs (1 December 1992): 2. Cited from files of the Department of Foreign Affairs and International Trade (DFAIT), 21-14-6-UNOSOM, vol. 7; and Colonel Douglas Fraser, "Somalia/UNOSOM Troop Contributors Meeting," COSICS message C-PRMNY-WKGR-1440 to External Affairs (7 December 1992): 3. Cited from files of DFAIT, 21-14-6-UNOSOM, vol. 8.

26 Vachon, "Somalia: Security Council Deliberations and Options for UNOSOM," 2.

27 Ibid., 3.

28 External Affairs, "Somalia: Secretary-General's Options," telex IDS-3026 to Permanent Mission in New York (1 December 1992): 3. Cited from files of DFAIT, 21-14-6-UNOSOM, vol. 7; and Embassy in Washington, "Somalia: Evolving United States Views," telex UNGR-2394 to External Affairs (2 December 1992): 3. Cited from files of DFAIT, 21-14-6-UNOSOM, vol. 7.

29 Kent Vachon, "Somalia: Situation Report 2 December, 8:00 p.m.," COSICS message C-PRMNY-WKGR-1403 to External Affairs (2 December 1992): 2. Cited from files of DFAIT, 21-14-6-UNOSOM, vol. 7.

30 Judd, interview, 31 August 2000.

31 Confidential interview with senior government official, 26 June 2000.

32 Ibid.

33 Judd, interview, 31 August 2000.

34 Interview with former Director-General of the International Security Bureau Mark J. Moher, at DFAIT in Ottawa, 21 December 2000; and Moher, interview, 21 February 2000.

35 Geoffrey York, "Ottawa Delays Sending Soldiers to Somalia," *Globe and Mail*, 3 December 1992: A2.

36 Barbara McDougall, "Letter to United Nations Secretary-General Boutros Boutros-Ghali" (11 December 1992): 1. Cited from files of DFAIT, 21-14-6-UNOSOM; and Moher, interview, 21 February 2000.

37 Moher, interview, 21 December 2000.

38 Charlotte Gray, "New Faces in Old Places: The Making of Canadian Foreign Policy," in *Canada among Nations 1992-93: A New World Order?* ed. Fen Osler Hampson and Christopher J. Maule (Ottawa: Carleton University Press, 1992), 20.

39 Interview with Dr. Gerry Wright, former special policy adviser to Secretary of State for External Affairs Barbara McDougall, in Ottawa, 23 August 2000.

40 George Bush, "Letter to Prime Minister Brian Mulroney" (3 December 1992): 1. Cited from files of DFAIT, 21-14-6-UNOSOM, vol. 7.

41 Editorial, "Canada Tags Along," *Calgary Herald*, 10 December 1992: A4.

42 Denis Stairs, "Architects or Engineers? The Conservatives and Foreign Policy," *Diplomatic Departures: The Conservative Era in Canadian Foreign Policy, 1984-93*, ed. Kim Nossal and Nelson Michaud (Vancouver: UBC Press, 2001), 32.

43 Cited in Louise Crosby, "Stronger Ties to the United States Hallmark of PM's New World Order," *Ottawa Citizen*, 21 November 1992: B5; and J.L. Granatstein, "The World Canada Faces in the 1990s," in *Canadian Forces and the Modern World*, ed. David E. Code and Ian Cameron (Ottawa: Conference of Defence Associations Institute, 1993), 22.

44 J.L. Granatstein, "Peacekeeping: Did Canada Make a Difference? And What Difference Did Peacekeeping Make to Canada?" in *Making a Difference? Canada's Foreign Policy in a Changing World Order*, ed. John English and Norman Hillmer (Toronto: Lester, 1992), 233; and Granatstein, "The World Canada Faces in the 1990s," 22-23.

45 Mary Collins, speech to Parliament, House of Commons, 3rd session, 34th Parliament, *Hansard* (7 December 1992): 14784.

46 Barbara McDougall and Marcel Masse, "Mission to Somalia," transcript of joint press conference, CBC Newsworld, special broadcast (4 December 1992): 2. Cited from files of DFAIT, 21-14-6-UNOSOM, vol. 7.

47 McDougall, speech to Parliament, 14773.

48 Editorial, "Somalia Poses New Moral Issues for United Nations," *Ottawa Citizen*, 5 December 1992: A10.

49 Glen Shortliffe, "Situation Report on Somalia, December 8, 1992," memorandum for the Prime Minister (8 December 1992): 3. Access to Information request, Privy Council Office.

50 "Somalia Poses New Moral Issues for United Nations," *Ottawa Citizen*, A10.

51 "Canada Tags Along," *Calgary Herald*, A4.

52 Confidential interview with senior government official, 26 June 2000.

53 John Holmes, "The New Agenda for Canadian Internationalism," in *Canada and the New Internationalism*, ed. John Holmes and John Kirton (Toronto: Canadian Institute of International Affairs, 1988), 20.

54 Bush, "Letter to Prime Minister Brian Mulroney," 1.

55 Glen Shortliffe, "Somalia – The Longer Term," memorandum for the Prime Minister (8 December 1992): 2.

56 McDougall and Masse, "Mission to Somalia," 2.

57 Tim Harper, "MPs Question Peacekeepers' Changing Role," *Toronto Star*, 9 December 1992: A2.

58 Boutros Boutros-Ghali, "Letter to President George Bush" (8 December 1992). Cited from *UN and Somalia*, 216.

59 Editorial, "Do It Right in Somalia," *New York Times*, 1 December 1992: A24.

60 Geoffrey York, "Somali Gun Raids Studied," *Globe and Mail*, 23 December 1992: A2.

61 Cox was promoted to Brigadier-General in early 1993 and for a time was Chief of Staff of UNOSOM II. See York, "Somali Gun Raids Studied," A1.

62 Interview with United States Marine Corps Lieutenant-General (ret'd) Robert Johnston, 29 August 2000.

63 Glen Shortliffe, "Somalia: Situation Report," memorandum for the Prime Minister (18 December 1992): 2. Access to Information request, Privy Council Office.

64 Editorial, "Disarming Somalia," *Toronto Star*, 16 December 1992: A20.

65 Embassy in Washington, "Somalia: State Department Update: Disarming the Factions," telex UNGR-2496 to External Affairs (23 December 1992): 1, 4. Cited from files of DFAIT, 21-14-6-UNOSOM, vol. 10.

66 External Affairs and International Trade Canada, "McDougall Comments on United Nations Secretary-General's Report on Somalia," *News Release* 246 (24 December 1992): 1.

Chapter 8: Unified Task Force
1 High Commission in Nairobi, "Mission to Somalia by High Commission Representatives, August 12-14," telex WADA-0786 to Canadian International Development Agency and NDHQ (18 August 1992): paras. 5, 7. Cited from *Information Legacy: A Compendium of Source Material from the Commission of Inquiry into the Deployment of Canadian Forces to Somalia* (Ottawa: Public Works and Government Services Canada, 1997), document DND002606. (Hereafter *Information Legacy*.)
2 Interview with former Secretary-General of the UN Boutros Boutros-Ghali, 11 August 2000.
3 Boutros Boutros-Ghali, "Empowering the United Nations," *Foreign Affairs* 72, 5 (Winter 1992): 91.
4 Ismat Kittani with Ian Johnstone, "First Person: The Lessons from Somalia," *UN Chronicle* 33, 3 (September 1996): 81.
5 Boutros Boutros-Ghali, "Letter from the Secretary-General to the President of the Security Council," S/24859 (27 November 1992). Cited in United Nations, *The United Nations and Somalia, 1992-1996* (New York: United Nations, 1996), 207. (Hereafter *UN and Somalia*.)
6 Interview with former second Special Representative of the Secretary-General to Somalia Ambassador Ismat Kittani, 28 July 2000.
7 High Commission in Nairobi, "Somalia: Visit to UNOSOM HQ," telex WAGR-1076 to External Affairs (16 November 1992): 6. Cited from files of the Department of Foreign Affairs and International Trade (DFAIT), 21-14-6-UNOSOM, vol. 6.
8 High Commission in Nairobi, "Somalia: Visit to UNOSOM HQ," 3.
9 High Commission in Nairobi, "Somalia: Meetings with Secretary-General's Special Representative (SRSG) Kittani," telex WAGR-1098 to External Affairs (20 November 1992): 1-2. Cited from files of DFAIT, 21-14-6-UNOSOM, vol. 6.
10 Imtiaz Shaheen et al., "Political and Military Events in Somalia from Cease-Fire Agreement to Resolution Multinational Force," unpublished ms (15 December 1992), 30. The author thanks Brigadier-General (ret'd) Jim Cox for providing the information.
11 High Commission in Nairobi, "Somalia: Meetings with Secretary-General's Special Representative (SRSG) Kittani," 2; and John Drysdale, *Whatever Happened to Somalia?* (London: HAAN Associates, 1994), 80-81.
12 High Commission in Nairobi, "Somalia: Meetings with Secretary-General's Special Representative (SRSG) Kittani," 1.
13 CBC, *Prime Time News* with Brian Stewart, "UN Bungling to Blame" (15 December 1992). Cited from files of DFAIT, 21-14-6-UNOSOM, vol. 9.
14 Boutros-Ghali, "Letter" (27 November 1992). Cited in *UN and Somalia*, 209.
15 Boutros Boutros-Ghali, "Letter from the Secretary-General to the President of the Security Council," S/24868 (30 November 1992). Cited in *UN and Somalia*, 210, 212.
16 Boutros-Ghali, "Letter" (30 November 1992). Cited in *UN and Somalia*, 211.
17 George Bush, "Humanitarian Mission to Somalia," *US Department of State Dispatch* 3, 49 (7 December 1992): 865.
18 Brian Mulroney, "World Peace Demands Stronger United Nations Role," *Canadian Speeches: Issues of the Day* 6, 4 (June-July 1992): 31, 33.
19 Reuters, Canadian Press, and Associated Press, "UN Votes to Use Force in Somalia," *Globe and Mail*, 4 December 1992: A1; and Tim Harper, "Canada Waiting for Call to Make 'Contribution,'" *Toronto Star*, 4 December 1992: A36.
20 Bush, "Humanitarian Mission to Somalia," 865.
21 CTV, *Question Period*, "Craig Oliver Interview with General John de Chastelain, Colonel (ret'd) Brian MacDonald, and Executive Director of the Canadian Institute of Strategic Studies Alex Morrison" (27 November 1992): 2. Cited from files of DFAIT, 21-14-6-UNOSOM, vol. 6.
22 Cited from John de Chastelain and Gaëtan Lavertu, "News Conference – The Suffering of the Somali People" (4 December 1992). Cited from *Information Legacy*, document NS079033.
23 Charles Oliviero, "Operation Deliverance: International Success or Domestic Failure?" *Canadian Military Journal* 2, 2 (Summer 2001): 52. Emphasis in original.

24 Jarat Chopra, Åge Eknes, and Toralv Nordbø, *Fighting for Hope in Somalia* (Oslo: Norwegian Institute of International Affairs, 1995), 11.
25 Cited in John de Chastelain, "Somalia – CDS Discussion with General Powell, 1250 hrs 2 December 1992," note to file on telephone conversation. Cited from *Information Legacy*, control no. 810800.
26 John de Chastelain, "CDS Call to General Powell, 4 December 1992," note to file on telephone conversation. Cited from *Information Legacy*, document DND000956.
27 Testimony of Colonel Serge Labbé to the Somalia Inquiry, 7 February 1997. Cited from *Information Legacy*, 161:32877.
28 Andrew Leslie, "Testimony in Support of *The Study of Canada's National Security Policy*," issue 4, eighth proceeding of the Standing Senate Committee on National Security and Defence, 1st session, 38th Parliament (29 November 2004), 82.
29 Edward J. Perkins, "Statement on Somalia on behalf of the United States to the Security Council," provisional verbatim record of Security Council meeting, S/PV.3145 (3 December 1992): 36.
30 Jean-Bernard Mérimée, "Statement on Somalia on behalf of France to the Security Council," provisional verbatim record of Security Council meeting, S/PV.3145 (3 December 1992): 30.
31 Testimony of acting Chief of the Defence Staff Vice-Admiral Larry Murray to the Somalia Inquiry, 4 February 1997. Cited from *Information Legacy*, 158:32121.
32 Interview with Commodore Ken McMillan, in Ottawa, 17 November 2000.
33 Ken McMillan, "Canadian Rules of Engagement – Operation Deliverance," cover letter to Colonel Serge Labbé, 3120-62 (COS J3) (16 December 1992), *De Faye Board of Inquiry on the Canadian Airborne Regiment Battle Group*, Exhibit 65, paras. 1, 4. Cited from *Information Legacy*.
34 Interview with Commodore Ken McMillan, 17 November 2000.
35 Testimony of Captain (N) Ken McMillan to the Somalia Inquiry, 30 October 1995. Cited from *Information Legacy*, 11:2144.
36 McMillan, interview, 17 November 2000.
37 *Dishonoured Legacy: The Lessons of the Somalia Affair*, Report of the Commission of Inquiry into the Deployment of Canadian Forces to Somalia, (Ottawa: Public Works and Government Services Canada, 1997), 5:1465. (Hereafter *Dishonoured Legacy*.)
38 Labbé, testimony. Cited from *Information Legacy*, vol. 162, 10 February 1997, 32917; vol. 163, 11 February 1997, 33259; and vol. 164, 12 February 1997, 33388.
39 Serge Labbé, "Letter to Deputy Chief of the Defence Staff Vice-Admiral Larry Murray" (26 April 1993): para. 3. Cited from *Information Legacy*, document DND017705.
40 Ibid., para. 7.
41 Dennis C. Tabbernor, "Operational Commanders, Orders and the Right to Choose," research essay (Toronto: Canadian Forces College, 1998), 30. Document obtained from Canadian Forces College on-line Information Resource Centre portal. Cited from wps.cfc. forces.gc.ca/en/cfcpapers/index.php.
42 Testimony of Vice-Admiral Larry Murray to the Somalia Inquiry, 30 January 1997. Cited from *Information Legacy*, 155:31664.
43 Ibid., 155:31656.
44 Chris Madsen, *Another Kind of Justice: Canadian Military Law from Confederation to Somalia* (Vancouver: UBC Press, 1999), 6, 122, 160; and Sandra Cumner, "Review of *Another Kind of Justice*," *Armed Forces and Society: An Interdisciplinary Journal* 27, 2 (Winter 2001): 307.
45 *Dishonoured Legacy*, 3:855-56.
46 *Dishonoured Legacy*, 5:1145.
47 Murray, testimony, 28 January 1997. Cited from *Information Legacy*, 153:31261.
48 Interview with former Commander of the Canadian Joint Force Somalia Colonel Serge Labbé, 24 March 2000; and interview with former Commander of the Canadian Airborne Regiment Battlegroup Lieutenant-Colonel (ret'd) Carol Mathieu, in Montreal, 9 May 2000.
49 Interview with Lieutenant-General (ret'd) Jim Gervais, in Ottawa, 7 March 2000.
50 Labbé, testimony, 7 February 1997. Cited from *Information Legacy*, 162:32923-24.

51 Testimony of Brigadier-General Ernest Beno to the De Faye Board of Inquiry, *Report of the De Faye Board of Inquiry on the Canadian Airborne Regiment Battle Group – Phase 1* (Ottawa: July 1993), 2:240. Cited from *Information Legacy*.
52 Interview with Brigadier-General (ret'd) Ernest B. Beno, in Kingston, 24 May 2000.
53 Beno, interview, 25 May 2000.
54 *Dishonoured Legacy*, 1:250.
55 Gervais, interview, 8 March 2000 and 12 July 2000.
56 Testimony. of Lieutenant-General (ret'd) Jim Gervais to the Somalia Inquiry, 15 February 1996. Cited from *Information Legacy*, 47:9426-55.
57 Interview with Lieutenant-General (ret'd) Paul Addy, in Ottawa, 26 November 1999.
58 Interview with Major-General (ret'd) Lewis MacKenzie, 5 September 2000.
59 Interview with Lieutenant-Colonel Bernd Horn and Lieutenant-Colonel (ret'd) Dr. William (Bill) Bentley, in Ottawa, 2 May 2000.
60 MacKenzie, interview, 5 September 2000.
61 *Dishonoured Legacy*, 2:698.
62 Testimony of Commodore David Cogdon to the Somalia Inquiry, 25 October 1995. Cited from *Information Legacy*, 9:1704.
63 Interview with Commodore (ret'd) David Cogdon, 4 March 2001.
64 Gervais, interview, 7 March 2000; MacKenzie, interview, 5 September 2000; and testimony of Brigadier-General Ernest Beno to the Somalia Inquiry, 29 January 1996. Cited from *Information Legacy*, 40:7855.
65 McMillan, interview, 17 November 2000.
66 Ken McMillan, "Military Planning Considerations," in *Multinational Naval Forces*, ed. Peter T. Haydon and Ann L. Griffiths (Halifax: Centre for Foreign Policy Studies, 1995), 88-89.
67 Ralph Lysyshyn, "Domestic Political Considerations of International Security Operations," in *Multinational Naval Forces*, ed. Peter T. Haydon and Ann L. Griffiths (Halifax: Centre for Foreign Policy Studies, 1995), 78.
68 Interview with Colonel (ret'd) John Bremner, in Ottawa, 31 July 2000.
69 Tim Addison, "CDS/DM Meeting to Discuss Somalia," Notebook 1992-1994, unpublished ms (3 December 1992). The author thanks Tim Addison for providing the information. Captain (Navy) Ken McMillan could not attend this meeting, and so Lieutenant-Commander Addison represented J3 Plans.
70 Michel Drapeau, "Record of Discussion of a Special Meeting on Somalia with the DM/CDS" (4 December 1992). Cited from *Information Legacy*, document DND127177.
71 Jeff Sallot, "Troops Approved without Policy on Use of Deadly Force," *Globe and Mail*, 8 December 1992: A11.
72 See John de Chastelain, "Note to File – 7 December 1992," para. 1. Cited from *Information Legacy*, document DND018951. The quotation marks are de Chastelain's.
73 Interview with United States Marine Corps Lieutenant-General (ret'd) Robert Johnston, 29 August 2000.
74 Addy, interview, 7 February 2000.
75 De Chastelain, "Note to File – 7 December 1992," para. 1.
76 Johnston, interview, 29 August 2000.
77 Ibid.
78 Labbé, interview, 24 March 2000.
79 Serge Labbé, "Somalia: Setting the Record Straight," unpublished ms (March 1994). The author thanks Colonel Serge Labbé for providing the information.

Chapter 9: Stay or Go?

1 Colin Powell with Joseph E. Persico, *My American Journey* (New York: Random House Large Print, 1995), 860-61.
2 See US government, "Report on the Activities of the Unified Task Force," attached to Edward J. Perkins, "Letter from the United States to the President of the Security Council," S/24976 (17 December 1992); Boutros Boutros-Ghali, "Report of the Secretary-General in Pursuance of Paragraphs 18 and 19 of Resolution 794 (1992)," S/24992 (19 December 1992): para.

22; and US government, "Report on the Progress Made by UNITAF," attached to Edward J. Perkins, "Letter from the United States to the President of the Security Council," S/25126 (19 January 1993). All documents cited from United Nations, *The United Nations and Somalia, 1992-1996* (New York: United Nations, 1996). (Hereafter *UN and Somalia*.)

3   Madeline Albright, "Statement on Somalia on behalf of the United States to the Security Council," provisional verbatim record of Security Council meeting, United Nations, S/PV.3188 (26 March 1993): 18.

4   Daniel P. Bolger, *Savage Peace: Americans at War in the 1990s* (Novato, CA: Presidio Press, 1995), 282.

5   Eric Schmitt, "U.S. Assesses Risks of Sending Troops to Somalia," *New York Times*, 1 December 1992: A10.

6   United Nations, S/RES/794 (3 December 1992): operative paras. 10, 19. Cited from *UN and Somalia*.

7   Diana Jean Schemo, "Somali Police Back on Duty, with U.S. Aid," *New York Times*, 1 February 1993: A7.

8   Boutros-Ghali, "Report of the Secretary-General" (19 December 1992): para. 38.

9   United Nations, S/RES/814 (26 March 1993): operative paras. 5, 8. Cited from *UN and Somalia*.

10 UNOSOM II's authorized strength was 20,000 combat troops and 8,000 support troops. UNITAF peaked at 38,300 in January 1993; it had 28,000 in March. See United Nations, "30,000-Strong UN Force Steps in to 'Restore Hope,'" *UN Chronicle* 30, 2 (June 1993): 15.

11 Albright, "Statement on Somalia on behalf of the United States," 19.

12 Krauthammer was a *Washington Post* columnist. See Charles Krauthammer, "Essay: The Immaculate Intervention," *Time* (26 July 1993): 56.

13 Editorial, "Somalia Poses New Moral Issues for UN," *Ottawa Citizen*, 5 December 1992: A10.

14 Editorial, "What Next in Somalia?" *Globe and Mail*, 17 December 1992: A24.

15 Glen Shortliffe, "Memorandum for the Prime Minister" (17 December 1992): 2. Access to Information request, Privy Council Office.

16 Glen Shortliffe, "Memorandum for the Prime Minister" (16 December 1992): 3. Access to Information request, Privy Council Office.

17 For example, see John de Chastelain and Gäetan Lavertu, "News Conference – The Suffering of the Somali People" (4 December 1992); and Barbara McDougall, "Letter to UN Secretary-General Boutros Boutros-Ghali" (11 December 1992). Both documents cited from *Information Legacy: A Compendium of Source Material from the Commission of Inquiry into the Deployment of Canadian Forces to Somalia* (Ottawa: Public Works and Government Services Canada, 1997), documents NS079033 and DND000911. (Hereafter *Information Legacy*.)

18 Interview with former Commander of the Canadian Joint Force Somalia Colonel Serge Labbé, 24 March 2000.

19 Henry Kolatacz, "Bulletin – Somalia: Disarmament," External Affairs document IDS-1255 (9 February 1993): 1.

20 Interview with Chief of the Defence Staff General Maurice Baril, at NDHQ in Ottawa, 18 August 2000.

21 Canada had agreed to provide up to fifteen staff officers for the first UN mission in Somalia. The offer had been carried over to the second UN effort. See Reid Morden and Gaétan Lavertu, "Action Memorandum for the Secretary of State for External Affairs" (8 February 1993): 1. Access to Information request, Department of Foreign Affairs and International Trade.

22 Edwards succeeded Larry Smith as High Commissioner in January 1993. Cited from interview with former High Commissioner to Nairobi Ambassador Lucie Edwards, 25 July 2000.

23 John Anderson and Robert Fowler, "Letter to Glen Shortliffe" (undated): 1. Cited from *Information Legacy*, document DND345994.

24 Gerry Wright, "Diplomacy and Peacekeeping: Part 2," *bout de papier* 13, 4 (Winter 1996): 28.

25 Canada was in the process of withdrawing from Cyprus at the time. Interview with former Canadian Deputy Permanent Representative to the United Nations Ambassador David Malone, in Ottawa, 30 September 2004.
26 Gaétan Lavertu, "Meeting of US Ambassador with Under-Secretary," attachment: "US Ambassador Talking Points," memorandum IFB-216 (12 December 1992): 1. Cited from files of the Department of Foreign Affairs and International Trade (DFAIT), 21-14-6-UNOSOM, vol. 9.
27 Morden and Lavertu, "Action Memorandum for the Secretary of State for External Affairs," 2.
28 Robert Fowler and John Anderson, "Update on the Transition from UNITAF to UNOSOM II," memorandum 3451-1 (DI Pol) (29 March 1993). Cited from *Information Legacy*, document NS008159.
29 The "post-settlement" mission would have implemented the Vance-Owen Plan (January 1993). The Bosnian Serbs rejected the plan. See Jim Judd, "Peacekeeping," memorandum to Privy Council Clerk Glen Shortliffe (31 March 1993): 1. Access to Information request, Privy Council Office.
30 The "recent major incidents" occurred during the week of 21 February 1993. See Boutros Boutros-Ghali, "Report of the Secretary-General in Pursuance of Paragraphs 18 and 19 of Resolution 794 (1992)," S/25354 (3 March 1993): paras. 6, 20, 21, 90. Cited from *UN and Somalia*.
31 Boutros-Ghali, "Report of the Secretary-General" (3 March 1993): para. 43.
32 The agreement included other provisions, but these two were the most important. See Conference on National Reconciliation in Somalia, "Addis Ababa Agreement concluded at the first session of the Conference on National Reconciliation in Somalia" (27 March 1993). Cited from *UN and Somalia*, 265-66.
33 John Hirsch and Robert Oakley, *Somalia and Operation Restore Hope: Reflections on Peacemaking and Peacekeeping* (Washington, DC: United States Institute of Peace, 1995), 97n8.
34 Commission of Inquiry, "Report of the Commission of Inquiry established pursuant to resolution 885 (1993) to investigate armed attacks on UNOSOM II personnel," S/1994/652 (1 June 1994): paras. 57, 61-63. Cited from *UN and Somalia*.
35 Glen Shortliffe, "Somalia: UN Mandate," memorandum for the Prime Minister (23 December 1992): 2. Access to Information request, Privy Council Office.
36 Glen Shortliffe, "Somalia: Recent Developments," memorandum for the Prime Minister (18 June 1993): 2. Access to Information request, Privy Council Office.
37 Boutros-Ghali, "Report of the Secretary-General" (3 March 1993): para. 30.
38 Reid Morden, handwritten comment on Morden and Lavertu, "Action Memorandum for SSEA" (8 February 1993): 1. Access to Information request, Department of Foreign Affairs and International Trade.
39 Daniel Dhavernas, "Canadian Contribution of Troops to Somalia," memorandum IDS-1200 to the Secretary of State for External Affairs (9 February 1993): 1. Cited from DFAIT/ATIP.
40 John Anderson and Robert Fowler, "Letter to Assistant Secretary to Cabinet for Foreign and Defence Policy Jim Judd" (4 May 1993). Cited from *Information Legacy*, document DND281790.
41 Glen Shortliffe, handwritten comment on "Somalia: Update," memorandum for the Prime Minister (4 March 1993): 2. Access to Information request, Privy Council Office. Also Duncan Miller, "Memorandum for Robert Fowler" (1 April 1993): 1. Cited from *Information Legacy*, document DND018048.
42 Interview with former Under-Secretary of State for External Affairs Reid Morden, in Ottawa, 21 July 2000.
43 Interview with former Clerk of the Privy Council Glen Shortliffe, in Ottawa, 21 July 2000.
44 Morden, interview, 21 July 2000.
45 There were 4,700 Canadian Forces personnel deployed overseas in early 1993, about 1,300 in Somalia.
46 Campbell succeeded Marcel Masse in January 1993. Her letter also discussed significant reductions to the Canadian Forces presence in the former Yugoslavia. See Kim Campbell, "Letter to Prime Minister Brian Mulroney" (8 March 1993): 1, 3. Cited from *Information Legacy*, document DND282823.

47 Anderson succeeded John de Chastelain in January 1993. Cited from interview with former Chief of the Defence Staff Admiral (ret'd) John Anderson, 11 September 2004.
48 The number of blue helmets peaked in December 1994 with 77,783 deployed. See United Nations, *The Blue Helmets: A Review of United Nations Peacekeeping* (New York: United Nations, 1996), 4.
49 Shortliffe, interview, 21 July 2000.
50 Anderson, interview, 11 September 2004.
51 Glen Shortliffe, "Somalia: Situation Report," memorandum for the Prime Minister (18 December 1992): 2; and "Somalia: Update on Recent Developments," memorandum for the Prime Minister (22 December 1992): 1. Access to Information request, Privy Council Office.
52 Morden and Lavertu, "Action Memorandum for the SSEA," 3.
53 Kenneth D. Bush, "Somalia: When Two Anarchies Meet," in *Canada and Missions for Peace: Lessons from Nicaragua, Cambodia, and Somalia*, ed. Gregory Wirick and Robert Miller (Ottawa: International Development Research Centre, 1998), 92.
54 MacDonald visited Somalia on a few occasions. His role was to gather information, form a personal impression of how the international and Canadian effort was proceeding, and report back to the prime minister. See David MacDonald, "Report of Honourable David MacDonald's Fact-Finding Mission" (29 January 1993): paras. 4. Cited from *Information Legacy*, document FA000771.
55 Interview with Deputy Minister of National Defence Jim Judd, at NDHQ in Ottawa, 31 August 2000.
56 There were four incidents involving Somalis shot and killed by Canadians, but the 16 March incident attracted the most media attention. The three other incidents were: on 17 February, in which a Somali was killed during a violent demonstration at a bridge; on 4 March, in which a Somali was killed after breaking into the Canadian camp; and 17 March, in which a Somali was killed during a riot in Beledweyne.
57 Shortliffe, interview, 21 July 2000.
58 Glen Shortliffe, "Somalia – Update," memorandum to the Prime Minister (17 March 1993): 2. Access to Information request, Privy Council Office.
59 UNOSOM II took command in Somalia the same day. See Anderson and Fowler, "Letter to Jim Judd" (4 May 1993).
60 R. Mark Hutchings, "List of Incidents" (1993). Cited from *Information Legacy*, document DND080212.
61 Confidential interview with former Canadian government official, 17 November 2005.
62 David Pugliese, "Campbell Accused of Hiding Somali's Death," *Ottawa Citizen*, 3 April 1993: A3.
63 Shortliffe, "Somalia – Update" (17 March 1993): 2.
64 Julian Beltrame, "Kim Campbell Finds Early Somalia Stance Now Hard to Defend," *Vancouver Sun*, 3 September 1993: A8; Hutchings, "List of Incidents"; and Serge Labbé, "Transcript of Press Conference" (23 June 1993). Last document cited from *Information Legacy*, document DND018303.
65 Day saw the soldier, Clayton Matchee, carried away on 19 March. Day was visiting the Canadian area of operations on a military-sponsored press junket. Personal computer problems and faulty telephone lines prevented Day from finishing and filing his report until the 31st, after his return to Canada. See Don Sellar, "Jim Day's Footnote in History," *Toronto Star*, 19 July 1997: C2; and Beltrame, "Kim Campbell Finds Early Somalia Stance Now Hard to Defend," A8.
66 For example, see Campbell's comment in Pugliese, "Campbell Accused of Hiding Somali's Death," A3; and Kim Campbell, speech to Parliament, House of Commons, 3rd session, 34th Parliament, *Hansard* (26 April 1993): 18448, 18457.
67 Kim Campbell, *Time and Chance: The Political Memoirs of Canada's First Woman Prime Minister* (Toronto: Doubleday Canada, 1996), 278-79, 283.
68 Pugliese, "Campbell Accused of Hiding Somali's Death," A3; Sarah Scott, "What Did Campbell Know? Is She Covering Up? MPs ask," *Edmonton Journal*, 1 May 1993: A4, and

Lloyd Axworthy, speech to Parliament by Liberal Party external affairs critic (29 April 1993).

69 Andrew Phillips, "A Few Bad Men," *Maclean's* (28 March 1994): 24.

70 Duncan Miller, "Memorandum for Glen Shortliffe" (7 May 1993): 2. Access to Information request, Privy Council Office. See also Associated Press and Staff, "Canadians Praised for Restoring Order in Somalia Town," *Globe and Mail* (10 May 1993): A11.

71 Daniel Terrance Hurley, "Turning around a Supertanker: Media-Military Relations in Canada in the CNN Age" (MJ diss., Ottawa, Carleton University, 2000), 28, 56, 180.

72 John Anderson and Robert Fowler, "Letter to Jim Judd" (4 May 1993).

73 See Fred Mifflin, speech to Parliament by Liberal Party national defence critic (26 April 1993): 18651-53; Axworthy, speech to Parliament (29 April 1993): 18458-60; and Harvie Andre, speech to Parliament by Leader of Government in the House (29 April 1993): 18639-44. All speeches from House of Commons, 3rd session, 34th Parliament, *Hansard*.

74 These rulings had been handed down in the Patti Starr case (Ontario) and the Westray Mine case (Nova Scotia). See Campbell, *Time and Chance*, 280; and De Faye Board of Inquiry, "Statement by the Board – Terms of Reference," *Report of the De Faye Board of Inquiry on the Canadian Airborne Regiment Battle Group – Phase 1* (Ottawa: July 1993), 11: para. 3. Cited from *Information Legacy*.

75 See Kim Campbell, "Letter to Deputy Minister Robert Fowler" (22 April 1993): 1. Cited from *Information Legacy*, document DND018092.

76 Campbell, *Time and Chance*, 281.

77 This was the De Faye Board of Inquiry chaired by Major-General Tom de Faye. It presented its Phase I report in July 1993. Phase II had to wait until completion of the court proceedings and military police investigations. Instead, Jean Chrétien's Liberal government created the Somalia Inquiry in spring 1995. See Campbell, speech to Parliament, House of Commons, 3rd session, 34th Parliament, *Hansard* (26 April 1993): 18458.

78 Mohamud A. Arush, "Canada and Somalia in the 21st Century: An Overview of the Performance of the Canadian Armed Forces in Somalia," *Strategic Datalink #60* (Canadian Institute of Strategic Studies, February 1997), 2.

79 Canadian International Development Agency, "Position on Development Assistance in Somalia in View of Upcoming MINA Visit," telex BFH-0085 to the High Commission in Nairobi (5 May 1993): 2. Cited from files of DFAIT, 20-1-2-Somali, vol. 6.

Chapter 10: The Canadian Joint Force Somalia

1 John Hirsch and Robert Oakley, *Somalia and Operation Restore Hope: Reflections on Peacemaking and Peacekeeping* (Washington, DC: United States Institute of Peace Press, 1995), 56.

2 Interview with former Special Envoy of the President to Somalia Ambassador (ret'd) Robert Oakley, 6 July 2000.

3 Hirsch and Oakley, *Somalia and Operation Restore Hope*, 67.

4 US government, "Report on the Progress Made by UNITAF," attached to Edward J. Perkins, "Letter from the United States to the President of the Security Council," S/25126 (19 January 1993). Cited from United Nations, *The United Nations and Somalia, 1992-1996* (New York: United Nations, 1996). (Hereafter *UN and Somalia*.)

5 Brian Gable, "The Somalia Campaign," editorial cartoon, *Globe and Mail*, 11 December 1992: A26.

6 Interview with Lieutenant-General (ret'd) Robert Johnston, 29 August 2000; interview with John Hirsch, former political adviser to Commander Unified Task Force and Deputy Special Envoy of the President to Somalia, New York, 21 June 2000; and S.L. Arnold, "Somalia: An Operation Other Than War," *Military Review* 73, 12 (December 1993): 28-29.

7 Cited in Geoffrey York, "'Why Do They Kill Each Other?' Clans Bind Somalis Together – As They Tear Somalia Apart," *Globe and Mail*, 13 February 1993: A1.

8 Arnold, "Somalia: An Operation Other Than War," 28-29.

9 Stackhouse was a development issues reporter for the *Globe and Mail*. In 2006 he was "Report on Business" editor. See John Stackhouse, *Out of Poverty and into Something More Comfortable* (Toronto: Vintage Canada, 2001), 58.

10 Sherene H. Razack, *Dark Threats and White Knights: The Somalia Affair, Peacekeeping, and the New Imperialism* (Toronto: University of Toronto Press, 2004), 9, 155-56.
11 Robert Oakley, "Press Briefing in Mogadishu," 16 December 1992. Cited from files of the Department of Foreign Affairs and International Trade (DFAIT), 21-14-6-UNOSOM, vol. 10.
12 Oakley, interview, 3 August 2000.
13 Hirsch, interview, 21 June 2000.
14 Oakley, interview, 6 July 2000.
15 Johnston, interview, 13 June 2005.
16 Jane Perlez, "Expectations in Somalia," *New York Times*, 4 December 1992: A1; Walter S. Clarke, "Testing the World's Resolve in Somalia," *Parameters* 23, 4 (Winter 1993): 42, 55-56; and John Elson, "Somalia: Warlord Country," *Time* (11 January 1993): 14.
17 Africa Rights, *Somalia – Operation Restore Hope: A Preliminary Assessment* (London: May 1993), 43; and Alex de Waal and Rakiya Omaar, "Doing Harm by Doing Good? The International Relief Effort in Somalia," *Current History* (May 1993): 198-202.
18 Geoffrey York, "Allied Convoy Reaches Hub of Somali Famine," *Globe and Mail*, 16 December 1992: A14.
19 "Playing the US against the UN," *Economist* (9 January 1993): 36.
20 Serge Labbé, "Somalia: Setting the Record Straight," unpublished ms. (March 2004). The author thanks Colonel Serge Labbé for providing the information.
21 Serge Labbé, "Operation Deliverance Situation Report #26" (9 January 1993): para. 5e. Cited from *Information Legacy: A Compendium of Source Material from the Commission of Inquiry into the Deployment of Canadian Forces to Somalia* (Ottawa: Public Works and Government Services Canada, 1997), document DND024278. (Hereafter *Information Legacy*.)
22 Labbé, "Somalia: Setting the Record Straight."
23 Ibid.
24 In the Canadian Forces context, joint operations involve the co-operation of two or more environmental doctrines (see also Chapter 3). In a combined operation, two or more national militaries are participating.
25 Serge Labbé, Foreword to *Canadian Joint Force Somalia: In the Line of Duty, 1992-1993*, ed. Ron Pupetz (Ottawa: Department of National Defence, 1994), viii.
26 In addition to ship-to-ship refuelling and other maritime duties, the *Preserver* would serve as a short-term rest centre for the contingent and provide medical, dental, and repair services for Canadians and NGOs.
27 Daniel P. Bolger, *Savage Peace: Americans at War in the 1990s* (Novato, CA: Presidio Press, 1995), 293.
28 Testimony of Serge Labbé to the Somalia Inquiry. Cited from *Information Legacy*, 162 (10 February 1997): 32980.
29 The United States battalion was the 2nd Battalion, 87th Infantry Regiment, 2nd Brigade, 10th Mountain Division. See Arnold, "Somalia: An Operation Other Than War," 32.
30 Labbé, "Somalia: Setting the Record Straight." The Hercules unit was known as the Canadian Air Transport Detachment Somalia. Based on the formerly independent Operation Relief airlift, it had been expanded from three to eight aircraft to support the movement to Beledweyne.
31 Department of National Defence (DND), "Operation Deliverance: Canadian Joint Forces Somalia," unclassified information package (1 May 1993): 3.3, 3.5. The author thanks Dr. Gerry Wright for providing the information.
32 "Technicals" was a name more commonly given to armed Somalis with civilian vehicles who might be affiliated with a faction. The United Nations and NGOs sometimes hired them as guards. See also Chapter 5. The "white" reference likely related to the skin colour of most Canadian Joint Force Somalia members, though it could also have related to the colour of their vehicles, which were painted white in anticipation of the now-cancelled first UN operation in Somalia. See Marsha Dorge and David Snashall, "The White Technicals Who Never Sleep," *Sentinel: Magazine of the Canadian Forces* 29, 2 (April-May 1993): 10.
33 Hirsch and Oakley, *Somalia and Operation Restore Hope*, 83.

34 DND, "Operation Deliverance: Canadian Joint Forces Somalia" (1 May 1993): "Introduction" (no page number), and page 3.3.
35 Serge Labbé, "Conclusion," in *Canadian Joint Force Somalia: In the Line of Duty, 1992-1993*, ed. Ron Pupetz (Ottawa: Department of National Defence, 1994), 268.
36 Robert Oakley, "Letter to Minister of National Defence Kim Campbell" (11 May 1993). Cited from *Information Legacy*, document DND320065.
37 Jonathan Manthorpe, "It's the Canadian Way: A Mix of Firmness, Kindness," *Ottawa Citizen*, 9 January 1993: B4.
38 Labbé, "Somalia: Setting the Record Straight."
39 Interview with former OXFAM-Quebec Program Co-ordinator in Beledweyne Guy Naud, in Brigham, Quebec, 25 September 2000.
40 Cited in Robert M. Press, "Canadian Troops Win Somali Kudos," *Christian Science Monitor*, 17 February 1993: 6; and Geoffrey York, "Laying a Fresh Foundation," *Globe and Mail*, 2 February 1993: A12.
41 York, "Laying a Fresh Foundation"; Andrew Phillips, "A Few Bad Men," *Maclean's* (28 March 1994): 24; and Marsha Dorge, "Humour Helps," *Sentinel: Magazine of the Canadian Forces* 29, 3 (June-July 1993): 26.
42 Guy Naud, "Letter to Chief of the Defence Admiral John Anderson" (10 May 1993). Cited from *Information Legacy*, document DND202189. Translated for the author by Mr. Naud in 2001.
43 Didier Roguet, letter to author (3 January 2000): 1.
44 Oakley, "Letter to Minister of National Defence Kim Campbell."
45 Press, "Canadian Troops Win Somali Kudos," 6.
46 Labbé, "Somalia: Setting the Record Straight."
47 Naud, interview, 25 September 2000.
48 Marsha Dorge and David Snashall, "Out of Africa," *Sentinel: Magazine of the Canadian Forces* 29, 2 (April-May 1993), 5.
49 Dorge and Snashall, "The White Technicals Who Never Sleep," 11.
50 R.H. Kennedy, "Battle Group Coming Home," in *Canadian Joint Force Somalia: In the Line of Duty, 1992-1993*, ed. Ron Pupetz (Ottawa: Department of National Defence, 1994), 240.
51 David Bercuson, *Significant Incident: Canada's Army, the Airborne, and the Murder in Somalia* (Toronto: McClelland and Stewart, 1996), 234.
52 Oakley, "Letter to Minister of National Defence Kim Campbell"; and Canadian Forces, "Operation Deliverance Briefs." The briefs in the document appear to have been for the Daily Executive Meetings held in National Defence Headquarters from December 1992-June 1993 (1993). Cited from *Information Legacy*, document DND310406.
53 Oakley, "Letter to Minister of National Defence Kim Campbell"; and Oakley, interview, 3 August 2000.
54 Razack, *Dark Threats and White Knights*, 14.
55 Alex de Waal, "US War Crimes in Somalia," *New Left Review* 230 (July 1998): 136-37; and Dana Priest, *The Mission: Waging War and Keeping Peace with America's Military* (New York: W.W. Norton, 2004), 290-91.
56 Andrew Leslie, e-mail to author, 9 February 2005.
57 Testimony of Vice-Admiral Larry Murray to the Somalia Inquiry, 29 January 1997. Cited from *Information Legacy*, 154:31499.
58 Interview with Major Steve McCluskey, in Velika Kladusa, Bosnia Herzegovina, 3 April 2000. Then a captain, McCluskey was G1 (Personnel) in CJFS Headquarters.
59 Interview with former High Commissioner to Nairobi Ambassador Lucie Edwards, 25 July 2000.
60 Operational control is authority delegated to a commander to accomplish missions or tasks and to deploy or reassign forces. It does not include logistic or administrative responsibilities. Tactical control involves the specific and usually local control of movements or manoeuvres needed to accomplish a task.
61 The Canadian contingent included the following units at one time or another: the Canadian Airborne Regiment Battlegroup, Canadian Air Transport Detachment Somalia (the former Operation Relief airlift), National Support Element Somalia (which had a detachment in

Nairobi), Canadian Joint Force Somalia Headquarters, HMCS *Preserver* (until it departed the theatre on 6 March 1993), 93 Rotary Wing Aviation Flight (a Twin Huey helicopter unit of six aircraft that replaced the Sea King assets on the *Preserver*), and 23 Field Squadron (created 1 May).

62 Serge Labbé, e-mail to author, 13 June 2005.
63 Leslie Green, "War Crimes, Crimes against Humanity, and Command Responsibility," *Naval War College Review* 50, 2 (Spring 1997): 26, 63, 64.
64 Interview with then Major-General Andrew Leslie, 19 May 2004. Leslie was also the deputy commander of the North Atlantic Treaty Organisation's International Stabilization Assistance Force, to which Canada's Task Force had been committed.
65 *Dishonoured Legacy: The Lessons of the Somalia Affair*, Report of the Commission of Inquiry into the Deployment of Canadian Forces to Somalia (Ottawa: Public Works and Government Services Canada, 1997), 5:1061-62. (Hereafter *Dishonoured Legacy*.)
66 Jean Boyle, "Canadian Airborne Regiment Battle Group in Somalia," briefing note for the Chief of the Defence Staff (23 December 1993): para. 12. Cited from *Information Legacy*, document DND202439.
67 Jean Boyle, "Information Briefing to the Minister of National Defence" (18 November 1993): n.p. Cited from *Information Legacy*, document DND335009.
68 *Dishonoured Legacy*, 5:1101-3.
69 Ibid., 5:1125.
70 Labbé, testimony. Cited from *Information Legacy*, 165 (13 February 1997): 33785-6; and 168 (19 February 1997): 34497, 34500.
71 Ibid., 166 (14 February 1997): 33890-91.
72 Ibid., 164 (12 February 1997): 33478; and 166 (14 February 1997): 33993.
73 Bercuson, *Significant Incident*, 238.
74 Stephen Harris, *Canadian Brass: The Making of a Professional Army, 1860-1939* (Toronto: University of Toronto Press, 1988), 3-4.
75 Bercuson, *Significant Incident*, 233.
76 Anthony Seward, "Letter to Colonel Ian H. Gray" (10 January 1993): 1. Cited from *Information Legacy*, document DND029963.
77 Seward, "Letter to Colonel Ian H. Gray," and Carol Mathieu, "Maj Seward Af, Inf 23a – Return To Canada," telex (25 March 1993): 2, para. 1. Cited from *Information Legacy*, document DND029974.
78 Anthony Seward, "Letter to Wife" (1 February 1993). Cited from *Information Legacy*, document DND015255.
79 Ibid.
80 Paul Dowd and Michel Côté, "Interview Analysis, Major Seward" (undated): paras. H and I. Cited from *Information Legacy*, document DND015095. Military Police Master Warrant Officer Dowd and Sergeant Côté interviewed Seward on 28 May 1993 in Toronto.
81 Canadian Forces Military Police, "March 16, 1993 Incident: Military Police Report – Chronology of Events" (undated): para. 7. Cited from *Information Legacy*, document DND015036.
82 Johnston, interview, 13 June 2005.
83 "Abuse of Iraqi POWs by GIs Probed," *60 Minutes II* with Dan Rather, CBS News, 28 April 2004. Cited from www.cbsnews.com.
84 Testimony of Major Michael Kampman to the De Faye Board of Inquiry (19 May 1993): evidence vol. 3, 570. Cited from *Information Legacy*.
85 Paul Watson, "Tense Vigil in Somalia," *Toronto Star*, 21 March 1993: F1.
86 Cited in Geoffrey York, "Campbell Ignoring Crisis in Somalia," *Globe and Mail*, 23 April 1993: A4.
87 Kim Campbell, speech to Parliament – Incidents in Somalia, House of Commons, 3rd session, 34th Parliament, *Hansard* (26 April 1993): 18457.
88 John Anderson, "A Mysterious Killing – The New Chief of Defence Faces His First Test," interview by Luke Fisher, *Maclean's* (26 April 1993): 12.
89 Robert Lewis, "Canada's Shame," editor comment, *Maclean's* (28 March 1994): 2.

90 Associated Press, "Canadians Praised for Restoring Order in Somali Town," *Globe and Mail*, 10 May 1993: A11; and Geoffrey York, "Racists in Military 'Not Acceptable,'" *Globe and Mail*, 12 May 1993: A3.

91 Labbé, "Somalia: Setting the Record Straight."

92 De Faye Board of Inquiry, *Report of the De Faye Board of Inquiry on the Canadian Airborne Regiment Battlegroup – Phase 1*, vol. 11, Annex A (Ottawa: July 1993): para. 35. Cited from *Information Legacy*.

93 Canadian Forces, "Canadian Humanitarian Relief Support Activities," in *Canadian Joint Force Somalia: In the Line of Duty, 1992-1993*, ed. Ron Pupetz (Ottawa: Department of National Defence, 1994), 62.

94 Testimony of Ambassador Lucie Edwards to De Faye Board of Inquiry (24 May 1993): evidence vol. 4, 890. Cited from *Information Legacy*.

95 Labbé, "Somalia: Setting the Record Straight."

96 Serge Labbé, "'Somalia Medal,' Letter to NDHQ Joint Staff J1 Co-ordination" (25 February 1993): 2, para. 6. Cited from *Information Legacy*, document DND231172.

97 Labbé, "Somalia: Setting the Record Straight."

98 Interview with Colonel (ret'd) Michael O'Brien, 11 October 2004.

99 Jim Cox, e-mail to author, 18 January 2005.

100 Labbé, "Somalia: Setting the Record Straight."

101 Ibid.

102 Ottawa did, however, consider prolonging its presence (see Chapter 9). Robert Astroff and David Meren, "Short-Term Gain, Long-Term Pain: An Assessment of United Nations Chapter VII Activities in Central Africa," in *Twisting Arms and Flexing Muscles: Humanitarian Intervention and Peacebuilding in Perspective*, ed. Natalie Mychajlyszyn and Timothy M. Shaw (Aldershot: Ashgate, 2005), 53.

103 Robert Oakley, "Somalia: An Envoy's Perspective," *Joint Force Quarterly* no. 2 (Autumn 1993): 54.

104 Interview with Lieutenant-Colonel (ret'd) Carol Mathieu, in Montreal, 9 May 2000.

105 Labbé, "Somalia: Setting the Record Straight."

106 Of the UN wounded, fifty-seven were Pakistani, one was Italian, and three were from the United States. See Commission of Inquiry, "Report of the Commission of Inquiry established pursuant to resolution 885 (1993) to investigate armed attacks on UNOSOM II personnel," S/1994/652 (1 June 1994): paras. 117-118. Cited from *UN and Somalia*.

107 Labbé, "Somalia: Setting the Record Straight"; and interview with Brigadier-General (ret'd) Jim Cox, in Ottawa, 16 August 2000.

Conclusion

1 Jennifer Welsh, *At Home in the World: Canada's Global Vision for the 21st Century* (Toronto: HarperCollins, 2004), 25-26.

2 Michael Schäfer, "European Security and Defence Policy and Transatlantic Relations," public lecture at Carleton University, Ottawa (4 November 2005). Schäfer was the Political Director of the German Foreign Ministry in Berlin at the time of his lecture.

3 Interview with former Commander of Canadian Joint Force Somalia Colonel Serge Labbé, Brussels, 12 December 2005.

4 Matthew Bryden, e-mail to author, 18 September 2000. Bryden was a Canadian-born Somali-speaking consultant with the High Commission in Nairobi.

5 Labbé, interview, 12 December 2005.

6 Lucie Edwards, "Letter to Colonel Serge Labbé" (2 June 1993). Cited from *Information Legacy: A Compendium of Source Material from the Commission of Inquiry into the Deployment of Canadian Forces to Somalia* (Ottawa: Public Works and Government Services Canada, 1997), document DND320075.

Bibliography

Primary Sources
Department of Foreign Affairs and International Trade Files
20-1-2-Somali, vol. 4
20-1-2-Somali, vol. 5
20-1-2-Somali, vol. 6
20-1-2-Somali, vol. 7
38-11-1-Somali, vol. 2
38-11-1-Somali, vol. 3
38-11-1-Somali, vol. 4
38-11-1-Somali-2, vol. 1
38-11-1-Somali-2, vol. 2
21-14-6-UNOSOM, vol. 2
21-14-6-UNOSOM, vol. 3
21-14-6-UNOSOM, vol. 4
21-14-6-UNOSOM, vol. 5
21-14-6-UNOSOM, vol. 6
21-14-6-UNOSOM, vol. 7
21-14-6-UNOSOM, vol. 8
21-14-6-UNOSOM, vol. 9
21-14-6-UNOSOM, vol. 10
38-11-UN, vol. 64
38-11-UN, vol. 65
38-11-UN, vol. 66

Press Releases and Media Reports
"Abuse of Iraqi POWs by GIs Probed." *60 Minutes II* with Dan Rather. CBS News. 28 April 2004. Cited from www.cbsnews.com.
Canada. "Canada to Withdraw Troops from Cyprus." *News Release* 231 (11 December 1992): 1-2.
Canada. Department of External Affairs and International Trade Canada. "Canada Contributes Largest Peacekeeping Force since 1974 to UN Operation in the Western Sahara." *News Release* 163 (18 July 1991): 1-2.
–. "McDougall Comments on UN Secretary-General's Report on Somalia." *News Release* 246 (24 December 1992): 1-2.
–. "McDougall to Meet UN Secretary-General, Dr. Boutros Boutros-Ghali in New York." *News Release* 9 (10 January 1992): 1.
Canada. Department of National Defence. "Air Transport Group Aircraft Leave for Somalia." *News Release* (4 September 1992): 1.
–. "Canada Ready to Send Troops to Somalia," *News Release* 92/51 (28 August 1992): 1.

–. "Canadian Airborne Regiment Going to Somalia." *News Release* 92/52 (2 September 1992): 1.

Canada. Office of the Prime Minister. "Canada to Provide Additional Help to Somalia." *News Release* (21 August 1992): 1.

Canadian Broadcasting Corporation. *The Journal* with Brian Stewart. Transcript, 5 March 1992.

Findlay, Gillian. "The Face of Famine." Part of episode "Somalia: The Desperate Struggle." *The National* with Peter Mansbridge. Canadian Broadcasting Corporation. 26 May 1992. Cited from http://archives.cbc.ca.

"Perot's Partisans; Lowering Your Guard; Misery's Cradle." *MacNeil-Lehrer NewsHour* with Robert MacNeil and James Lehrer. Transcript 4383. Public Broadcasting Service. 22 July 1992.

"Somalia: War and Starvation." *News in Review* with Knowlton Nash. Canadian Broadcasting Corporation. October 1992.

"UN Head Charges Yugoslavia Bias." *Facts on File* 52, 2700 (20 August 1992): 623.

United Nations. "More World Food Programme Aid Arrives in Somalia." Press release WFP/801. 12 June 1992.

–. "Secretary-General Addresses First International Youth Leadership Conference, in Montreal, on 'Nationalism and Globalization.'" Press release SG/SM/4756. 22 May 1992.

–. "Secretary-General Opens Photo Exhibit on 'Somalia's Cry.'" Press release SG/SM/4855. 17 November 1992.

–. "Secretary-General Sends Message of Hope and Reassurance to Somali People, Saying UN Mandate is One of Peace and Co-operation." Press release SG/SM/4854. 13 November 1992.

–. "Secretary-General 'Shocked and Concerned' over Situation in Somalia." Press release SG/SM/4682. 27 December 1991.

–. "Transcript of Press Conference by Secretary-General Boutros Boutros-Ghali, held at Headquarters Today." Press release SG/SM/4718. 19 March 1992.

–. "UN Calls on Somali People to Co-operate with Special Representative to Save Lives, Defeat Famine and Strife, Pave Way for Reconciliation." Press release SG/SM/4848. 2 November 1992.

Reports and Document Collections

Adibe, Clement. *Managing Arms in Peace Processes: Somalia.* UN Institute for Disarmament Research. UNIDIR/95/30. New York: United Nations, 1995.

Annan, Kofi. "Report of the Secretary-General Pursuant to General Assembly Resolution 53/35: The Fall of Srebrenica." United Nations document A/54/549. 15 November 1999. www.un.org.

Boutros-Ghali, Boutros. "An Agenda For Peace: Preventive Diplomacy, Peacemaking and Peacekeeping." United Nations document A/47/277-S/24111. 17 June 1992. Cited from www.un.org.

Brahimi, Lakhdar. "Report of the Panel on United Nations Peace Operations." United Nations document A/55/305-S/2000/809. 21 August 2000. Cited from www.un.org.

Canada. Commission of Inquiry into the Deployment of Canadian Forces to Somalia. *Dishonoured Legacy: The Lessons of the Somalia Affair.* Report of the Commission of Inquiry into the Deployment of Canadian Forces to Somalia. 5 vols. Ottawa: Public Works and Government Services Canada, 1997.

–. *Information Legacy: A Compendium of Source Material from the Commission of Inquiry into the Deployment of Canadian Forces to Somalia.* CD-ROM. Ottawa: Public Works and Government Services Canada, 1997.

Canada. Department of National Defence. "Operation Deliverance: Canadian Joint Forces Somalia." Unclassified information package. 1 May 1993.

–. Special Joint Committee of the Senate and of the House of Commons. *Canadian Foreign Policy: Principles and Priorities for the Future.* Report of the Special Joint Committee of the Senate and of the House of Commons Reviewing Canadian Foreign Policy. Ottawa: Canada Communications Group for the Speaker of the House of Commons, 1994.

–. Standing Senate Committee on Foreign Affairs. *Meeting New Challenges: Canada's Response to a New Generation of Peacekeeping.* Report of Standing Senate Committee on Foreign Affairs, Subcommittee on Security and National Defence. 3rd session, 34th Parliament. Ottawa: Canada Communications Group, 1993.

Donaghy, Greg, ed. *Documents on Canadian External Relations: 1956-57.* Vol. 22. Ottawa: Public Works and Government Services Canada, 2001.

United Nations. "Assessment of Member States' Contributions for the Financing of the United Nations Operation in Somalia (UNOSOM) from 1 May 1992 to 30 April 1993." ST/ADM/SER.B/393. 22 December 1992. 1-14.

–. *Index to Proceedings of the Security Council, 47th Year.* New York: United Nations, 1993.

–. *The United Nations and Somalia, 1992-1996.* New York: United Nations, 1996.

–. Special Emergency Programme for the Horn of Africa. *Consolidated Inter-Agency Appeal.* New York: United Nations, February 1992.

Statements

Albright, Madeline. "Statement on Somalia on behalf of the United States to the Security Council." Provisional verbatim record of Security Council meeting. United Nations, S/PV.3188, 26 March 1993.

Canada. House of Commons. *Hansard.* 3rd session, 34th Parliament. 7 December 1992; 26 April 1993; and 29 April 1993.

de Chastelain, John. "Testimony in Support of *The Study of Peacekeeping.*" Issue 9, Eighth proceeding of the Standing Senate Committee on Foreign Affairs, Subcommittee on Security and National Defence. 3rd session, 34th Parliament. 25 November 1992.

Fréchette, Louise. "Statement to the Donor's Meeting for the Special Emergency Programme for the Horn of Africa." New York, 28 January 1992, 1-4.

Hannay, David. "Statement on Somalia on behalf of the United Kingdom to the Security Council." Provisional verbatim record of Security Council meeting. United Nations, S/PV.3060, 17 March 1992.

Hassan, Fatun Mohammed. "Approaches to the Problems of Somalia." Annex to "Letter from the Chargé d'affaires A.I. of the Permanent Mission of Somalia to the UN to the President of the Security Council." United Nations, S/23507, 3 February 1992, 1-5.

Hohenfellner, Peter. "Statement on Somalia on behalf of Austria to the Security Council." Provisional verbatim record of Security Council meeting. United Nations, S/PV.3060, 17 March 1992.

Leslie, Andrew. "Testimony in Support of *The Study of Canada's National Security Policy.*" Issue 4, Eighth proceeding of the Standing Senate Committee on National Security and Defence. 1st session, 38th Parliament. 29 November 2004.

McDougall, Barbara. "Address entitled 'Peacekeeping and the Limits of Sovereignty' to a Seminar of the Centre Québécois des Relations Internationales." External Affairs and International Trade Canada, *Statement 92/58,* 2 December 1992, 1-8.

–. "Address entitled 'Peacekeeping, Peacemaking and Peacebuilding' to the Standing House of Commons Committee on External Affairs and International Trade." External Affairs and International Trade Canada, *Statement 93/11,* 17 February 1993, 1-6.

–. "Address to the London Peace Conference on the Former Socialist Federal Republic of Yugoslavia." External Affairs and International Trade Canada, *Statement 92/36,* 26 August 1992, 1-4.

–. "Address to the Primrose Club of Toronto." External Affairs and International Trade Canada, *Statement 92/43,* 17 September 1992, 1-8.

Masse, Marcel. "Testimony in Support of *The Study of Peacekeeping.*" Issue 9, Eighth proceeding of the Standing Senate Committee on Foreign Affairs, Subcommittee on Security and National Defence. 3rd session, 34th Parliament. 25 November 1992.

Mérimée, Jean-Bernard. "Statement on Somalia on behalf of France to the Security Council." Provisional verbatim record of Security Council meeting. United Nations, S/PV.3145, 3 December 1992.

Mulroney, Brian. "Address entitled 'Global Report: World Political Review' to the Commonwealth Heads of Government Meeting." Harare, Zimbabwe, 16 October 1991, 1-4.

–. "Address on the Occasion of the Centennial Anniversary Convocation of Stanford University." Stanford, California, 29 September 1991, 1-6.

–. "World Peace Demands a Stronger United Nations Role." *Canadian Speeches: Issues of the Day* 6, 4 (June-July 1992): 29-33.

Nwachukwu, Ike O.S. "Statement on Somalia on behalf of the Organization of African Unity to the Security Council." Provisional verbatim record of Security Council meeting. United Nations, S/PV.3060, 17 March 1992.

Perkins, Edward J. "Statement on Somalia on behalf of the United States to the Security Council." Provisional verbatim record of Security Council meeting. United Nations, S/PV.3145, 3 December 1992.

United Nations. General Assembly Resolution. A/RES/289 (IV). 21 November 1949.

Watson, Alexander F. "Statement on Somalia on behalf of the United States to the Security Council." Provisional verbatim record of Security Council meeting. United Nations, S/PV.3060, 17 March 1992.

Other Sources

Africa Rights. *Somalia – Operation Restore Hope: A Preliminary Assessment.* London: May 1993.

Allen, Robin W. "Combined and Joint Operations in Somalia." In *Multinational Naval Forces*, edited by Peter T. Haydon and Ann L. Griffiths, 203-30. Halifax: Dalhousie University Centre for Foreign Policy Studies, 1996.

Anderson, John. "A Mysterious Killing – The New Chief of Defence Faces His First Test." Interview by Luke Fisher *Maclean's*, 26 April 1993, 12.

Arnold, S.L. "Somalia: An Operation Other Than War." *Military Review* 73, 12 (December 1993): 26-35.

Arush, Mohamud A. "Canada and Somalia in the 21st Century: An Overview of the Performance of the Canadian Armed Forces in Somalia," *Strategic Datalink #60* (Canadian Institute of Strategic Studies, February 1997): 1-4.

Astroff, Robert, and David Meren. "Short-Term Gain, Long-Term Pain: An Assessment of United Nations Chapter VII Activities in Central Africa." In *Twisting Arms and Flexing Muscles: Humanitarian Intervention and Peacebuilding in Perspective*, edited by Natalie Mychajlyszyn and Timothy M. Shaw, 53-73. Aldershot: Ashgate, 2005.

Baril, Maurice. "Le Canada, les Casques bleus et le maintien de la paix." Interview by Francois Taschereau. *bout de papier* 12, 4 (Winter 1995): 17-19. Translated for author by Alex Lazarow.

Bercuson, David. *Significant Incident: Canada's Army, the Airborne, and the Murder in Somalia.* Toronto: McClelland and Stewart, 1996.

Berdal, Mats, and Michael Leifer. "Cambodia." In *The New Interventionism, 1991-1994: The United Nations Experience in Cambodia, Former Yugoslavia, and Somalia*, edited by James Mayall, 25-58. Cambridge: Cambridge University Press, 1996.

Besteman, Catherine. *Unravelling Somalia: Race, Violence, and the Legacy of Slavery.* Philadelphia: University of Pennsylvania Press, 1999.

Bilski, Andrew. "Wings of Hope." *Maclean's*, 28 September 1992, 34-35.

Bland, Douglas. *Chiefs of Defence: Government and the Unified Command of the Canadian Armed Forces.* Toronto: Canadian Institute of Strategic Studies, 1995.

Bolger, Daniel P. *Savage Peace: Americans at War in the 1990s.* Novato, CA: Presidio Press, 1995.

Boulden, Jane. *The United Nations and Mandate Enforcement: Congo, Somalia, and Bosnia.* Martello Paper #20. Kingston-Quebec City: Queen's University-Université Laval, 1999.

Boutros-Ghali, Boutros. "Empowering the United Nations." *Foreign Affairs* 72, 5 (Winter 1992): 89-102.

–. "Setting a New Agenda for the United Nations." Interview by Carolyn Reynolds et al. *Journal of International Affairs* 46, 2 (Winter 1993): 289-98.

–. *Unvanquished: A US-UN Saga.* New York: Random House, 1999.

Brauman, Rony. "When Suffering Makes a Good Story." In *Somalia, Rwanda, and Beyond: The Role of the International Media in Wars and Humanitarian Crises,* edited by Edward R. Girardet, 135-48. Dublin: Crosslines Communications, 1995.

Bush, George H.W. "Humanitarian Mission to Somalia." *US Department of State Dispatch* 3, 49 (7 December 1992): 865-66.

Bush, George H.W., and Brent Scowcroft. *A World Transformed.* New York: Knopf, 1998.

Bush, Kenneth D. "Somalia: When Two Anarchies Meet." In *Canada and Missions for Peace: Lessons from Nicaragua, Cambodia, and Somalia,* edited by Gregory Wirick and Robert Miller, 79-109. Ottawa: International Development Research Centre, 1998.

Campbell, Kim. *Time and Chance: The Political Memoirs of Canada's First Woman Prime Minister.* Toronto: Doubleday Canada, 1996.

Canada. Department of National Defence. *Canadian Defence Policy 1992.* Ottawa: Department of National Defence, 1992.

–. *Challenge and Commitment: A Defence Policy for Canada.* Ottawa: Supply and Services Canada, 1987.

–. *Defence Policy 1991.* Ottawa: Department of National Defence, 1991.

Canadian Forces. "Canadian Humanitarian Relief Support Activities." In *Canadian Joint Force Somalia: In the Line of Duty, 1992-1993,* edited by Ron Pupetz, 60-63. Ottawa: Department of National Defence, 1994.

Carment, David B. "Rethinking Peacekeeping: The Bosnia and Somalia Experience." In *Canada among Nations 1996: Big Enough to Be Heard,* edited by Fen Osler Hampson and Maureen Appel Molot, 221-49. Ottawa: Carleton University Press, 1996.

Carment, David, Patrick James, and Zeynep Taydas. *Who Intervenes? Ethnic Conflict and Interstate Crisis.* Columbus: Ohio State University Press, 2006.

Casper, Lawrence E. *Falcon Brigade: Combat and Command in Somalia and Haiti.* Boulder, CO: Lynne Rienner, 2001.

Chopra, Jarat, Åge Eknes, and Toralv Nordbø. *Fighting for Hope in Somalia.* Oslo: Norwegian Institute of International Affairs, 1995.

Clapham, Christopher. "Being Peacekept." In *Peacekeeping in Africa,* edited by Oliver Murray and Roy May, 303-19. Sydney: Ashgate, 1998.

Clark, Joe. "Canada's New Internationalism." In *Canada and the New Internationalism,* edited by John Holmes and John Kirton, 3-11. Toronto: Canadian Institute of International Affairs, 1988.

Clarke, Walter S. "Testing the World's Resolve in Somalia." *Parameters* 23, 4 (Winter 1993): 42-58.

Claude, Innis. "Peace and Security: Prospective Roles for the Two United Nations." *Global Governance* 2 (1996): 289-98.

Cohen, Andrew. "Pearsonianism." In *Pearson: The Unlikely Gladiator,* edited by Norman Hillmer, 153-59. Montreal and Kingston: McGill-Queen's University Press, 1999.

Cohen, Herman J. *Intervening in Africa: Superpower Peacemaking in a Troubled Continent.* New York: St. Martin's, 2000.

–. "Intervention in Somalia." In *The Diplomatic Record, 1992-93,* edited by Allan E. Goodman, 51-80. Boulder, CO: Westview Press, 1995.

Colombo, Furio. "The Media and Operation Restore Hope in Somalia." In *Somalia, Rwanda, and Beyond: The Role of the International Media in Wars and Humanitarian Crises,* edited by Edward R. Girardet, 85-90. Dublin: Crosslines Communications, 1995.

Cooper, Andrew. *Canadian Foreign Policy: Old Habits and New Directions.* Toronto: Prentice Hall, 1997.

Cortright, David, and George A. Lopez. *The Sanctions Decade: Assessing UN Strategies in the 1990s.* Boulder, CO: Lynne Rienner, 2000.

Corwin, Phillip. *Dubious Mandate: A Memoir of the UN in Bosnia, Summer 1995.* Durham: Duke University Press, 1999.

Coulon, Jocelyn. *Soldiers of Diplomacy: The United Nations, Peacekeeping, and the New World Order,* translated by Phyllis Aronoff and Howard Scott. Toronto: University of Toronto Press, 1994.

Cox, David. "Peacekeeping: The Canadian Experience." In *Peacekeeping: International Challenge and Canadian Response*, with Alastair Taylor and J.L. Granatstein. Toronto: Canadian Institute of International Affairs, 1968.

Cumner, Sandra. Review of *Another Kind of Justice* by Chris Madsen. *Armed Forces and Society: An Interdisciplinary Journal* 27, 2 (Winter 2001): 306-8.

Dawson, Grant. "In Support of Peace: Canada, the Brahimi Report and Human Security." In *Canada among Nations 2001: The Axworthy Legacy*, edited by Fen Osler Hampson, Norman Hillmer and Maureen Appel Molot, 294-317. Toronto: Oxford University Press, 2001.

–. "Still Committed: Canada's Response to the Changes in UN and non-UN Peacekeeping in the 1990s." In *Mémoire de Guerre et Construction de la Paix. Mentalités et Choix Politiques, Belgique-Europe-Canada*, edited by Serge Daumain and Eric Remacle, 201-16. New York: Peter Lang, 2006.

Delvoie, Louis A. "Canada and Peacekeeping: A New Era?" *Canadian Defence Quarterly* 20, 2 (October 1990): 9-14.

de Waal, Alex. "U.S. War Crimes in Somalia." *New Left Review* 230 (July 1998): 131-44.

de Waal, Alex, and Rakiya Omaar. "Doing Harm By Doing Good? The International Relief Effort in Somalia." *Current History* (May 1993): 131-44.

Diehl, Paul F. *International Peacekeeping*. 2nd ed. Baltimore: Johns Hopkins University Press, 1994.

–. "With the Best of Intentions: Lessons from UNOSOM I and II." *Studies in Conflict and Terrorism* 19, 2 (April-June 1996): 153-76.

Dorge, Marsha. "Humour Helps." *Sentinel: Magazine of the Canadian Forces* 29, 3 (June-July 1993): 26.

Dorge, Marsha, and David Snashall. "Out of Africa," *Sentinel: Magazine of the Canadian Forces* 29, 2 (April-May 1993): 2-5.

–. "The White Technicals Who Never Sleep." *Sentinel: Magazine of the Canadian Forces* 29, 2 (April-May 1993): 10-12.

Drysdale, John. *Whatever Happened to Somalia?* London: HAAN Associates, 1994.

Durch, William. "Epilogue: Peacekeeping in Uncharted Territory." In *The Evolution of UN Peacekeeping: Case Studies and Comparative Analysis*, edited by William Durch, 463-77. New York: St. Martin's, 1993.

–. "Introduction to Anarchy: Humanitarian Intervention and 'State-Building' in Somalia." In *UN Peacekeeping, American Policy and the Uncivil Wars of the 1990s*, edited by William Durch, 311-65. New York: St. Martin's, 1996.

Durch, William, and James A. Schear. "Faultlines: UN Operations in the Former Yugoslavia." In *UN Peacekeeping, American Policy and the Uncivil Wars of the 1990s*, edited by William Durch, 193-274. New York: St. Martin's, 1996.

Economides, Spyros, and Paul Taylor. "Former Yugoslavia." In *The New Interventionism, 1991-1994: The United Nations Experience in Cambodia, Former Yugoslavia and Somalia*, edited by James Mayall, 59-93. Cambridge: Cambridge University Press, 1996.

Economist. "Playing the U.S. against the U.N." *Economist*, 9 January 1993, 36.

Elson, John. "Somalia: Warlord Country." *Time*, 11 January 1993, 14-15.

Fitzgerald, Todd, and Michael A. Hennessy. "An Expedient Reorganization: The NDHQ J-Staff System in the Gulf War." *Canadian Military Journal* 4, 1 (Spring 2003): 23-28.

Fortier, Yves. "Canada and the United Nations: A Half-Century Partnership." O.D. Skelton Memorial Lecture. Montreal, 6 March 1996. Cited from www.dfait-maeci. gc.ca/skelton/lectures-en.asp.

Gammer, Nicholas. *From Peacekeeping to Peacemaking: Canada's Response to the Yugoslav Crisis*. Montreal and Kingston: McGill-Queen's University Press, 2001.

Garnett, Gary. "The Evolution of the Canadian Approach to Joint and Combined Operations at the Strategic and Operation Level." *Canadian Military Journal* 3 (Winter 2002-3): 3-8.

Gervais, Jim. "Land Force in Transition: Challenges and Opportunities, II." *Canadian Defence Quarterly* 22, 2 (October 1992): 6-11.

Goulding, Marrack. "The Evolution of United Nations Peacekeeping." *International Affairs* 69, 3 (1993): 451-64.

–. *Peacemonger*. London: John Murray, 2002.

Granatstein, J.L. "Canada: Peacekeeper – A Survey of Canada's Participation in Peacekeeping Operations." In *Peacekeeping: International Challenge and Canadian Response*, with Alastair Taylor and David Cox, 93-187. Toronto: Canadian Institute of International Affairs, 1968.

–. "Peacekeeping: Did Canada Make a Difference? And What Difference Did Peacekeeping Make to Canada?" *Making a Difference? Canada's Foreign Policy in a Changing World Order*, edited by John English and Norman Hillmer, 222-36. Toronto: Lester, 1992.

–. "The World Canada Faces in the 1990s." In *Canadian Forces and the Modern World*, edited by David E. Code and Ian Cameron, 11-23. Ottawa: Conference of Defence Associations Institute, 1993.

Granatstein, J.L., and Norman Hillmer. *For Better or For Worse: Canada and the United States to the 1990s*. Toronto: Copp Clark Pitman, 1991.

Gray, Charlotte. "New Faces in Old Places: The Making of Canadian Foreign Policy." In *Canada among Nations 1992-93: A New World Order?* edited by Fen Osler Hampson and Christopher J. Maule, 15-28. Ottawa: Carleton University Press, 1992.

Green, Leslie. "War Crimes, Crimes against Humanity, and Command Responsibility." *Naval War College Review* 50, 2 (Spring 1997): 26-68.

Haas, Ernst B. "Collective Conflict Management: Evidence for a New World Order?" *Collective Security in a Changing World*, edited by Thomas G. Weiss, 63-117. Boulder, CO: Lynne Rienner, 1993.

Hammarskjöld, Dag. "The UNEF [UN Emergency Force I] Experience Report, October-November 1958." In *The Public Papers of the Secretaries-General of the United Nations*. Vol. 4, *Dag Hammarskjöld, 1958-1960*, edited and compiled by Andrew W. Cordier and Wilder Foote, 230-91. New York: Columbia University Press, 1974.

Hampson, Fen Osler. "The Pursuit of Human Rights: The United Nations in El Salvador." In *UN Peacekeeping, American Policy and the Uncivil Wars of the 1990s*, edited by William Durch, 69-102. New York: St. Martin's, 1996.

Harris, Stephen. *Canadian Brass: The Making of a Professional Army, 1860-1939*. Toronto: University of Toronto Press, 1988.

Hillmer, Norman. "Canadian Peacekeeping and the Road Back to 1945." In *Canada and Italy in the World: Current Opportunities, Future Possibilities*, edited by Fabrizio Ghilardi, 145-58. Pisa: University of Pisa Press, 1993.

–. "Canadian Peacekeeping: New and Old," *Peacekeeping 1815 to Today*. Proceedings of the 21st Colloquium of the International Commission of Military History. 20-26 August 1995. Ottawa: Canadian Commission of Military History, 1995. 539-48.

–. "Mike Was Right: The Pearson Impulse in Canadian Peacekeeping." Briefing Paper of the Lester B. Pearson Canadian International Peacekeeping Training Centre. Presented to Public Fora in Halifax, Montreal, Ottawa, Toronto, Winnipeg, Calgary and Victoria, September-October 2000.

–. "Peacekeeping: Canadian Invention, Canadian Myth." In *Welfare States in Trouble: Historical Perspectives on Canada and Sweden*, edited by Sune Akerman and J.L. Granatstein, 159-70. Uppsala: Swedish Science Press, 1995.

–. "Peacekeeping: The Inevitability of Canada's Role." In *War in the Twentieth Century: Reflections at Century's End*, edited by Michael A. Hennessy and B.J.C. McKercher, 145-65. London: Praeger, 2003.

–. "Peacemakers, Blessed and Otherwise." *Canadian Defence Quarterly* 19, 1 (August 1989): 55-58.

Hillmer, Norman, and Grant Dawson. "Canada and Peacekeeping in the 1990s: A Search for Strategy." Unpublished manuscript. 2002. Author's collection.

Hillmer, Norman, and J.L. Granatstein. *Empire to Umpire: Canada and the World to the 1990s*. Toronto: Copp Clark Longman, 1994.

Hillmer, Norman, and Dean Oliver. "The NATO-United Nations Link: Canada and the Balkans, 1991-95." In *A History of NATO: The First Fifty Years*, edited by Gustav Schmidt, 1:71-84. Houndmills, Hampshire, England: Palgrave, 2001.

Hinton, D. "Where There's a Need ATG Crews Will Travel." *Air Transport Group Newsletter* 4, 1 (1992): 11-12.

Hirsch, John L., and Robert B. Oakley. *Somalia and Operation Restore Hope: Reflections on Peacemaking and Peacekeeping*. Washington, DC: United States Institute of Peace Press, 1995.

Hoey, Brian Patrick. "Humanitarian Intervention in Somalia, 1992-1994: Elite Newspaper Coverage, Public Opinion, and US Foreign Policy." PhD diss., University of Maryland, College Park, 1995.

Hoffmann, Stanley. "The Hell of Good Intentions." *Foreign Policy* 29 (Winter 1977): 3-26.

Holmes, John. "The New Agenda for Canadian Internationalism." In *Canada and the New Internationalism*, edited by John Holmes and John Kirton, 12-23. Toronto: Canadian Institute of International Affairs, 1988.

Hooglund, Eric. "Government and Politics." In *Somalia: A Country Study*, edited by Helen Chapin Metz, 151-78. 4th ed. Washington, DC: Federal Research Division, 1993.

Horn, Bernd. *Bastard Sons: An Examination of Canada's Airborne Experience, 1942-1995*. St. Catharines: Vanwell, 2001.

Hurley, Daniel Terrance. "Turning around a Supertanker: Media-Military Relations in Canada in the CNN Age." MJ diss., Carleton University, Ottawa, 2000.

Ignatieff, Michael. "The Stories We Tell: Television and Humanitarian Aid." In *Hard Choices: Moral Dilemmas in Humanitarian Intervention*, edited by Jonathan Moore, 287-302. New York: Rowman and Littlefield, 1998.

Institute on Governance. "Government Decision-Making in Canada – Players, Processes, Institutions: Central Agencies in Decision-Making." Report of Study Tour by the Secretariat of the Cabinet of Ministers of Ukraine. Ottawa: January 2001. Cited from www.igvn.ca.

International Committee of the Red Cross. *The Fundamental Principles of the Red Cross and Red Crescent*. 1 July 1996. Cited from www.icrc.org.

James, Alan. "The History of Peacekeeping: An Analytical Perspective." *Canadian Defence Quarterly* 23, 1 (September 1993): 10-17.

–. "Humanitarian Aid Operations and Peacekeeping," *The Politics of International Humanitarian Aid Operations*, edited by Eric A. Belgrad and Nitza Nachmias, 53-64. Westport, CT: Praeger, 1997.

–. *Peacekeeping in International Politics*. New York: St. Martin's, 1990.

–. "Problems of Internal Peacekeeping." *Diplomacy and Statecraft* 5, 1 (March 1994): 21-46.

James, Stephen L. "The Air Force's Cold War Struggle with Its National Purpose." *Proceedings of the 3rd Annual Air Force Historical Conference*, edited by William March and Don Pearsons, 83-92. Winnipeg: Department of National Defence, 1998.

–. "The Formation of Air Command: A Struggle for Survival." MA diss., Royal Military College, Kingston, 1989.

Jensen, John P. "Airlift Control Element (ALCE) I." In *Canadian Joint Force Somalia: In the Line of Duty, 1992-1993*, edited by Ron Pupetz, 36-38. Ottawa: Department of National Defence, 1994.

Johnston, Philip. *Somalia Diary: The President of CARE Tells One Country's Story of Hope*. Atlanta: Longstreet Press, 1994.

Keating, Tom. *Canada and World Order: The Multilateralist Tradition in Canadian Foreign Policy*. 2nd ed. Toronto: Oxford University Press, 2002.

Kennedy, R.H. "Battle Group Coming Home." In *Canadian Joint Force Somalia: In the Line of Duty, 1992-1993*, edited by Ron Pupetz, 240. Ottawa: Department of National Defence, 1994.

Kern, David. "Incentives and Disincentives for Violence." In *Greed and Grievance: Economic Agendas in Civil Wars*, edited by Mats Berdal and David M. Malone, 19-41. Boulder, CO: Lynne Rienner, 2000.

Kittani, Ismat, with Ian Johnstone. "First Person: The Lessons from Somalia." *UN Chronicle* 33, 3 (September 1996): 80-81.

Krauthammer, Charles. "Essay: The Immaculate Intervention." *Time*, 26 July 1993, 56.

Labbé, Serge. Foreword to *Canadian Joint Force Somalia: In the Line of Duty, 1992-1993*, edited by Ron Pupetz, viii. Ottawa: Department of National Defence, 1994.

–. "Conclusion." In *Canadian Joint Force Somalia: In the Line of Duty, 1992-1993*, edited by Ron Pupetz, 266-69. Ottawa: Department of National Defence, 1994.

–. "Somalia: Setting the Record Straight." Unpublished ms. 1994. Author's collection.

Laitin, David D. "The Economy." In *Somalia: A Country Study*, edited by Helen Chapin Metz, 121-49. 4th ed. Washington, DC: Federal Research Division, 1993.

–. "Somalia: Civil War and International Intervention." In *Civil Wars, Insecurity and Intervention*, edited by Barbara F. Walter and Jack Snyder, 146-80. New York: Columbia University Press, 1999.

Lewis, Ioan, and James Mayall. "Somalia." In *The New Interventionism, 1991-1994: The United Nations Experience in Cambodia, Former Yugoslavia, and Somalia,* edited by James Mayall, 94-124. Cambridge: Cambridge University Press, 1996.

Lewis, Robert. "Canada's Shame." Editor comment. *Maclean's*, 28 March 1994, 2.

Liu, F.T. *United Nations Peacekeeping and the Non-Use of Force*. International Peace Academy Occasional Paper. Boulder, CO: Lynne Rienner, 1992.

Lyons, Terrance, and Ahmed I. Samatar. *Somalia: State Collapse, Multilateral Intervention, and Strategies for Political Reconstruction*. Washington, DC: Brookings, 1995.

Lysyshyn, Ralph. "Domestic Political Considerations of International Security Operations." In *Multinational Naval Forces*, edited by Peter T. Haydon and Ann L. Griffiths, 71-82. Halifax: Centre for Foreign Policy Studies, 1995.

MacDonald, Jane. "The First ALCE Commander." In *Canadian Joint Force Somalia: In the Line of Duty, 1992-1993*, edited by Ron Pupetz, 34-35. Ottawa: Department of National Defence, 1994.

–. "Operation Relief." In *Canadian Joint Force Somalia: In the Line of Duty, 1992-1993*, edited by Ron Pupetz, 26-7. Ottawa: Department of National Defence, 1994.

McDougall, Barbara. "Canada and the New Internationalism." *Canadian Foreign Policy* 1, 1 (Winter 1992-93): 1-6.

–. "A Few Parting Shots." Interview by Anthony Wilson-Smith and E. Kaye Fulton. *Maclean's*, 5 July 1993, 10.

–. "Meeting the Challenge of the New World Order." *International Journal* 47, 3 (Summer 1992): 463-78.

MacKenzie, Lewis. "Peacekeeping: Into the Grey Zone." In *Canadian Forces and the Modern World*, edited by David E. Code and Ian Cameron, 24-43. Ottawa: Conference of Defence Associations Institute, 1993.

McLaughlin, Greg. *The War Correspondent*. London: Pluto Press, 2000.

McMillan, Ken. "Military Planning Considerations." In *Multinational Naval Forces*, edited by Peter T. Haydon and Ann L. Griffiths, 83-90. Halifax: Centre for Foreign Policy Studies, 1995.

Madsen, Chris. *Another Kind of Justice: Canadian Military Law from Confederation to Somalia*. Vancouver: UBC Press, 1999.

Makinda, Samuel M. *Seeking Peace from Chaos: Humanitarian Intervention in Somalia*. Boulder, CO: Lynne Rienner, 1993.

Maloney, Sean M. *Canada and UN Peacekeeping: Cold War by Other Means, 1945-1970*. St. Catharines: Vanwell, 2002.

–. "Purple Haze: Joint Planning in the Canadian Forces from Mobile Command to J-Staff, 1975-1991 (Part 1)." *Army Doctrine and Training Bulletin* 5, 4 (Winter 2002-3): 57-72.

Moeller, Susan D. *Compassion Fatigue: How the Media Sell Disease, Famine, War and Death*. New York: Routledge, 1999.

Mohamed, Hassan A. "The Socio-Cultural Adaptation of Somali Refugees in Toronto: An Explanation of Their Integration Experiences." DEd diss., University of Massachusetts, Amherst, 2001.

Moorhead, Caroline. *Dunant's Dream: War, Switzerland and the History of the Red Cross*. New York: Carroll and Graf, 1999.

Morin, Jean. "The Command and Control of the Air Transport Group during the Gulf War." In *Proceedings of the 3rd Annual Air Force Historical Conference*, edited by William March and Don Pearsons, 117-24. Winnipeg: Department of National Defence, 1998.

Morin, Jean, and Richard H. Gimblett. *The Canadian Forces in the Persian Gulf: Operation Friction 1990-1991*. Toronto: Dundurn Press, 1997.

Mouafo, Dieudonné, Nadia Ponce Morales, and Jeff Heynen, eds. *Building Cross-Border Links: A Compendium of Canada-U.S. Government Collaboration*. Canada School of Public Service Action-Research Roundtable on Managing Canada-U.S. Relations. Ottawa: Canada School of Public Service, 2004.

Natsios, Andrew S. "Humanitarian Relief Intervention in Somalia: The Economics of Chaos." In *Learning from Somalia: The Lessons of Humanitarian Intervention*, edited by Walter Clarke and Jeffery Herbst, 77-95. Boulder, CO: Westview Press, 1997.

–. "U.S. Relief Effort in Somalia." Statement to the House Foreign Affairs Committee, Subcommittee on Africa. *US Department of State Dispatch* 3, 39 (28 September 1992): 738-40.

Newman, Peter C. *The Secret Mulroney Tapes: Unguarded Confessions of a Prime Minister*. Toronto: Random House Canada, 2005.

Oakley, Robert. "Somalia: An Envoy's Perspective." *Joint Force Quarterly* no. 2 (Autumn 1993): 44-55.

Ofcansky, Thomas. "National Security." In *Somalia: A Country Study*, edited by Helen Chapin Metz, 181-226. 4th ed. Washington, DC: Federal Research Division, 1993.

Oliviero, Charles. "Operation Deliverance: International Success or Domestic Failure?" *Canadian Military Journal* 2, 2 (Summer 2001): 51-58.

Omaar, Rakiya. "Somalia: At War with Itself." *Current History* (May 1992): 230-34.

Parsons, Anthony. "The UN and the National Interests of States." In *United Nations, Divided World: The UN's Roles in International Relations*, edited by Adam Roberts and Benedict Kingsbury, 104-24. 2nd ed. Oxford: Clarendon, 1996.

Pearson, Geoffrey. "Canadian Attitudes toward Peacekeeping." In *Peacekeeping: Appraisals and Proposals*, edited by Henry Wiseman, 118-29. New York: Pergamon, 1983.

–. *Seize the Day: Lester B. Pearson and Crisis Diplomacy*. Ottawa: Carleton University Press, 1993.

Pearson, Lester B. *Mike: The Memoirs of the Right Honourable Lester B. Pearson*. Vol. 2, *1948-57*, edited by John A. Munro and Alex I. Inglis. Toronto: Signet, 1975.

Phillips, Andrew. "A Few Bad Men." *Maclean's*, 28 March 1994, 24-25.

Potter, Evan. "A Question of Relevance: Canada's Foreign Policy and Foreign Service in the 1990s." In *Canada Among Nations, 1993-94: Global Jeopardy*, edited by Christopher J. Maule and Fen Osler Hampson, 37-56. Ottawa: Carleton University Press, 1993.

Powell, Colin, with Joseph E. Persico. *My American Journey*. New York: Random House Large Print, 1995.

Priest, Dana. *The Mission: Waging War and Keeping Peace with America's Military*. New York: W.W. Norton, 2004.

Ratner, Steven R. *The New UN Peacekeeping: Building Peace in Lands of Conflict after the Cold War*. New York: St. Martin's, 1996.

Razack, Sherene H. *Dark Threats and White Knights: The Somalia Affair, Peacekeeping, and the New Imperialism*. Toronto: University of Toronto Press, 2004.

Roberts, Adam. "From San Francisco to Sarajevo: The UN and the Use of Force." *Survival* 37, 4 (Winter 1995-96): 7-28.

Robertson, Jamie. "Canada – Please Help Us!" *Sentinel* 27, 6 (1991): 2-4.

Robinson, Piers. "The Policy-Media Interaction Model: Measuring Media Power during Humanitarian Crisis." *Journal of Peace Research* 37, 5 (September 2000): 613-33.

Sahnoun, Mohamed. "Flashlights over Mogadishu." *New Internationalist* no. 262 (December 1994): 9-11.

–. "Prevention in Conflict Resolution: The Case of Somalia." *Irish Studies in International Affairs* 5 (1994): 5-13.

–. *Somalia: The Missed Opportunities*. Washington, DC: United States Institute of Peace Press, 1994.

Samatar, Said S. "Historical Setting." In *Somalia: A Country Study*, edited by Helen Chapin Metz, 3-53. 4th ed. Washington, DC: Federal Research Division, 1993.

–. *Somalia: A Nation in Turmoil*. 1991. London: Minority Rights Group International, 1995.

–. "The Society and Its Environment." In *Somalia: A Country Study*, edited by Helen Chapin Metz, 57-118. 4th ed. Washington, DC: Federal Research Division, 1993.

Savoie, Donald J. *Governing from the Centre: The Concentration of Power in Canadian Politics.* Toronto: University of Toronto Press, 2001.

Schacter, Mark, with Phillip Haid. "Cabinet Decision-Making in Canada: Lessons and Practice." Institute on Governance research paper. Ottawa: April 1999. Cited from www.igvn.ca.

Schäfer, Michael. "European Security and Defence Policy and Transatlantic Relations." Public lecture at Carleton University, Ottawa, 4 November 2005.

Schear, James A. "Riding the Tiger: The United Nations and Cambodia's Struggle for Peace." In *UN Peacekeeping, American Policy and the Uncivil Wars of the 1990s,* edited by William Durch, 135-91. New York: St. Martin's, 1996.

Shearer, David. "Aiding or Abetting? Humanitarian Aid and Its Economic Role in Civil War." In *Greed and Grievance: Economic Agendas in Civil Wars,* edited by Mats Berdal and David M. Malone, 189-203. Boulder, CO: Lynne Rienner, 2000.

Schmitz, Gerald J. "CIDA as Peacemaker: Integration or Overload?" *Aid as Peacemaker: Canadian Development Assistance and Third World Conflict,* edited by Robert Miller, 89-106. Ottawa: Carleton University Press, 1992.

Schraeder, Peter J. "The Horn of Africa: U.S. Foreign Policy in an Altered Cold War Environment." *Middle East Journal* 46, 4 (Autumn 1992): 571-93.

Sens, Allen G. *Somalia and the Changing Nature of Peacekeeping: The Implications for Canada.* Study prepared for the Commission of Inquiry into the Deployment of Canadian Forces to Somalia. Ottawa: Public Works and Government Services Canada, 1997.

Simonds, Charles R. "External Military Involvement in the Provision of Humanitarian Relief in Ethiopia." In *Humanitarian Emergencies and Military Help in Africa,* edited by Thomas G. Weiss, 61-73. New York: St. Martin's, 1990.

Simpson, Jeffrey. *Discipline of Power: The Conservative Interlude and the Liberal Restoration.* 2nd ed. Toronto: University of Toronto Press, 1996.

Smith, Brian D., and William Durch. "UN Observer Group in Central America." In *The Evolution of UN Peacekeeping: Case Studies and Comparative Analysis,* edited by William Durch, 436-62. New York: St. Martin's, 1993.

Smith, Gordon S. "Establishing Canada's Priorities." In *Canada among Nations 2004: Setting Priorities Straight,* edited by David Carment, Fen Osler Hampson, and Norman Hillmer, 42-54. Montreal and Kingston: McGill-Queen's University Press, 2005.

Stackhouse, John. *Out of Poverty and into Something More Comfortable.* Toronto: Vintage Canada, 2001.

Stairs, Denis. "Architects or Engineers? The Conservatives and Foreign Policy." *Diplomatic Departures: The Conservative Era in Canadian Foreign Policy, 1984-93,* edited by Kim Richard Nossal and Nelson Michaud, 25-42. Vancouver: University of British Columbia Press, 2001.

–. "Canada in the 1990s: Speak Loudly and Carry a Bent Twig." *Policy Options* 22, 1 (January-February 2001): 43-49.

–. "Choosing Multilateralism: Canada's Experience after World War II." Presentation to the North-South Co-operative Security Dialogue, Beijing, June 1982. *CANCAPS Paper #4,* 1-6. Toronto: Canadian Consortium on Asia-Pacific Security, 1994.

–. "Lester B. Pearson and the Meaning of Politics." In *Pearson: The Unlikely Gladiator,* edited by Norman Hillmer, 30-50. Montreal and Kingston: McGill-Queen's University Press, 1999.

Stevenson, Brian. *Canada, Latin America, and the New Internationalism: A Foreign Policy Analysis, 1968-1990.* Montreal and Kingston: McGill-Queen's University Press, 2000.

Stevenson, Jonathan. "Hope Restored in Somalia?" *Foreign Policy* 91 (Summer 1993): 138-54.

–. *Losing Mogadishu: Testing US Policy in Somalia.* Annapolis, MD: Naval Institute Press, 1995.

Tabbernor, Dennis C. "Operational Commanders, Orders and the Right to Choose." Research essay, Canadian Forces College, Toronto, November 1998. Document obtained from Canadian Forces College on-line Information Resource Centre portal, http://wps.cfc.forces.ca/en/cfcpapers/index.php.

Taylor, Alastair. "Peacekeeping: The International Context." In *Peacekeeping: International Challenge and Canadian Response*, with David Cox and J.L. Granatstein, 1-40. Toronto: Canadian Institute of International Affairs, 1968.

Tessier, Manon, and Michel Fortmann. "The Conservative Approach to International Peacekeeping." In *Diplomatic Departures: The Conservative Era in Canadian Foreign Policy, 1984-93*, edited by Kim Richard Nossal and Nelson Michaud, 113-27. Vancouver: University of British Columbia Press, 2001.

Tharoor, Shashi. "Should UN Peacekeeping Go 'Back to Basics'?" *Survival* 37, 4 (Winter 1995-96): 52-64.

United Nations. *The Blue Helmets: A Review of United Nations Peacekeeping*. 3rd ed. New York: United Nations, 1996.

–. "Peacekeeping Fatalities by Mission and Incident Type." 30 June 2005. Cited from www.un.org/Depts/dpko/fatalities/.

–. "Security in Somalia." *Secretariat News* (July-August 1993): 12.

–. "Somalia Peace Elusive." *Secretariat News* (February 1992): 11.

–. "Somalia too Deadly, Immediate Evacuation Urged by Staff Union." *Secretariat News* (January 1992): 5, 7.

–. "30,000-strong UN Force Steps in to 'Restore Hope.'" *UN Chronicle* 30, 2 (June 1993): 13-17.

–. "United Nations Interim Force in Lebanon (UNIFIL)." *The Blue Helmets: A Review of United Nations Peacekeeping*, 83-112. 3rd ed. New York: United Nations, 1996.

–. "United Nations Operation in Somalia I and II (UNOSOM I and II)." In *The Blue Helmets: A Review of United Nations Peacekeeping*, 285-318. 3rd ed. New York: United Nations, 1996.

Wallensteen, Peter. *Understanding Conflict Resolution: War, Peace and the Global System*. London: Sage, 2002.

Weiss, Thomas G. *Military-Civilian Interactions: Intervening in Humanitarian Crisis*. Boulder, CO: Rowman and Littlefield, 1999.

Welsh, Jennifer. *At Home in the World: Canada's Global Vision for the 21st Century*. Toronto: HarperCollins, 2004.

Wright, Gerry. "Canada and Bosnia: A Ten-Year Retrospective." Presentation to the Queen's University-Royal Military College conference "Give Peace a Chance? Implications of a Decade of Western Conflict Management in Bosnia (1992-2002)." 14 June 2002.

–. "Diplomacy and Peacekeeping: Part 2." *bout de papier* 13, 4 (Winter 1996): 25-28.

Index